Summary Guides

Maths 9

Michael Loh

First published in 2024, reprinted in 2025.

Insight Publications Pty Ltd
3/350 Charman Road
Cheltenham Victoria 3192
Australia

Tel: +61 3 8571 4950
Email: books@insightpublications.com.au
www.insightpublications.com.au

Summary Guides – Maths 9 / Michael Loh

ISBN: 9781923154568

Edited by Dr Geoffrey Marnell
Proofread by Sage Napthine-Morrison
Artwork by Artin Education
Typesetting by Aptara®, Inc.
Cover design by Melisa Paredes
Printed by Markono Print Media Pte Ltd

Table of contents

Introduction

The *Summary Guides – Maths* series has been written by practising teachers who are passionate about creating user-friendly, accessible guides on mathematics.

The explanations and exercises in these guides develop core numeracy skills for personal, work and civic life, and provide the base knowledge for professional applications of maths as well as mathematical specialisations. Maths is part of your daily life no matter what you choose to do as an adult – it is important for thinking critically and making sense of the world.

This book summarises key concepts in a clear and comprehensive way. It includes examples with worked solutions and step-by-step explanations, as well as exercises for you to complete. The best way to use this book is to make a habit of it, regularly working through the exercises and examples and comparing your answers with those provided. Whether you commit to a daily, weekly or fortnightly routine, consistent practice is the key to your success.

The content of this book is based on years of experience making mathematics comprehensible to students in the classroom. By working through this book you will be able to practise your skills, grow in confidence and reap the rewards that come from a solid understanding of maths.

Michael Loh and Insight Publications

Michael Loh BE (Hons), MEngSc, GradDipEdu (Secondary) is a Senior Mathematics teacher at Shenton College in Perth, where he also coordinates the Gifted and Talented Program. He has taught in the secondary and tertiary sectors for many years and is a regular presenter at conferences, including the Google Education Conference, the EdTech Summit and conferences held by the Mathematical Association of Western Australia. Michael has co-authored Years 11 and 12 mathematics textbooks for use in schools in Western Australia. He is also a marker of WACE Mathematics Applications examinations.

Chapter 1 – Financial mathematics

When we deposit money into a bank account (make an investment), we expect it to grow, because the bank will be paying us money based on a percentage (the interest). Similarly, when we borrow money from the bank (take out a loan), the bank will charge us interest on the amount we borrow.

The amount of interest is dependent on the initial amount of money, the interest rate and the duration of the investment (or loan).

Definitions

- Principal (P) – the amount of money initially invested or borrowed
- Interest (I) – the amount of money paid by the bank (investment) or that we pay the bank (loan)
- Rate (R) – the percentage that determines the interest, usually quoted as a percentage per annum (% p.a.)
- Time (T) – the duration of the investment or loan (usually in years)
- Final amount (A) – the final value of the investment or loan

1.1 Simple interest

In Year 9, we are concerned only with simple interest.

For simple interest:

$$I = PRT \quad \text{and} \quad A = P + I$$

Example

How much interest would I have to pay if I borrowed \$3000 for 8 years at a simple interest rate of 10% p.a.?

✓ Solution

Working	Explanation
$P = \$3000$ $R = 10\%$ p.a. $T = 8$ years	List the information given, i.e. P, R and T.
$I = (3000)\left(\frac{10}{100}\right)(8)$ $= 2400$	Substitute the information into the simple interest formula to determine the amount of interest.
I would have to pay interest of \$2400.	Answer the question with a sentence.

Example

What is the final value of an investment of $4000 after 6.5 years at a simple interest rate of 6% p.a.?

✓ Solution

Working	Explanation
$P = \$4000$ $R = 6\%$ p.a. $T = 6.5$ years	List the information given, i.e. P, R and T.
$I = (4000)\left(\frac{6}{100}\right)(6.5)$ $= 1560$	Substitute the information into the simple interest formula to determine the amount of interest.
$A = P + I$ $= 4000 + 1560$ $= 5560$	Add the principal to the interest to determine the final value.
The final value of the investment is $5560.	Answer the question with a sentence.

You may be required to determine the principal of an investment or loan, the rate of interest or the duration (i.e. time). These can be found by rearranging the interest formula: $I = PRT$.

Principal	Rate	Duration
$P = \frac{I}{RT}$	$R = \frac{I}{PT}$	$T = \frac{I}{PR}$

Example

Money was borrowed over a period of 10 years at a simple interest rate of 5% p.a. The interest paid on the loan was $2000. What was the principal?

✓ Solution

Working	Explanation
$I = \$2000$ $R = 5\%$ p.a. $T = 10$ years	List the information given, i.e. I, R and T.
$P = \frac{2000}{(0.05)(10)} = 4000$	Substitute the information into a rearranged simple interest formula to determine the amount of principal. Note that in the calculation, the decimal form of the interest rate is used instead of a fraction.
The principal was $4000.	Answer the question with a sentence.

Example

The interest from an investment of $P = \$5100$ was $\$1147.50$. Given a simple interest rate of 3% p.a., determine the duration of the investment.

✓ ***Solution***

Working	Explanation
$I = \$1147.50$ $R = 3\%$ p.a. $P = \$5100$	List the information given, i.e. I, R and P.
$T = \dfrac{1147.50}{(0.03)(5100)} = 7.5$	Substitute the information into a rearranged simple interest formula to determine the duration.
The duration of the investment was 7.5 years (or 7 years and 6 months).	Answer the question with a sentence.

Example

Mark borrowed $3000 from his parents to buy a motorbike. He paid a simple interest rate on the loan. After 5 years he paid back a total of $3600. What was the interest rate?

✓ ***Solution***

Working	Explanation
$A = \$3600$ $P = \$3000$ $T = 5$ years	List the information given, i.e. A, P and T.
$I = A - P$ $= 3600 - 3000$ $= 600$	Determine the interest paid on the loan.
$R = \dfrac{600}{(3000)(5)} = 0.04$	Substitute the information into a rearranged simple interest formula to determine the rate.
The simple interest rate was 4% p.a.	Answer the question with a sentence and remember to convert the rate to a percentage.

Hint: when you calculate the principal or interest you may not get a whole number. In these cases always round the result to 2 decimal places.

Exercise 1.1

a. Grace invested $5000 in an account that paid simple interest at the rate of 6% p.a. for 5 years. Determine the interest and the final value of the investment.

b. Ari bought a gaming computer for $3000. He had a savings of $1250 and his parents lent him the balance at a rate of 2% p.a. simple interest. It took Ari 3 years to pay his parents back. Determine the interest he paid.

c. The interest paid on a loan was $4500. The simple interest rate was 2% p.a. and the duration of the loan was 5.5 years. Determine the principal.

d. The final value of an investment with a principal of $3650 and a duration of 8 years is $4672. Determine the simple interest rate for the loan.

e. Chris borrowed $15 000 to purchase a car at a simple interest rate of 5.5% p.a. He paid interest of $7425. Determine the duration of the loan.

1.2 Budgeting

When you start to work, you may want to buy a new smartphone (or a car or even a house). But how do you know how much money you have to save up?

Budgeting is the activity of **recording** your income (what you earn) and your expenditure (what you spend) over a period of time to see if you are saving money or spending more than you earn. You can also **estimate** your future income and expenditure to see if you are likely to achieve your goal of buying a new smartphone (or whatever you want to buy).

Suppose you work part-time and earn $100 a week after tax. You could spend less than, exactly the same as, or more than the amount you earn. Consider the diagram below.

Income = $100/week Expenditure = $100/week	In this situation, income equals expenditure. You spend what you earn, and you won't save money.
Income = $100/week Expenditure = $70/week	$30/week	In this situation, income is greater than expenditure. You spend less than what you earn and will save money. If you spend $70 a week, you will save $30 a week.
Income = $100/week Expenditure = $120/week $20/week	In this situation, income is less than expenditure. You spend more than what you earn and you won't save money (and may be in debt). In this case, you are over-spending by $20/week.

If you are going to save money to buy a new smartphone, you need to spend less than you earn. However, if you are spending all the money you earn (or more), you will have no savings. To save money, you may need to modify your spending habits. For example, if you spend \$50 on chocolate each week, you may need to reduce your expenditure to just \$10/week to save some money.

Example

Mandy wants to save up for a dress for her Year 12 ball. She works part-time and earns \$120 a week after tax. She spends a third of her earnings on snacks and half of her earnings on going out with friends.

How much money would she be able to save after one year (52 weeks)?

✓ Solution

Working	Explanation
Weekly income $= \$120$	List the weekly income.
Weekly expenditure: • snacks $= \frac{1}{3} \times 120 = \$40$ • going out $= \frac{1}{2} \times 120 = \$60$ Total weekly expenditure $= \$100$	Calculate the total weekly expenditure from the information given.
Weekly savings $= 120 - 100 = \$20$	Calculate the weekly savings.
Yearly savings $= 20 \times 52 = \$1040$	Calculate the savings after 52 weeks.
After a year Mandy can save \$1040.	Answer the question with a sentence.

Example

Marcus would like to save \$1200 in 6 months. He works part-time at Bunnings. His monthly expenditure is:

- \$40 – phone bill
- \$100 – board
- \$160 – entertainment (going out, snacks etc.).

How much will Marcus have to earn after tax each month in order to reach his target savings of \$1200?

✓ ***Solution***

Working	Explanation
Total expenditure $= 40 + 100 + 160$ $= 300$	Calculate total monthly expenditure.
Savings/month $= \frac{1200}{6} = 200$	Calculate the required savings each month.
Monthly earnings after tax $= 300 + 200$ $= 500$	Determine the monthly earnings by adding together the savings and total expenditure.
Marcus would have to earn a monthly income of \$500 after tax.	Answer the question with a sentence.

Exercise 1.2

a. Jane wants to buy an Xbox Series X which costs \$800. She was told that if she saved up half the amount, her brother Jake would provide the rest of the money. She works in a café and earns \$18 per hour after tax. She works 8 hours per week and spends \$80 on entertainment. How long will she have to save for before she can afford to buy the Xbox?

b. Vincent is given a weekly allowance of \$80 by his parents. He spends \$12 each day during the school week to buy snacks and lunch.

i. Determine Vincent's weekly savings.

ii. How much is he able to save after 10 weeks?

iii. Suggest a way that he can save more money.

Answers

Exercise 1.1

a. $I = \$1500, A = \$6500$

b. $I = \$105$

c. $P = \$40\ 909.09$

d. $R = 3.5\%$ p.a.

e. $T = 9$ years

Exercise 1.2

a. 7 weeks. Jane can save \$64 a week, so after 6 weeks she will have saved \$384. However, this is less than half of the cost of the Xbox. After 7 weeks, she will have saved \$448, which is more than half the cost of the Xbox. So Jane will be able to buy the Xbox after 7 weeks.

b.

i. Weekly savings = \$20.

ii. Vincent is able to save \$200 after 10 weeks.

iii. Spend less on snacks and lunches.

Chapter 2 – Linear relationships

A linear relationship is a relationship between two sets of data that, when plotted on the Cartesian plane, form a straight line. An example of a linear relationship is the relationship between the amount of money earned and the number of hours worked.

2.1 Distance between two points on the Cartesian plane

The distance, d, between two points on the Cartesian plane with the coordinates (x_1, y_1) and (x_2, y_2) – as shown on the diagram below – is given by the formula

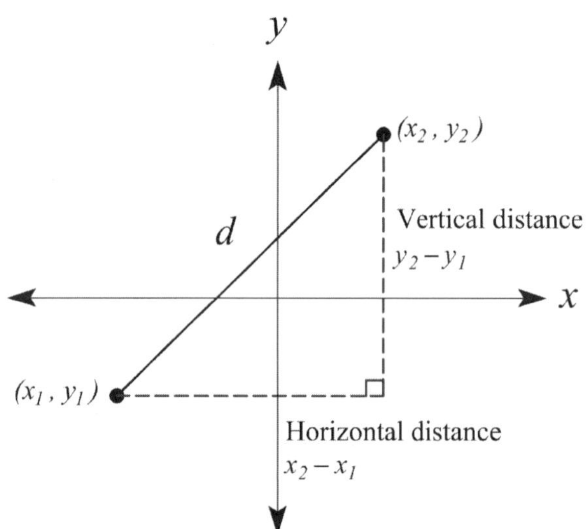

$$d = \sqrt{(x_2 - x_1)^2 + (y_2 - y_1)^2}$$

This equation is derived using Pythagoras' theorem, which will be discussed in Chapter 7.

In this formula, $y_2 - y_1$ is the vertical distance and $x_2 - x_1$ is the horizontal distance between the two points.

Therefore, the distance between two points with the same y-coordinate will be the difference between the two x-coordinates. This is because a line between the two points will be horizontal. Similarly, the distance between two points with the same x-coordinate will be the difference between the two y-coordinates, as a line between the two points will be vertical.

Example

Determine the distance between the points $(3, 4)$ and $(-2, -5)$.

✓ *Solution*

Working	Explanation
$d = \sqrt{(3-(-2))^2 + (4-(-5))^2}$ $= \sqrt{5^2 + 9^2}$ $= \sqrt{25 + 81}$ $= \sqrt{106}$ $= 10.30$ units	Substitute the values of the respective x- and y-coordinates into the distance formula. **Note:** make sure that you include the negative sign for any negative numbers. Calculate the distance to 2 decimal places or as an exact value if and when appropriate. **Note**: the distance from point 1 to point 2 is the same as from point 2 to point 1.

Example

Suppose that the distance between two points on the Cartesian plane is 5 units. If one point has coordinates of $(5, 9)$ and the other point has coordinates of $(a, 12)$, determine the possible values of a.

✓ Solution

Working	Explanation
$5 = \sqrt{(5-a)^2 + (9-12)^2}$ $25 = (5-a)^2 + (-3)^2$ $25 = (5-a)^2 + 9$ $16 = (5-a)^2$ $5 - a = \pm 4$ $a = 1$ or 9	Substitute the given information into the distance formula. Square both sides of the equation and collect like terms. Since the square of $5 - a$ is 16, $5 - a$ will be the square root of 16, which is ± 4. Therefore $a = 5 \pm 4$.

Exercise 2.1.1

Determine the distance between the following points. Give your answers to 2 decimal places.

a. $(-10, 2)$ and $(4, 8)$

b. $(7, -3)$ and $(0, -7)$

Exercise 2.1.2

The distance between $(1, -2)$ and $(4, b)$ on the Cartesian plane is $\sqrt{73}$ units. Determine the possible values of b.

2.2 Midpoint between two points on the Cartesian plane

The diagram below shows the midpoint, $M(x_m, y_m)$, between two points on the Cartesian plane with coordinates (x_1, y_1) and (x_2, y_2).

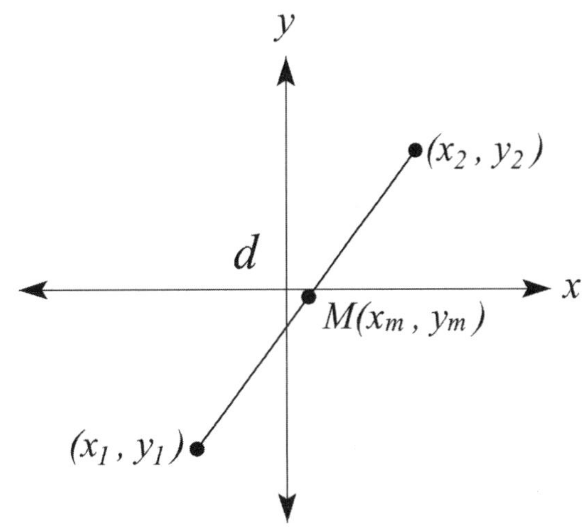

The coordinates of M are given by

$$(x_m, y_m) = \left(\frac{x_1 + x_2}{2}, \frac{y_1 + y_2}{2}\right)$$

If you know the coordinates of one point and the coordinates of the midpoint, you can rearrange the midpoint formula to find the coordinates of the unknown point.

For example:

$$(x_2, y_2) = (2x_m - x_1, 2y_m - y_1)$$

Example

Determine the coordinates of the midpoint between the following two points.

a. $(3, 4)$ and $(-5, -2)$

b. $(-3, 7)$ and $(4, -8)$

✓ Solution

Working	Explanation
a. $(x_m, y_m) = \left(\frac{3 + (-5)}{2}, \frac{4 + (-2)}{2}\right)$ $= \left(\frac{-2}{2}, \frac{2}{2}\right)$ $= (-1, 1)$	Substitute the respective coordinates in the midpoint equation and determine the coordinates of the midpoint. **Notes:** • To avoid confusion always enclose a negative number in brackets. • It is acceptable to leave the coordinates in fraction format.
b. $(x_m, y_m) = \left(\frac{(-3) + 4}{2}, \frac{7 + (-8)}{2}\right)$ $= \left(\frac{1}{2}, \frac{-1}{2}\right)$ $= \left(\frac{1}{2}, -\frac{1}{2}\right)$	

Example

Given that the coordinates of the midpoint are $(5, 2)$ and the coordinates of one of the points are $(-2, 1)$, determine the coordinates of the other point.

✓ Solution

Working	Explanation
$(x_2, y_2) = (2(5) - (-2), 2(2) - 1)$ $= (12, 3)$	Substitute the respective coordinates into the equation and determine the coordinates of the other point.

Exercise 2.2.1

Determine the coordinates of the midpoint between the following points.

a. $(2, 3)$ and $(20, -8)$

b. $(-2, -4)$ and $(-12, -8)$

Exercise 2.2.2

Given that the coordinates of the midpoint are $(1, 2)$ and the coordinates of one of the points are $(-4, -1)$, determine the coordinates of the other point.

2.3 Gradient of a straight line on the Cartesian plane

The diagram to the right shows a straight line plotted on the Cartesian plane.

Where the straight line meets the y-axis is known as the y-axis intercept (shortened to y-intercept). Where the straight line meets the x-axis is known as the x-axis intercept (shortened to x-intercept).

The general equation for a straight line is

$$y = mx + c$$

where m = the gradient of the line, and

c = the y-coordinate of the y-intercept.

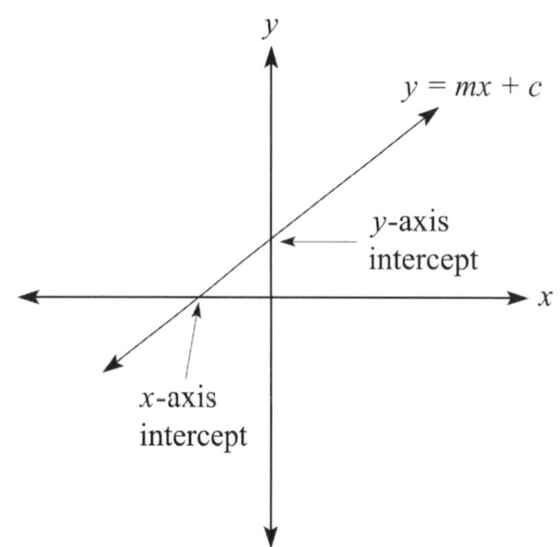

Note that $y = mx + c$ can also be written as $y = ax + b$.

The four types of gradient that a straight line can have are shown in the diagrams below. Note that the gradient is also known as the slope.

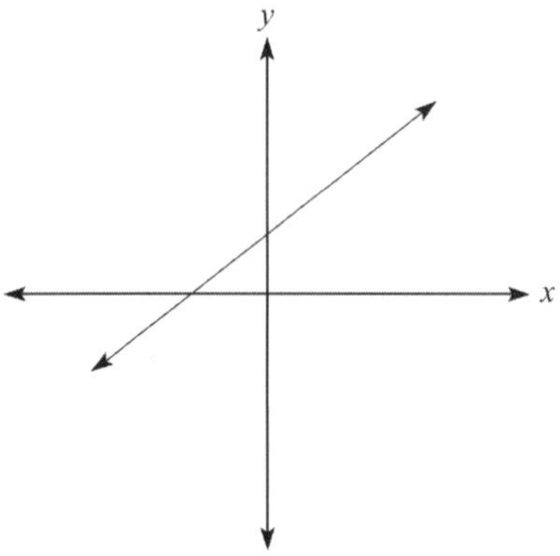

Positive gradient	Negative gradient
Horizontal line (slope = 0)	Vertical line (undefined gradient)

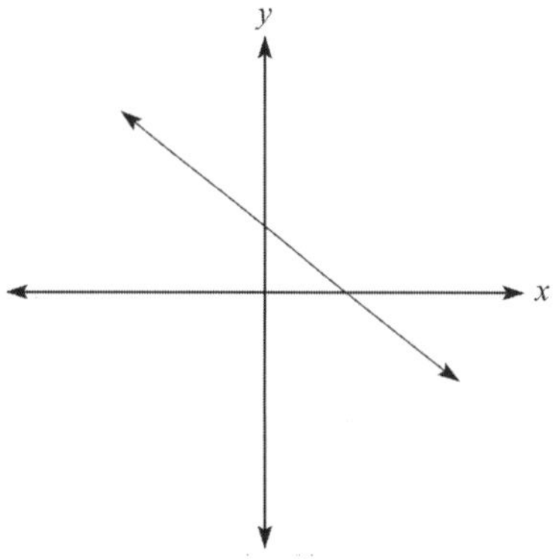

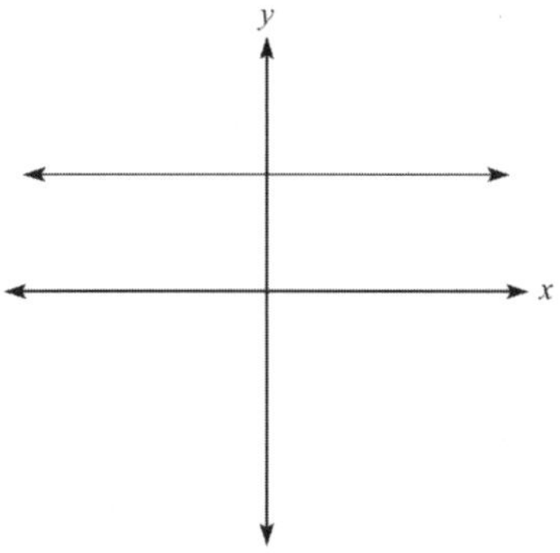

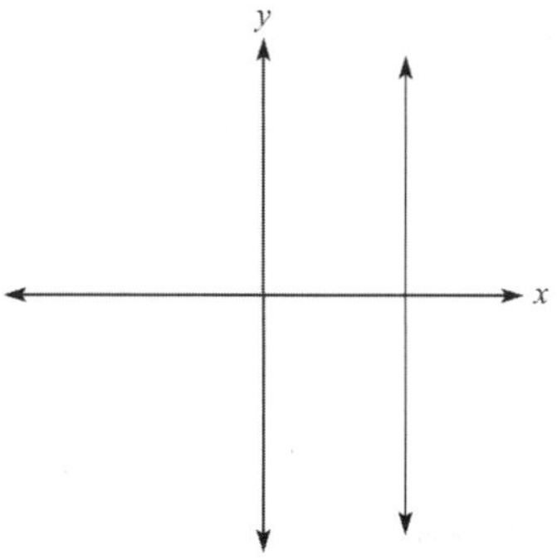

To determine the gradient of a straight line, the coordinates of two points on the line are required. Consider the diagram at the right. The gradient of the line, m, can be determined from the following formula.

$$m = \frac{rise}{run} = \frac{y_2 - y_1}{x_2 - x_1}$$

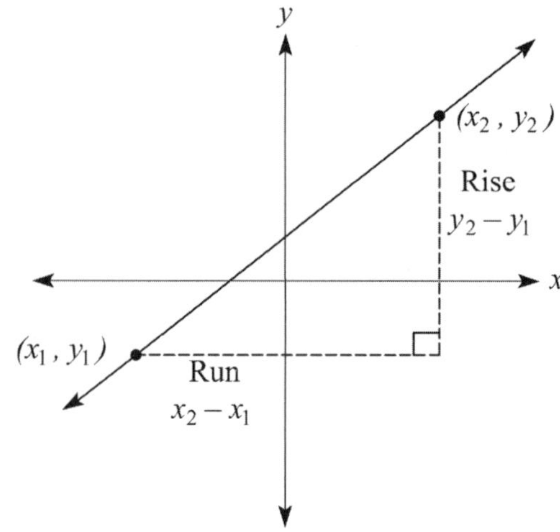

Note the following:

- For a horizontal line, the y-coordinates do not change. Therefore $y_2 - y_1 = 0$ and the gradient, m, is 0.
- For a vertical line, the x-coordinates do not change. Therefore $x_2 - x_1 = 0$ and the gradient, m, is undefined (as the denominator of the formula is 0).
- Parallel lines have the same gradient.

Instead of writing the equation of a straight line as $y = mx + c$ (the **gradient–intercept form**), the equation can also be expressed as $ax + by = d$.

This is known as the **general form**.

Example

Determine the gradient of the straight line between the following points.

a. (7, 4) and (10, 28)

b. (2, 3) and (8, −7)

✓ Solution

Working	Explanation
a. $m = \frac{28 - 4}{10 - 7} = \frac{24}{3} = 8$	Determine the rise ($y_2 - y_1$) and run ($x_2 - x_1$) and calculate the gradient.
b. $m = \frac{(-7) - 3}{8 - 2} = \frac{-10}{6} = -\frac{5}{3}$	

Example

A straight line passes through the point (2, 6) and has a gradient of $\frac{2}{3}$. Determine:

a. the x-coordinate of a point on the line with the y-coordinate of 10

b. the y-coordinate of a point on the line with the x-coordinate of −13.

✓ ***Solution***

Working	Explanation
a. $\frac{2}{3} = \frac{10-6}{x-2}$ $\frac{2}{3} = \frac{4}{x-2}$ $x - 2 = \frac{12}{2}$ $x = 8$	Substitute the gradient and the known values of the coordinates into the gradient equation. Then solve for the value of the unknown coordinate.
b. $\frac{2}{3} = \frac{y-6}{-13-2}$ $\frac{2}{3} = \frac{y-6}{-15}$ $\frac{-30}{3} = y - 6$ $y = -4$	

Exercise 2.3.1

Determine the gradient of a straight line between the following points.

a. $(4, 7)$ and $(1, 8)$

b. $(5, -2)$ and $(-2, -6)$

Exercise 2.3.2

A straight line passes through the point $(2, 3)$ and has a gradient of 4. Determine:

a. the x-coordinate of a point on the line with the y-coordinate of -1

b. the y-coordinate of a point on the line with the x-coordinate of 5.

2.4 Plotting or sketching a linear graph

Plotting involves drawing a line on a grid so that you can precisely pinpoint the points you are plotting. Sketching also refers to drawing a line, but it can be less precise. However, it still requires you to show the general form of the graph – such as the gradient – and the critical points (e.g. the x- and y-intercepts).

There are four ways of plotting or sketching a linear relationship (that is, a straight line) on the Cartesian plane:

- using a table of values
- using the y-intercept and the gradient of the line
- using two points on the line
- using the two intercepts (i.e. the Two-Intercept Method).

Example

Complete the table of values below and then plot the graph of $y = 2x + 3$.

x	-2	-1	0	1	2
y					

✓ *Solution*

<table>
<tr><th>Working</th><th>Explanation</th></tr>
<tr><td>

x	-2	-1	0	1	2
y	-1	1	3	5	7

</td><td>By substituting the values of x into the equation of the line, determine the corresponding values of y.</td></tr>
<tr><td> 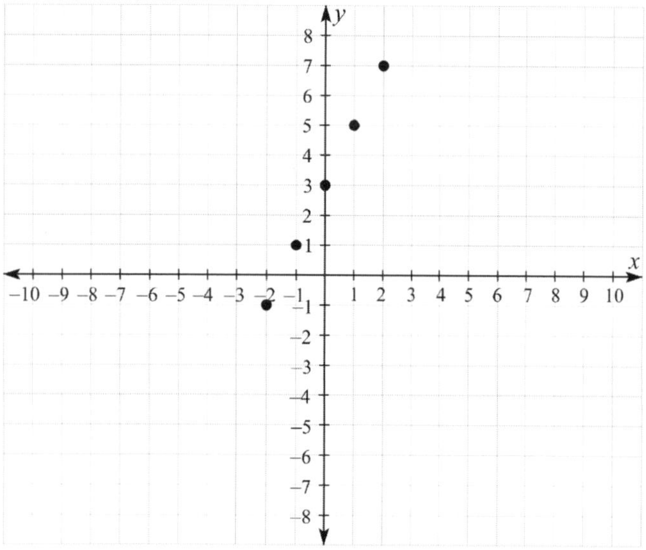

</td><td>Using a sheet of grid paper:
1. Draw the x- and y-axes, clearly labelling them.
2. Label the axes with an appropriate scale.
3. Plot the points from the table of values.</td></tr>
<tr><td> 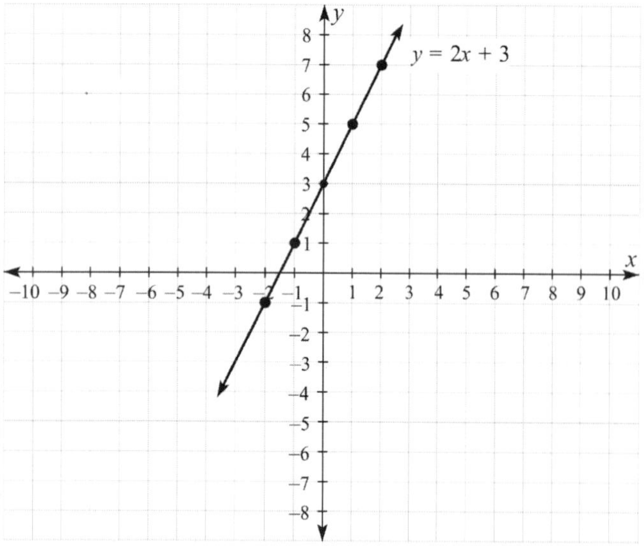

</td><td>4. Join all the points with a straight line.
5. Draw arrows at both ends of the line.
6. Add the equation of the line next to the line.</td></tr>
</table>

Example

Plot $y = -3x + 1$ using the gradient and intercept information provided by the equation.

✓ *Solution*

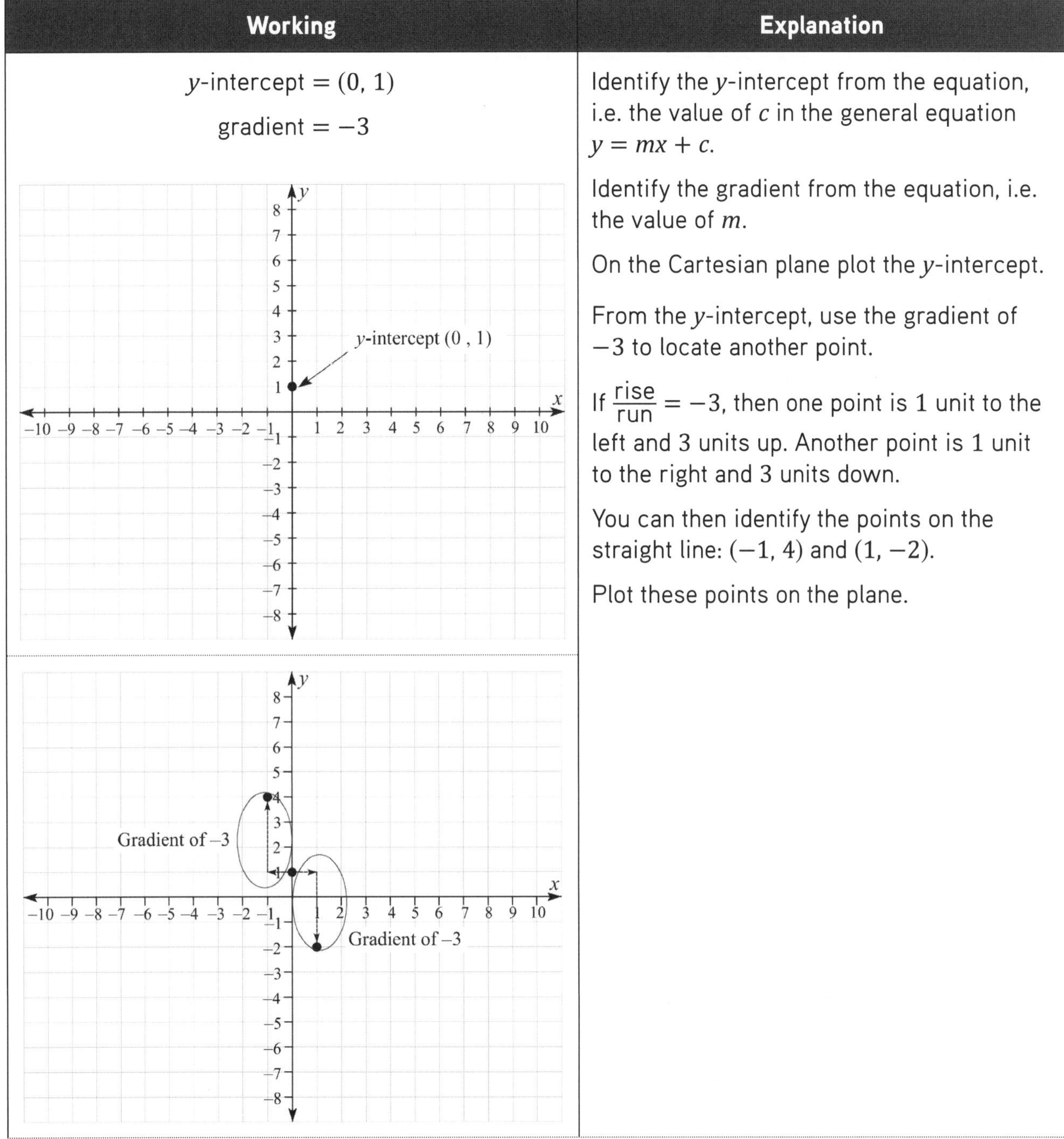

Working	Explanation
y-intercept = (0, 1) gradient = −3	Identify the y-intercept from the equation, i.e. the value of c in the general equation $y = mx + c$. Identify the gradient from the equation, i.e. the value of m. On the Cartesian plane plot the y-intercept. From the y-intercept, use the gradient of −3 to locate another point. If $\frac{\text{rise}}{\text{run}} = -3$, then one point is 1 unit to the left and 3 units up. Another point is 1 unit to the right and 3 units down. You can then identify the points on the straight line: $(-1, 4)$ and $(1, -2)$. Plot these points on the plane.

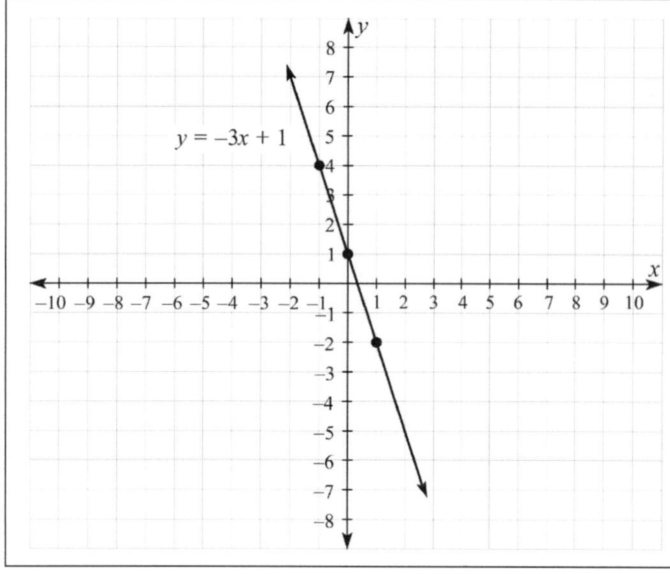	Draw a straight line between these points (which must pass through the y-intercept) and extend it in both directions. Add arrows at both ends of the line and label the line with the equation.

Example

Plot $y = -2x - 4$ by finding any two points on the line.

✓ Solution

Working	Explanation
When $x = -3$ $y = -2(-3) - 4 = 6 - 4 = 2$ Hence one of the points is $(-3, 2)$.	Pick any two values for x. Let's start with $x = -3$ and solve for y.
When $x = 2$ $y = -2(2) - 4 = -4 - 4 = -8$ Hence another point is $(2, -8)$.	Let's continue with $x = 2$ and solve for y.
(–3 , 2) • • (2 , –8)	Locate and plot the two points on the Cartesian plane.

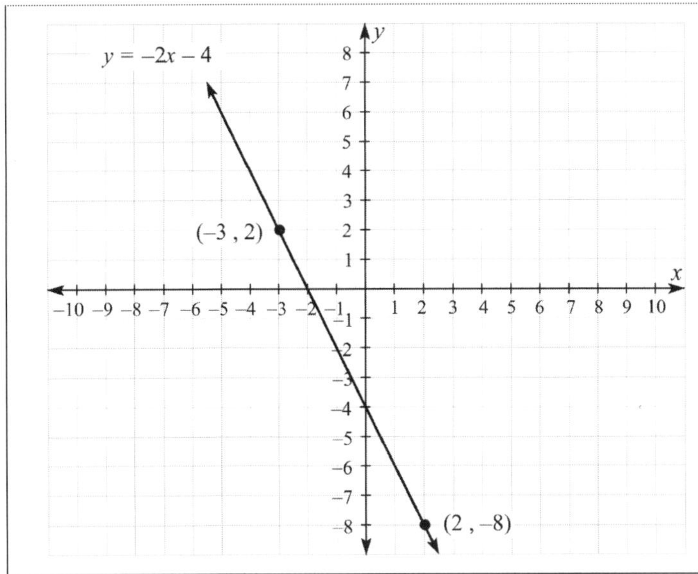

Connect the two points with a straight line. Extend the line beyond the points.

Remember to add arrows to the ends of the line and label the line with the equation.

Example

Plot $2y - x = 4$ by first determining the two intercepts.

✓ ***Solution***

Working	Explanation
Substitute $x = 0$ into the equation. $$2y - 0 = 4$$ $$y = 2$$	The y-intercept occurs when $x = 0$.
The y-intercept is $(0, 2)$.	You now have the coordinates of the y-intercept.
Substitute $y = 0$ into the equation. $$2(0) - x = 4$$ $$x = -4$$	The x-intercept occurs when $y = 0$.
The x-intercept is $(-4, 0)$.	You now have the coordinates of the x-intercept.
(−4 , 0) (0 , 2)	Locate and plot the two intercepts on the Cartesian plane.

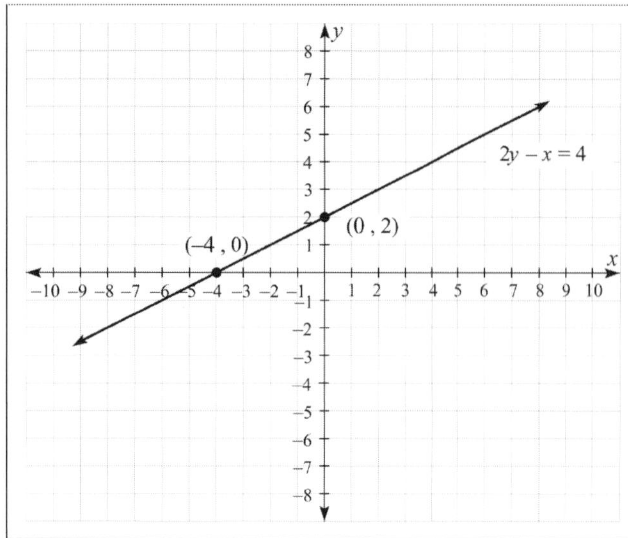

Draw a straight line through the two intercepts and extend the line. Remember to add arrows at both ends of the line and label the line with the equation.

Note: this is generally a very good method to use, especially when you are given the equation in the general form.

Exercise 2.4.1

Complete the table of values below according to the equation $y = -4x - 2$ and then plot the equation on the Cartesian plane.

x	-2	-1	0	1	2
y					

Exercise 2.4.2

Sketch the graph of $y = \frac{3x}{2} + 1$ by first identifying its gradient and the y-intercept.

Exercise 2.4.3

By substituting $x = -2$ and $x = 10$ into the linear relationship of $y = -x + 5$, determine two points on the line, then sketch a graph of the line.

Exercise 2.4.4

Determine the x- and y-intercepts of $-3y + 2x = 6$ and then sketch a graph of the equation on the Cartesian plane.

2.5 Equation of a straight line

A linear relationship is represented by a straight line on the Cartesian plane. Its equation can be written as follows.

$$y = mx + c \text{ (gradient–intercept form) or } ax + by = d \text{ (general form)}$$

To determine the equation of a straight line, we need the coordinates of two points on the line, or the y-intercept and the gradient of the line.

Example

Determine the equation of the straight line passing through the point $(0, 5)$ with a gradient of -2.

✓ ***Solution***

Working	Explanation
$c = 5$ $m = -2$	$(0, 5)$ must be the y-intercept because the y-intercept is the point where the x-coordinate is 0. Hence, we have a value for c in the equation $y = mx + c$. The gradient, m, is given as -2.
Therefore the equation is $y = -2x + 5$.	Substitute c and m into $y = mx + c$ to determine the equation.

Example

Determine the equation of the straight line passing through points $(-2, -9)$ and $(4, 18)$.

✓ ***Solution***

Working	Explanation
$m = \frac{18-(-9)}{4-(-2)} = \frac{27}{6} = \frac{9}{2}$ The equation is $y = \frac{9x}{2} + c$.	Determine the gradient of the line from the coordinates of the two points. Once the gradient is known, you can add it to the equation $y = mx + c$.
Substitute $(4, 18)$ into the equation. $18 = \frac{9(4)}{2} + c$ $18 = 18 + c$ $c = 0$ The equation is $y = \frac{9x}{2}$.	Substitute one of the points into the equation and solve for c. **Note:** you will get the same answer if you substitute the other point into the equation. Write out the equation in full. **Note:** there is no need to add $+0$ to the equation if c is 0.

Exercise 2.5.1

Determine the equation of the straight line with a gradient of -3 passing through the point $(0, 2)$.

Exercise 2.5.2

Determine the equation of the straight line that passes through the following points.

a. $(2, 3)$ and $(4, -5)$

b. $(-3, -4)$ and $(1, 8)$

2.6 Horizontal and vertical lines

The equations of horizontal and vertical lines are unique. The gradient of a horizontal line is zero and the gradient of a vertical line is undefined.

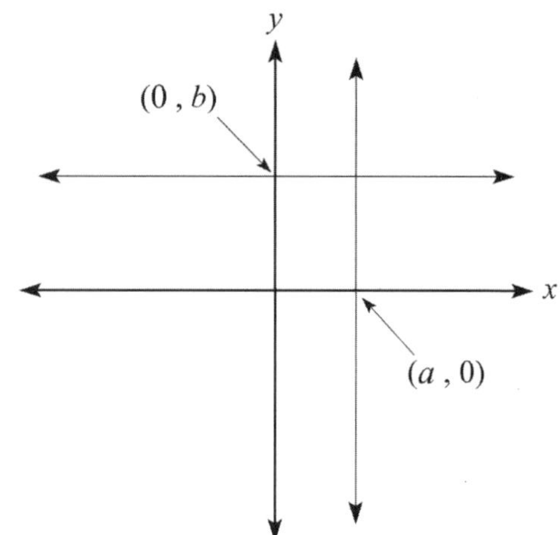

For a horizontal straight line going through a particular point (e.g. $(0, b)$ on the diagram at the right), the equation of the line is $y = b$. This is because all the y-coordinates on the line have the same value, i.e. b.

For a vertical straight line going through a particular point (e.g. $(a, 0)$ on the diagram at the right), the equation of the line is $x = a$. This is because all the x-coordinates on the line have the same value, i.e. a.

Example

a. State the equation of the vertical straight line passing through the point $(4, 5)$.

b. State the equation of the horizontal straight line passing through the point $(-2, -9)$.

✓ *Solution*

Working	Explanation
a. $x = 4$	The x-coordinates of points on this vertical line are always 4.
b. $y = -9$	The y-coordinates of points on this horizontal line are always -9.

2.7 Modelling using linear relationships

Many real-life situations can be modelled using linear relationships.

One practical example of a linear relationship is the cost of engaging an electrician.

To use $y = mx + c$ to model the cost of engaging an electrician, we can define the variables as:

y = the total cost of engaging the electrician

x = the number of hours the electrician works

m = the rate the electrician charges, in $ per hour

c = the electrician's call-out fee.

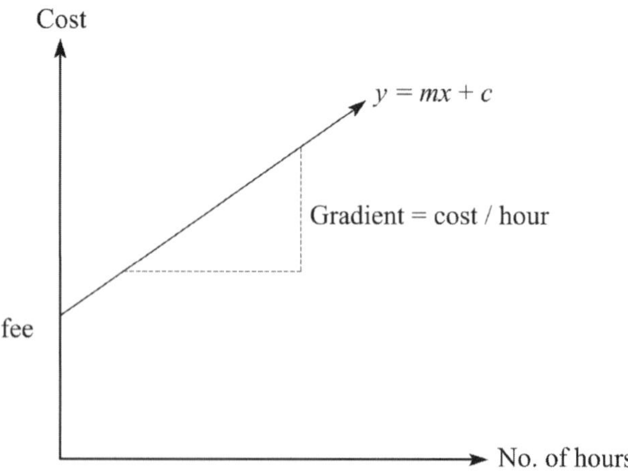

Example

Chris the Plumber charges \$40 for every 30 minutes of labour and a \$40 call-out fee. Chris' cost (b) can be modelled using a linear relationship in which t is the number of hours worked.

a. State the equation of the total cost in terms of t.

b. How much would it cost to use Chris if the plumbing job took a total of 4 hours?

c. If Brendan paid Chris \$600 for a plumbing job, how long did Chris spend on the job?

✓ Solution

Working	Explanation
a. y-intercept $= 40$ rate $= \frac{40}{0.5} = 80$/hour $b = 80t + 40$	Determine the value of the y-intercept and the rate/hour (i.e. the gradient). Substitute the values of the rate (gradient) and y-intercept into $y = mx + c$.
b. $b = 80(4) + 40 = 360$ The cost of using Chris for 4 hours is \$360.	Substitute $t = 4$ into the equation to determine the total cost for 4 hours.
c. $600 = 80t + 40$ $560 = 80t$ $t = 7$ Chris spent 7 hours on the job.	Substitute $b = 600$ into the equation to determine the number of hours Chris spent on the job.

Example

David is organising the Year 9 trip to the zoo. The cost of the trip is shown in the table below.

Number of students (n)	0	50	100	150
Total cost in \$ (c)	300	1300	2300	3300

a. Plot a graph of the total cost (c) against the number of students (n) on the axes provided at the right.

b. State the y-intercept and the cost per student.

c. Hence state the equation of the total cost (c).

d. Use the equation to determine the total cost of 120 students going on this trip.

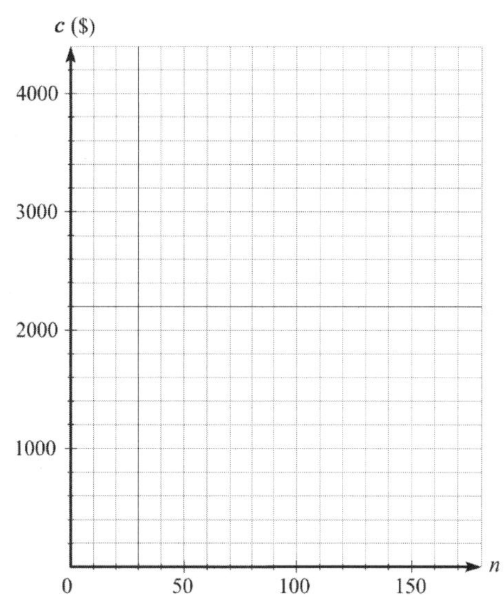

✓ *Solution*

Working	Explanation
a. 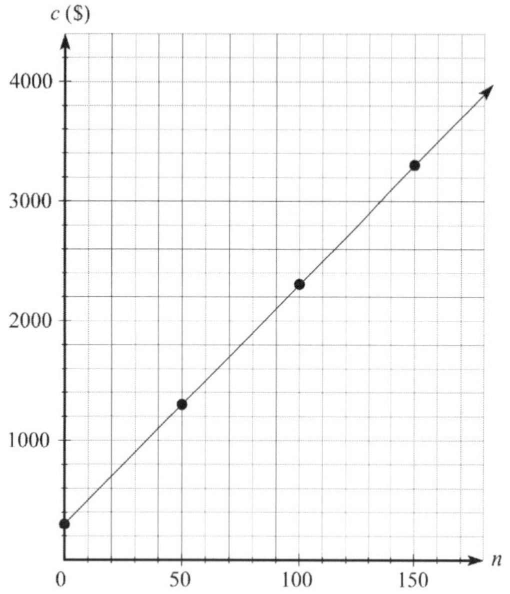	On the axes provided, plot the data given. Join the dots with a straight line.
b. y-intercept is (0, 300) Gradient $= \frac{2300 - 1300}{100 - 50} = \frac{1000}{50} = 20$ Cost per student = \$20	The y-intercept occurs when $n = 0$. To determine the cost per student, use any two points given to determine the gradient of the line. The gradient of the line is the cost/student.
c. $c = 20n + 300$	Substitute the values of the rate (gradient) and the y-intercept into $y = mx + c$.
d. $c = 20(120) + 300 = 2700$ The total cost of 120 students going on the trip is \$2700.	Substitute $n = 120$ into the equation to determine the total cost for 120 students.

Exercise 2.7.1

Star Taxi charges an initial cost (also known as the flag fall) of \$4.50 and then \$1.20 per kilometre travelled. The cost of using Star Taxi can be modelled using a linear relationship.

a. Derive the relationship between the cost (c) of using Star Taxi and the distance travelled (d).

b. Determine the cost of using Star Taxi for a distance of 20 km.

c. Mandy spent \$24.30 on her trip from her house to the airport using Star Taxi Company. Determine the distance between her house and the airport.

Exercise 2.7.2

The cost to a baker of baking up to 30 cakes is shown by the graph on the right.

a. State the fixed cost and the cost/cake.

b. Hence, or otherwise, derive a linear relationship between the cost (c) and the number of cakes baked (n).

c. Use the equation to determine the cost to the baker of baking 20 cakes.

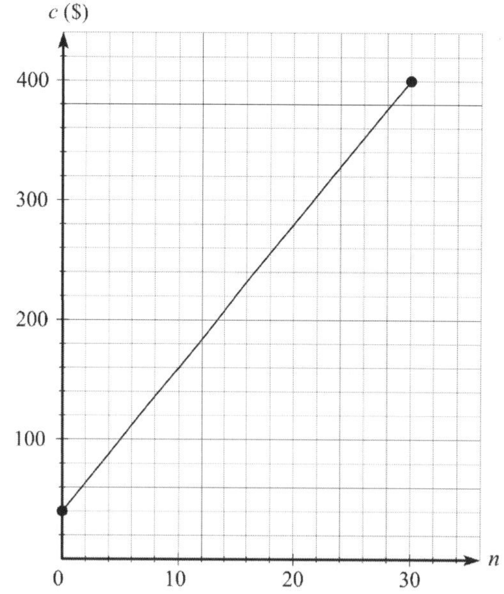

2.8 Direct proportion

Direct proportion is a linear relationship where the y-intercept is the origin: (0, 0). An example is when you work for a fixed amount per hour. The total amount you earn is directly proportional to the number of hours you work. Your hourly rate is the constant multiplier of the number of hours you work. So if your hourly rate is \$15 and you work for 10 hours, you earn $15 \times 10 = \$150$, as shown in the graph below.

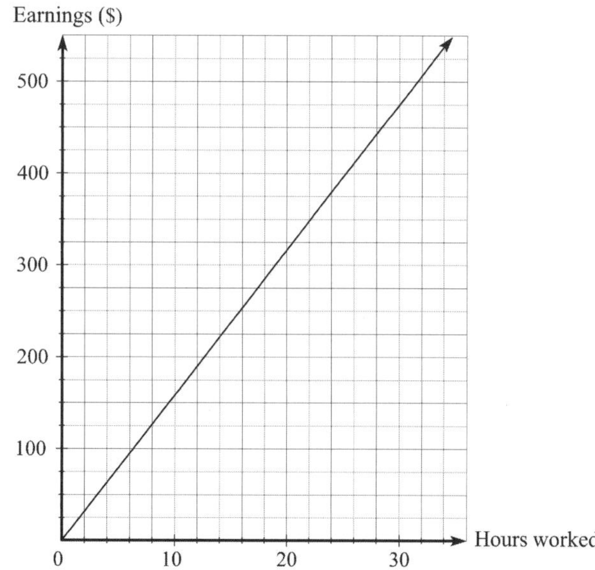

The gradient of the straight line – in this example the hourly rate – is also known as the **constant of proportionality** (k).

If y is directly proportional to x, we can express this statement mathematically as

$$y \propto x$$

where the symbol $\propto$ means 'directly proportional to'. This is known as the **statement of proportionality**.

We can write the equation as

$$y = kx$$

where k is the constant of proportionality (i.e. the gradient or rate).

Example

Marcus is renovating his house and wants to buy a particular type of carpet. He knows that the cost (C) of this type of carpet is directly proportional to the length (l). If 16 m of the carpet costs \$2400, determine:

a. the formula for C in terms of l

b. the cost of 30 m of this type of carpet.

✓ *Solution*

Working	Explanation
a. $C \propto l$	Write the statement of proportionality.
$C = kl$	Rewrite the equation to incorporate the constant of proportionality, k.
$2400 = k(16)$	Substitute $C = 2400$ and $l = 16$ into the equation to determine k.
$k = 150$	**Note:** in this case, $k = 150$ means that the carpet cost is $\$150/\text{m}$.
$C = 150l$	Write the equation relating C and l.
b. $C = 150(30) = 4500$ The cost of 30 m of this type of carpet is \$4500.	Substitute $l = 30$ into the equation to determine the cost of the carpet.

Example

Jenny is driving from Melbourne to Perth via the Nullarbor Plain. The distance (D) she travels is directly proportional to the time (t).

a. Assuming that she travels at a constant speed, determine the equation relating D and t given that she travelled 225 km in 2 hours and 15 minutes.

b. Jenny would like to stay overnight in Adelaide, which is 725 km from Melbourne. How long will it take Jenny to drive to Adelaide if she stops for an hour on the way to have lunch?

✓ ***Solution***

Working	Explanation
a. $D \propto t$	Write the statement of proportionality.
$D = kt$	Rewrite the equation to incorporate k.
$225 = k(2.25)$	Substitute $D = 225$ and $t = 2.25$ into the equation to determine k.
$k = 100$	**Note:**
$D = 100t$	1. The time has been converted from 2 hours 15 minutes to 2.25 hours. 2. In this case, $k = 100$ means that Jenny's speed is 100 km/h. Write the equation relating D and t.
b. $725 = 100t$ $t = 7.25$	Substitute $D = 725$ into the equation to determine the driving time. The driving time is 7.25 hours (i.e. 7 hours and 15 minutes).
It would take Jenny 8 hours and 15 minutes to get to Adelaide.	Add the 1 hour of stopping time to the driving time.

Exercise 2.8.1

Mary works part-time in a restaurant. She is paid based on the number of hours she works. When she worked 9 hours last week, she earned \$193.50.

a. Determine the equation that relates the amount Mary earns (A) to the number of hours (H) she works.

b. How much will Mary earn if she works 20 hours this week?

c. In the last two weeks of February, Mary earned \$1204. How many hours did she work during this period?

Exercise 2.8.2

Matthew is designing an electrical circuit that uses the power supply from his home. He knows that the voltage (V) is directly proportional to the resistance (R). He also knows that when the voltage is 120 volts, the resistance is 40 ohms. The maximum voltage for Australia is 240V.

a. Determine the equation that relates V and R.

b. Determine the resistance of the circuit when $V = 180$.

c. Determine the voltage of the circuit if the resistance is 200 ohms. Is this situation possible? Justify your answer.

2.9 Transformation of $y = x$ to $y = ax + b$

In this section we consider the following transformations of a straight line (either by themselves or in combination with other transformations):

- vertical translation – moving the straight line up or down the y-axis
- dilation – changing the gradient of the straight line
- reflection about the x-axis.

Vertical translation

When the straight line $y = x$ is transformed to $y = x \pm b$, the right-hand side of the equation, $\pm b$, indicates how far the line is translated (i.e. moved) up or down the y-axis.

Consider the diagram below where three straight lines are plotted.

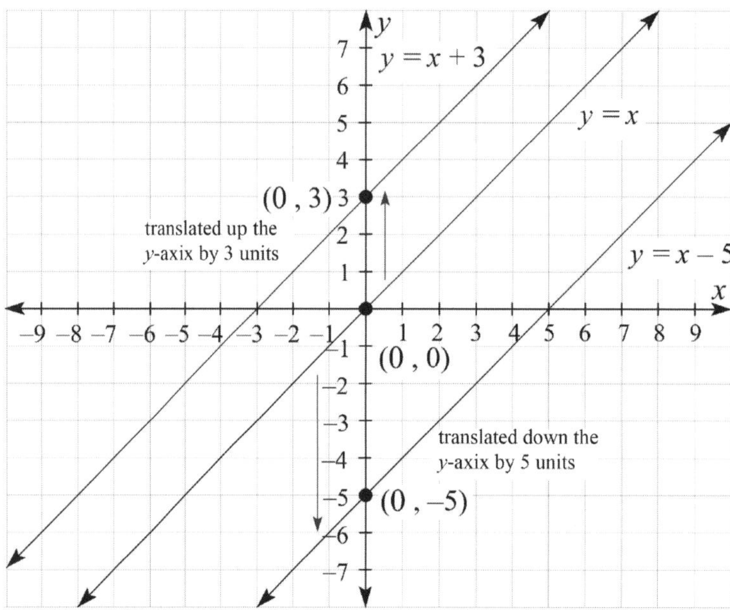

In a transformation from $y = x \rightarrow y = x + 3$, the line is translated up the y-axis by 3 units.

In a transformation from $y = x \rightarrow y = x - 5$, the line is translated down the y-axis by 5 units.

Dilation

When the straight line $y = x$ is transformed to $y = ax$, the line is dilated by multiplying the x-coordinates by $\frac{1}{a}$.

Consider the diagram below where three straight lines are plotted.

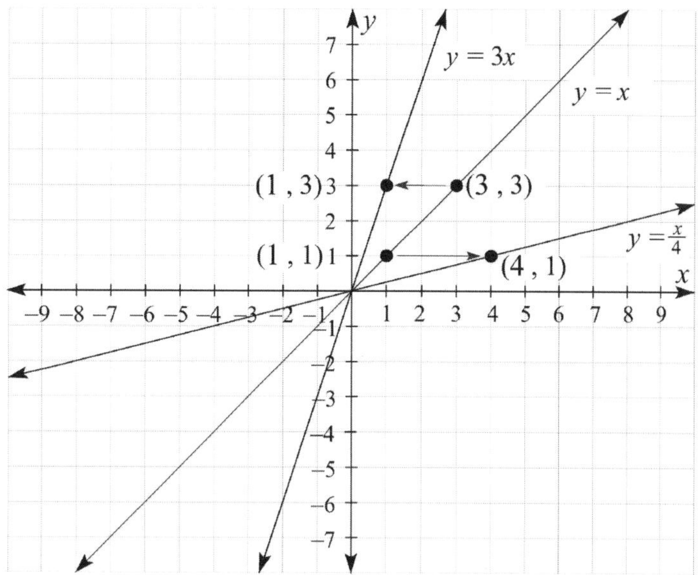

In the transformation from $y = x \rightarrow y = 3x$, the line is dilated by multiplying all the x-coordinates by $\frac{1}{3}$. Taking point (3, 3) as an example, the dilation has transformed the point to (1, 3) and the gradient is steeper.

In the transformation from $y = x \rightarrow y = \frac{x}{4}$, the line is dilated by multiplying all the x-coordinates by 4. Taking point (1, 1) as an example, the dilation has transformed the point to (4, 1) and the gradient is flatter.

Reflection

When the straight line $y = x$ is transformed to $y = -x$, the negative sign indicates that we need to multiply all the y-coordinates by -1. This means that all the y-coordinates will be reflected about the x-axis.

This is shown in the diagram below.

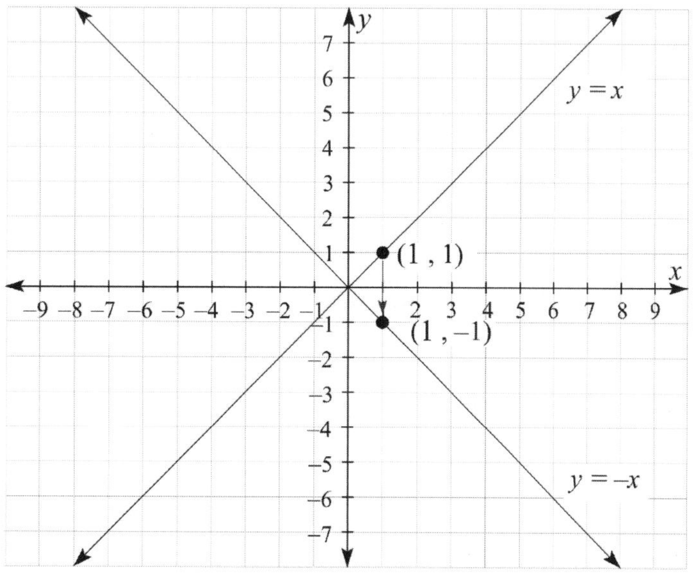

Combining transformations

When transforming $y = x \rightarrow y = ax + b$, always follow these steps:

1. Multiply the x coordinates by $\frac{1}{a}$ to determine the new x-coordinates. [DILATION]
2. If a is negative, reflect the straight line about the x-axis. [REFLECTION]
3. Move the line up and down the y-axis by b units. [TRANSLATION]

Consider the following three lines.

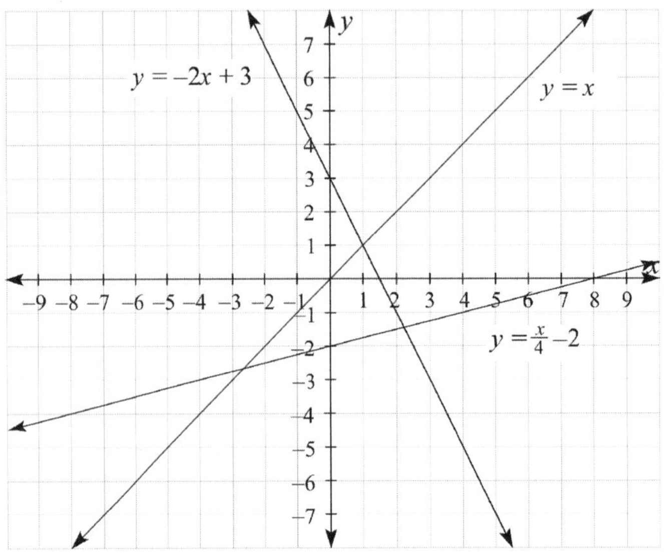

To transform $y = x \rightarrow y = -2x + 3$:

1. Dilate the line by multiplying all the x-coordinates by $\frac{1}{2}$.
2. Reflect the line about the x-axis.
3. Translate the line up by 3 units.

To transform $y = x \rightarrow y = \frac{x}{4} - 2$:

1. Dilate the line by multiplying all the x-coordinates by 4.
2. No reflection is required.
3. Translate the line down by 2 units.

Exercise 2.9.1

Describe the steps required to transform $y = x \rightarrow y = -\frac{2x}{3} + 2$.

Exercise 2.9.2

Describe the steps required to transform $y = x \rightarrow y = 4x - 5$.

Exercise 2.9.3

Describe the steps required to transform $y = x \rightarrow y = 2x + 4$.

Answers

Exercise 2.1.1

a. 15.23 units

b. 8.06 units

Exercise 2.1.2

6 and -10

Exercise 2.2.1

a. $\left(11, -\frac{5}{2}\right)$

b. $(-7, -6)$

Exercise 2.2.2

$(6, 5)$

Exercise 2.3.1

a. $-\frac{1}{3}$

b. $\frac{4}{7}$

Exercise 2.3.2

a. $x = 1$

b. $y = 15$

Exercise 2.4.1

x	-2	-1	0	1	2
y	6	2	-2	-6	-10

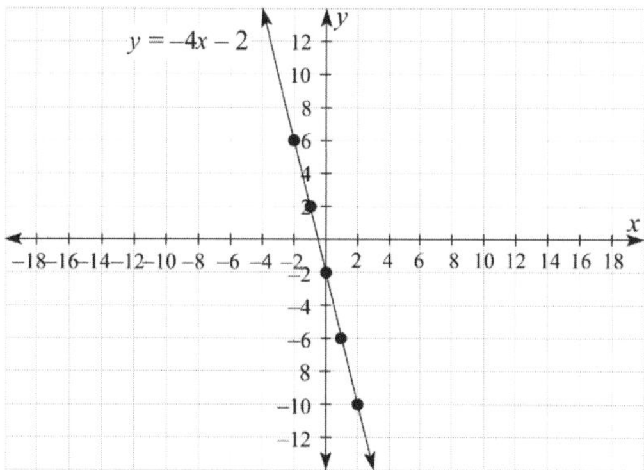

Exercise 2.4.2

$m = \frac{3}{2}$, y-intercept $= (0, 1)$

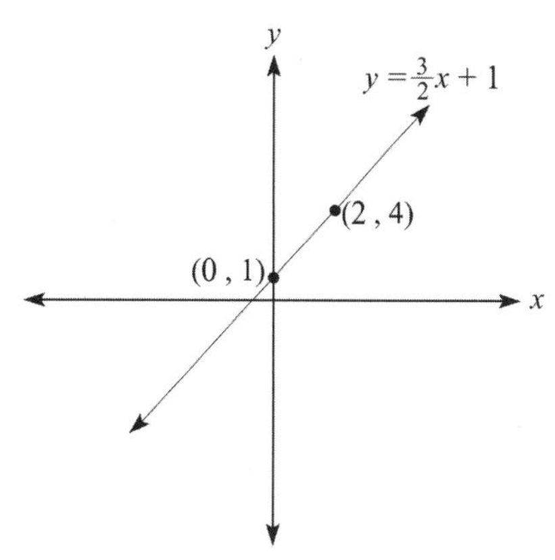

Exercise 2.4.3

$(-2, 7)$, $(10, -5)$

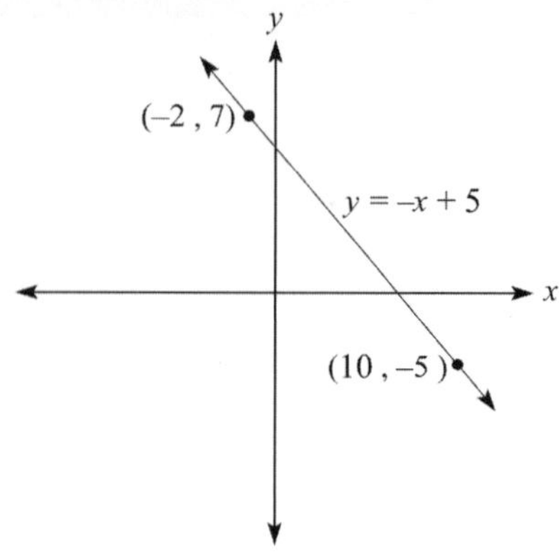

Exercise 2.4.4

y-intercept $= (0, -2)$, x-intercept $= (3, 0)$

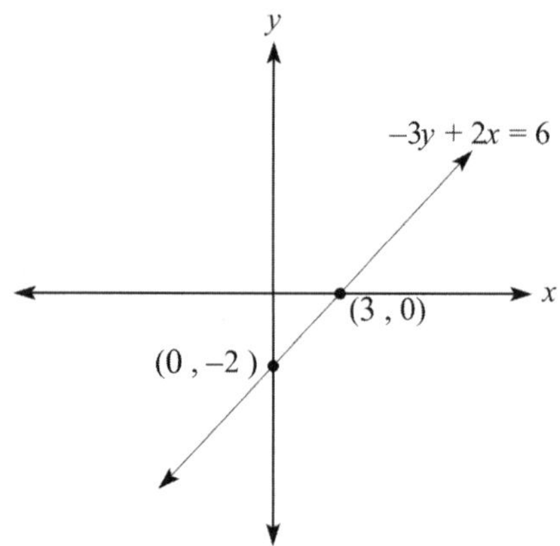

Exercise 2.5.1

$y = -3x + 2$

Exercise 2.5.2

a. $y = -4x + 11$

b. $y = 3x + 5$

Exercise 2.7.1

a. $c = 1.2d + 4.5$

b. $28.50

c. 16.5 km

Exercise 2.7.2

a. Fixed cost = $40
Cost/cake = $12

b. $c = 12n + 40$

c. $280

Exercise 2.8.1

a. $A = 21.5H$

b. $430

c. 56 hours

Exercise 2.8.2

a. $V = 3R$

b. 60 ohms

c. $V = 600$ volts.

This situation is not possible because in Australia electricity runs on 240 volts.

Exercise 2.9.1

Multiply the x-coordinates by $\frac{3}{2}$. Reflect the line about the x-axis.

Translate the line up by 2 units.

Exercise 2.9.2

Multiply the x-coordinates by $\frac{1}{4}$. Translate the line down by 5 units.

Exercise 2.9.3

Multiply the x-coordinates by $\frac{1}{2}$. Translate the line up by 4 units.

Chapter 3 – Algebraic techniques

3.1 Key concepts of algebra

The following is an example of an algebraic expression.

$$8x^2 - \frac{xy}{4} - 13$$

- It has three terms: $8x^2$, $-\frac{xy}{4}$ and -13.
- x and y are known as the **pronumerals** or **variables**. They can take any value.
- -13 is the **constant** term.
- 8 is the **coefficient** of x^2 while $-\frac{1}{4}$ is the **coefficient** of xy.
- Some terms are a combination of a number and one or more pronumerals. These are linked together by arithmetic signs (such as the signs for multiplication, division, addition or subtraction).

An expression is different from an equation.

Expression

$$x - 2$$

- There is no equals sign.
- x can take any value.

Equation

$$x = 2$$

- There is an equals sign.
- x can only be one value: 2 in this case.

Example

Consider the expression $-\frac{xy}{5} + 6x - 8y^2 + 2$. State:

a. the number of terms

b. the constant term

c. the pronumerals

d. the coefficients of xy and y^2.

✓ *Solution*

Working	Explanation
a. There are 4 terms.	The terms are: $-\frac{xy}{5}$, $+6x$, $-8y^2$and $+2$.
b. $+2$	The constant term is the only term without any pronumeral.
c. x and y	These are the only two variables in this expression. (**Note:** xy is not a pronumeral. It is a combination of pronumerals, in this case the product of x and y.)
d. xy: $-\frac{1}{5}$ y^2: -8	xy is multiplied by $-\frac{1}{5}$ y^2 is multiplied by -8

We can evaluate an expression if we are given the values of its pronumerals.

Example

Evaluate the expression $y + 2x - 3$ if $y = 4$ and $x = -2$.

✓ ***Solution***

Working	Explanation
$y + 2x - 3 = 4 + 2(-2) - 3$ $= 4 - 4 - 3$ $= -3$	Substitute $y = 4$ and $x = -2$ into the expression to evaluate it.

Like terms

Like terms are terms with the same pronumeral and same **index**.

Like terms can be added and subtracted. This is called **collecting like terms**.

Examples

Simplify the following expressions by collecting like terms.

a. $5a + 7a$ **b.** $12x^2y - 16x^2y$ **c.** $4gh^2 + 3h^2g$ **d.** $\frac{2x}{7} + \frac{5x}{3}$

✓ ***Solution***

Working	Explanation
a. $5a + 7a = 12a$	Add the coefficients of a.
b. $12x^2y - 16x^2y = -4x^2y$	Subtract the coefficients of x^2y.
c. $4gh^2 + 3h^2g = 4gh^2 + 3gh^2$ $= 7gh^2$	gh^2 is the same as h^2g. Therefore the coefficients can be added.
d. $\frac{2x}{7} + \frac{5x}{3} = \frac{2x}{7}\left(\frac{3}{3}\right) + \frac{5x}{3}\left(\frac{7}{7}\right)$ $= \frac{6x + 35x}{21}$ $= \frac{41x}{21}$	For both addition and subtraction, first give both terms the same denominator by multiplying each term by a fraction that equates to 1.

When writing an expression or equation, the multiplication and division symbols (× and ÷) are not usually shown, as in the examples below.

$$(4 \times a \times b) \times (2 \times a) = 4ab \times 2a = 8a^2b$$

$$12m^2n \div 4mn = \frac{12m^2n}{4mn} = 3m$$

Exercise 3.1.1

Consider the expression $xy - 4x^2 + \frac{y}{3} - 4$.

a. State the number of terms.

b. State the coefficients of xy and x^2.

c. State the constant term.

d. Evaluate the expression if $x = -2$ and $y = 3$.

Exercise 3.1.2

Simplify the following expressions where possible.

a. $4b - 2ab + 2ba - 3b$

b. $x^2 - 2x + 4$

c. $\frac{x}{2} - 2 + 4x - 3$

d. $4t - \frac{t}{6}$

e. $5x^3 - 4x^2 - 6x^3$

f. $\frac{4xy^2}{9} \times \frac{3}{2xy}$

g. $\frac{4x}{3} \div \frac{2x}{15}$

h. $\frac{6a}{7b} \div \frac{3ab}{4} \times \frac{a}{3}$

3.2 The distributive law

This distributive law is used to expand and remove brackets. Whatever pronumerals (or numbers) are outside the brackets multiply all the pronumerals (or numbers) inside the brackets.

$h(a + b) = ah + bh$	$h(a - b) = ah - bh$
$-h(a + b) = -ah - bh$	$-h(a - b) = -ah + bh$

Example

Expand the following expressions by using the distributive law.

a. $5(a + 4b)$

b. $y(12 - x)$

c. $-4(g + 3h)$

d. $-\frac{2}{3}\left(-3x + \frac{9}{4}\right)$

e. $2a(4a - 3a^2 + 7)$

f. $6t(2t + 1) - 4t$

✓ ***Solution***

Working	Explanation
a. $5(a+4b)=5a+20b$	
b. $y(12-x)=12y-xy$	
c. $-4(g+3h)=-4g-12h$	Multiply the pronumeral (or number) outside the brackets by each of the pronumerals (or numbers) inside the brackets.
d. $-\frac{2}{3}\left(-3x+\frac{9}{4}\right)=2x-\frac{3}{2}$	
e. $2a(4a-3a^2+7)=8a^2-6a^3+14a$	Collect like terms where possible.
f. $6t(2t+1)-4t=12t^2+6t-4t$ $=12t^2+2t$	

Exercise 3.2

Expand the following expressions using the distributive law.

a. $2(x+4)$ **b.** $4(d-3)$ **c.** $-3(4-r)$

d. $5(a+1)+a$ **e.** $-\frac{1}{3}(x-6)$ **f.** $-3y(y-2x)$

g. $2x(x-2y)$ **h.** $5(a+1)-2(a-4)$

3.3 Binomial expansion

A binomial expression is an expression with two terms, e.g. $(x+3)$. We can multiply two or more binomial expressions and use the distributive law to expand the product.

Consider the two binomial expressions $(x+3)$ and $(x+5)$.

The multiplication of the two expressions can be written as $(x+3)(x+5)$.

Using the distributive law and expanding, the product can be written as

$$\begin{aligned}(x+3)(x+5) &= x(x+5)+3(x+5)\\ &= (x^2+5x)+(3x+15)\\ &= x^2+8x+15\end{aligned}$$

The **FOIL** method is useful for doing binomial expansions:

- **F**irst: multiply the first terms in each binomial.
- **O**utermost: next multiply the two outermost terms.
- **I**nnermost: now multiply the two innermost terms.
- **L**ast: finally, multiply the second terms in each binomial.

The generalised binomial expansion can be represented graphically, as shown.

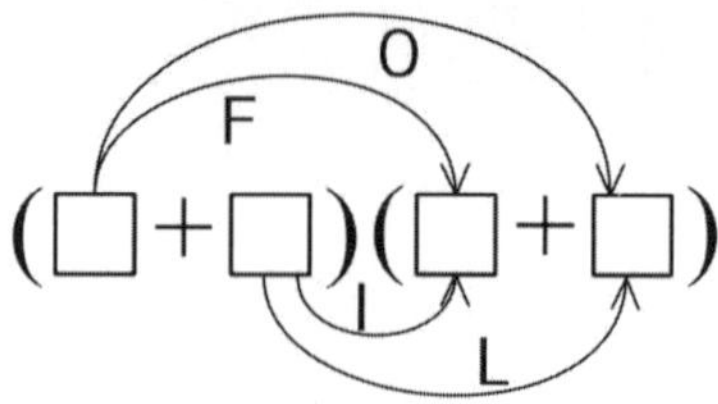

Examples

Expand the following binomial products.

a. $(4a + 3)(a - 12)$ b. $(2 - c)(4c + 2)$ c. $(x - 2)(x - 6)$

d. $(a + 3)^2$ e. $(x + 6)(x - 6)$

✓ *Solutions*

<table>
<tr><th>Working</th><th>Explanation</th></tr>
<tr><td>a. $(4a + 3)(a - 12)$
$= (4a \times a) + (4a \times (-12)) + (3 \times a) + (3 \times -12)$
$= 4a^2 - 48a + 3a - 36$
$= 4a^2 - 45a - 36$</td><td rowspan="3">Using the FOIL method:
• multiply both first terms (F)
• multiply the first term of the first binomial expression by the last term of the second binomial expression (O)
• multiply the second term of the first binomial expression by the first term of the second binomial expression (I)
• multiply both second terms (L).
Collect like terms.</td></tr>
<tr><td>b. $(2 - c)(4c + 2)$
$= (2 \times 4c) + (2 \times 2) + ((-c) \times 4c) + ((-c) \times 2)$
$= 8c + 4 - 4c^2 - 2c$
$= -4c^2 + 6c + 4$</td></tr>
<tr><td>c. $(x - 2)(x - 6)$
$= (x \times x) + (x \times (-6)) + ((-2) \times x) + (-2) \times (-6)$
$= x^2 - 6x - 2x + 12$
$= x^2 - 8x + 12$</td></tr>
<tr><td>d. $(a + 3)^2 = (a + 3)(a + 3)$
$= (a \times a) + (a \times 3) + (3 \times a) + (3 \times 3)$
$= a^2 + 6a + 9$</td><td>Note: the result of multiplying two identical binomial expressions (as shown in this example) is called a perfect square.</td></tr>
<tr><td>e. $(x + 6)(x - 6)$
$= (x \times x) + (x \times (-6)) + (6 \times x) + (6 \times (-6))$
$= x^2 - 36$</td><td>Note: the resulting expression in this example is called a difference of two squares (DOTS). Each term is a square number.</td></tr>
</table>

Note: you must always take the sign of the term into account when multiplying terms.

Exercise 3.3

Expand the following expressions.

a. $(x + 4)(2x - 2)$ b. $(3k - 2)(k + 4)$ c. $(n + 7)(n - 7)$
d. $(2a - 3)^2$ e. $(5 + r)(5 + r)$ f. $(3k + 2)(3k - 2)$
g. $(f + 2)(3 - f)$ h. $(4y + 1)(4y - 1)$ i. $(3e - 2)(e - 4)$

3.4 Factorising

Factorising is the process of rewriting an expression as the product of its factors. In the previous section, we explored how to expand expressions. To factorise an expanded expression is simply to find the expressions that were multiplied together to form it.

Factorised Form		Expanded Form
$2(x + 5)$	=	$2x + 10$
$(x + 2)(x + 5)$	=	$x^2 + 7x + 10$

In this section we will consider the following factorisation topics:

- factorising by taking out the highest common factor (HCF)
- factorising by grouping
- factorising monic quadratic expressions
- factorising perfect squares
- factorising a difference of two squares (DOTS).

Factorising by taking out the highest common factor (HCF)

With this method of factorising, you need to identify the highest common factor (HCF) of all the terms in the expression. This is the largest number and/or pronumeral that can divide into each term without leaving a remainder. You make the HCF one factor and the other factor is what you get when you divide the original expression by the HCF.

Example

Factorise the following expressions by determining the HCF and making it a factor.

a. $2x + 10$ b. $3x^2 + 6x$ c. $4xy + 8y^2 - 2y$

✓ ***Solution***

Working	Explanation
a. $2x + 10 = 2\left(\frac{2x}{2} + \frac{10}{2}\right)$ $= 2(x + 5)$	Identify the HCF, which is 2. Rewrite the expression as shown. The HCF is outside the brackets and each term in the expression is divided by the HCF. Simplify the expression.
b. $3x^2 + 6x = 3x\left(\frac{3x^2}{3x} + \frac{6x}{3x}\right)$ $= 3x(x + 2)$	Identify the HCF, which is $3x$. Rewrite the expression as shown. The HCF is outside the brackets and each term in the expression is divided by the HCF. Simplify the expression.
c. $4xy + 8y^2 - 2y = 2y\left(\frac{4xy}{2y} + \frac{8y^2}{2y} - \frac{2y}{2y}\right)$ $= 2y(2x + 4y - 1)$	Identify the HCF, which is $2y$. Rewrite the expression as shown. The HCF is outside the brackets and each term in the expression is divided by the HCF. Simplify the expression.

Note: step 2 can be skipped once you are familiar with this factorisation technique.

Factorising by grouping

When an algebraic expression has many terms and there is no factor common to all of them, you may be able to group terms that do share a HCF and then factorise each group.

Example

Factorise the following expressions by grouping.

a. $3ax + 12x - a - 4$ **b.** $gh - 6 + 2g - 3h$

✓ ***Solution***

Working	Explanation
a. $3ax + 12x - a - 4 = 3ax - a + 12x - 4$ $= a(3x - 1) + 4(3x - 1)$ $= (a + 4)(3x - 1)$	By rearranging the terms of the expression, you can easily see that there are groups of terms that share a HCF. One group has a HCF of a and the other has a HCF of 4. Factorise by taking out the HCF $(3x - 1)$ from each group, leaving two factorised expressions: $(a + 4)$ and $(3x - 1)$.

Alternative method $3ax + 12x - a - 4 = 3x(a + 4) - 1(a + 4)$ $= (3x - 1)(a + 4)$	Look for the HCF of consecutive terms without rearranging the expression. **Note:** • the first and second terms have a HCF of $3x$ • the third and fourth terms have a HCF of -1. Factorise by taking out each HCF and then simplify.
b. $gh - 6 + 2g - 3h = gh + 2g - 3h - 6$ $= g(h + 2) - 3(h + 2)$ $= (g - 3)(h + 2)$	Rearrange the terms so that there are two groups, one with a HCF of g and the other with a HCF of -3. Factorise by taking out the HCF from each group, leaving two factorised expressions: $(g - 3)$ and $(h + 2)$.
Alternative method $gh - 6 + 2g - 3h = gh - 3h + 2g - 6$ $= h(g - 3) + 2(g - 3)$ $= (h + 2)(g - 3)$	Rearrange the terms so that there are two groups, one with a HCF of h and the other with a HCF of 2. Factorise by taking out the HCF from each group, leaving two factorised expressions: $(g - 3)$ and $(h + 2)$.

Factorising monic quadratic expressions

The product of two linear binomial expressions is a quadratic expression. It is usually written as

$$\boldsymbol{ax^2 + bx + c}$$

where a, b and c are any real numbers. When $a = 1$, we have a **monic quadratic expression**: $x^2 + bx + c$.

Note from our discussion on binomial expansion that

$$\boldsymbol{(x + p)(x + q) = x^2 + (p + q)x + pq}$$

This can be rewritten as

$$\boldsymbol{x^2 + (p + q)x + pq = x^2 + bx + c}$$

From this we can conclude that to factorise a monic quadratic expression, we need to look for two numbers (p and q) such that

$$\boldsymbol{p + q = b \text{ (the coefficient of } x)}$$

and

$$\boldsymbol{pq = c \text{ (the constant term)}}$$

The important consideration in factorising a monic quadratic expression is the factors of the constant term. Always start by determining these factors.

Note: in Year 9 we are not concerned with factorising non-monic quadratic expressions except where a non-monic quadratic can be factorised by first taking out the HCF.

Example

Factorise the following expressions.

a. $x^2 + 7x + 12$ b. $x^2 + 4x - 12$ c. $x^2 - 3x - 18$

d. $x^2 - 6x + 8$ e. $2x^2 - 14x + 24$ f. $-x^2 - 8x - 7$

✓ ***Solution***

Working	Explanation
a. $x^2 + 7x + 12 = (x + 4)(x + 3)$	Start by looking for factors of the constant term: 12. The possible factors are: • ± 1 and ± 12 • ± 2 and ± 6 • ± 3 and ± 4. In this case, the negative factors can be ignored because both the coefficient of x and the constant term are positive numbers. Hence, we only have three pairs of numbers to consider, all positive. Now look for pairs that add up to the coefficient of the x term: 7. From the three pairs, only $3 + 4 = 7$. Hence the factors are $(x + 3)$ and $(x + 4)$.
b. $x^2 + 4x - 12 = (x + 6)(x - 2)$	The possible factors of -12 are: • ± 1 and ∓ 12 • ± 2 and ∓ 6 • ± 3 and ∓ 4. From the six pairs, only $+6 + (-2) = 4$. Hence the factors are $(x + 6)$ and $(x - 2)$.
c. $x^2 - 3x - 18 = (x - 6)(x + 3)$	The possible factors of -18 are: • ± 1 and ∓ 18 • ± 2 and ∓ 9 • ± 3 and ∓ 6. From the six pairs, only $-6 + 3 = -3$. Hence the factors are $(x - 6)$ and $(x + 3)$.

d. $x^2 - 6x + 8 = (x - 4)(x - 2)$	The possible factors of +8 are: • ±1 and ±8 • ±2 and ±4. From the four pairs, only $-4 + (-2) = -6$. Hence the factors are $(x - 4)$ and $(x - 2)$.
e. $2x^2 - 14x + 24 = 2(x^2 - 7x + 12)$ $= 2(x - 3)(x - 4)$	Identify the HCF, which is 2, and rewrite the expression. The possible factors of +12 are: • ±1 and ±12 • ±3 and ±4 • ±2 and ±6. From the six pairs, only $-3 + (-4) = -7$. Hence the factors are 2, $(x - 3)$ and $(x - 4)$.
f. $-x^2 - 8x - 7 = -(x^2 + 8x + 7)$ $= -(x + 1)(x + 7)$	Identify the HCF, which is −1, and rewrite the expression. The only possible factors of +7 are ±1 and ±7. From the two pairs, only $1 + 7 = 8$. Hence the factors are −1, $(x + 1)$ and $(x + 7)$.

Note: the order of the linear binomial terms is not important. The signs (positive or negative) are important.

Factorising perfect squares

A perfect square is the result of multiplying two identical binomial expressions. Here are two examples.

$$(x + a)(x + a) = x^2 + 2ax + a^2$$

$$(x - a)(x - a) = x^2 - 2ax + a^2$$

In factorising perfect squares, it is important to recognise that the constant term (a^2) is a square number (e.g. 4, 9, 16 etc.) and the coefficient of x, ($2a$), is double the square root of the constant term.

Example

Factorise the following expressions.

a. $x^2 + 2x + 1$ **b.** $x^2 - 6x + 9$ **c.** $4x^2 + 32x + 64$

✓ Solution

Working	Explanation
a. $x^2 + 2x + 1 = (x + 1)(x + 1)$ $= (x + 1)^2$	Recognise that 1 is 1^2 and $2 = 2 \times 1$. Hence the expression can be factorised as a perfect square.
b. $x^2 - 6x + 9 = (x - 3)(x - 3)$ $= (x - 3)^2$	Recognise that 9 is 3^2 and $6 = 2 \times 3$. Hence the expression can he factorised as a perfect square.
c. $4x^2 + 32x + 64 = 4(x^2 + 8x + 16)$ $= 4(x + 4)(x + 4)$ $= 4(x + 4)^2$	Recognise that each term has a HCF: 4. First factorise by taking out the HCF. Now note that 16 is 4 and $6 = 2 \times 4$. Hence the bracketed expression can be factorised as a perfect square.

Factorising a difference of two squares

A difference of two squares (DOTS) is one square number minus another square number. Its general form is $x^2 - a^2$. Notice from the example below that a DOTS can be factorised by first taking the square root of each of its terms. The constant in one factor will be **plus** the square root of the constant term and the other factor will be **minus** the square root of the constant term.

$$\mathbf{x^2 - a^2 = (x + a)(x - a)}$$

Example

Factorise the following expressions.

a. $x^2 - 49$

b. $25x^2 - 16$

✓ Solution

Working	Explanation
a. $x^2 - 49 = (x - 7)(x + 7)$	Recognise that the expression is a difference of two squares and that the factors can be obtained by taking the square root of the terms: $x^2 = x \times x$ and $49 = 7^2$.
b. $25x^2 - 16 = (5x - 4)(5x + 4)$	Recognise that the expression is a difference of two squares and that the factors can be obtained by taking the square root of the terms: $25x^2 = (5x)^2$ and $16 = 4^2$.

Exercise 3.4

Factorise the following algebraic expressions.

a. $4a + 12$
b. $6xy - 18x$
c. $-50 - 25x$
d. $4ax - 2a + 6x - 3$
e. $6g^2 + 3g - 2gh - h$
f. $4x + 2xy + y^2 + 2y$
g. $x^2 + 4x - 140$
h. $x^2 - 12x + 35$
i. $x^2 - 13x + 22$
j. $x^2 + 2x - 63$
k. $2x^2 + 2x - 12$
l. $-3x^2 + 18x - 24$
m. $x^2 + 14x + 49$
n. $x^2 - 22x + 121$
o. $-x^2 + 12x - 36$
p. $x^2 - 64$
q. $x^2 - 144$
r. $16d^2 - 1$

3.5 Simplifying algebraic fractions

Algebraic fractions are fractions with algebraic expressions as the numerator and/or denominator. Some examples of algebraic fractions are:

$$\frac{3x}{5} \qquad \frac{5}{2x-3} \qquad \frac{x^2-2x}{4x+3}$$

Simplifying single algebraic fractions

Sometimes it is possible to simplify a single algebraic fraction. This requires you to know the techniques of factorisation.

Example

Simplify the following algebraic fractions.

a. $\frac{2x^2+6}{4}$
b. $\frac{x^2+7x+12}{x^2-4x-32}$
c. $\frac{x^2-xy}{x^2-y^2}$

✓ Solution

Working	Explanation
a. $\frac{2x^2+6}{4} = \frac{2(x^2+3)}{4}$ $= \frac{x^2+3}{2}$	Factorise the numerator by taking out the HCF: 2. Simplify the rewritten fraction.
b. $\frac{x^2+7x+12}{x^2-4x-32} = \frac{(x+3)(x+4)}{(x+4)(x-8)}$ $= \frac{x+3}{x-8}$	Factorise both the numerator and denominator. Notice that both the numerator and denominator have the expression $x + 4$ in common. These expressions can be cancelled, thus simplifying the fraction.
c. $\frac{x^2-xy}{x^2-y^2} = \frac{x(x-y)}{(x+y)(x-y)}$ $= \frac{x}{x+y}$	Factorise both the numerator and denominator. Notice that both the numerator and denominator have the expression $x - y$ in common. These expressions can be cancelled, thus simplifying the fraction.

Adding and subtracting algebraic fractions

Algebraic fractions can be added or subtracted if they have a common denominator. If two algebraic fractions do not have a common denominator, you need to convert the fractions so that they have a common denominator before adding or subtracting. You do this by multiplying each fraction by another fraction that is equivalent to 1.

Examples

Simplify the following algebraic fractions.

a. $\frac{2x}{5}+\frac{3x}{8}$ b. $\frac{4x-8}{3}-\frac{3x}{2}$ c. $\frac{2}{5x}+\frac{3x}{8}$ d. $-\frac{2}{3(k+2)}+\frac{3k}{4}$

✓ *Solution*

Working	Explanation
a. $\frac{2x}{5}+\frac{3x}{8}=\frac{2x}{5}\left(\frac{8}{8}\right)+\frac{3x}{8}\left(\frac{5}{5}\right)$ $=\frac{16x}{40}+\frac{15x}{40}$ $=\frac{31x}{40}$	Since the denominators are different, convert both fractions so that they have the same denominator. Note that the conversion fractions, shown in brackets, are equivalent to 1, so there is no actual change to the value of the fractions after multiplying. Add the numerators.
b. $\frac{4x-8}{3}-\frac{3x}{2}=\frac{4x-8}{3}\left(\frac{2}{2}\right)-\frac{3x}{2}\left(\frac{3}{3}\right)$ $=\frac{8x-16}{6}-\frac{9x}{6}$ $=\frac{8x-16-9x}{6}$ $=\frac{-x-16}{6}$	Since the denominators are different, convert both fractions so that they have the same denominator. Add the numerators.
c. $\frac{2}{5x}+\frac{3x}{8}=\frac{2}{5x}\left(\frac{8}{8}\right)+\frac{3x}{8}\left(\frac{5x}{5x}\right)$ $=\frac{16}{40x}+\frac{15x^2}{40x}$ $=\frac{15x^2+16}{40x}$	Since the denominators are different, convert both fractions so that they have the same denominator. Note that one of the denominators has a pronumeral, so the common denominator must also have a pronumeral. Add the numerators.
d. $-\frac{2}{3(k+2)}+\frac{3k}{4}$ $=-\frac{2}{3(k+2)}\left(\frac{4}{4}\right)+\frac{3k}{4}\left(\frac{3(k+2)}{3(k+2)}\right)$ $=-\frac{8}{12(k+2)}+\frac{9k(k+2)}{12(k+2)}$ $=-\frac{8}{12(k+2)}+\frac{9k^2+18k}{12(k+2)}$ $=\frac{9k^2+18k-8}{12(k+2)}$	Since the denominators are different, convert both fractions so that they have the same denominator. One of the denominators has an algebraic expression, so the common denominator must also have an algebraic expression. Add the numerators. It is not necessary to expand the denominator in this case.

Multiplying and dividing algebraic fractions

Algebraic fractions can be multiplied and divided. The rules for numerical operations apply in the same way they do for ordinary numbers. Sometimes it is easier to factorise algebraic fractions before multiplication.

Example

Simplify the following algebraic fractions.

a. $\frac{2x}{3} \times \frac{3x+2}{5}$

b. $\frac{2x}{3} \div \frac{4y}{9}$

c. $\frac{y^2 - 3y - 10}{y^2 - 5y} \times \frac{2y^2 - 2y}{y^2 - y - 6}$

d. $\frac{x^2 - 1}{x^2 + 2x + 1} \div \frac{x^2 - 2x + 1}{x^2 + 3x + 2}$

✓ *Solution*

Working	Explanation
a. $\frac{2x}{3} \times \frac{3x+2}{5} = \frac{2x \times (3x+2)}{3 \times 5}$ $= \frac{2x(3x+2)}{15}$ $= \frac{6x^2 + 4x}{15}$	Multiply the numerators together. Multiply the denominators together. Expand the result according to the distributive law.
b. $\frac{2x}{3} \div \frac{4y}{9} = \frac{2x}{3} \times \frac{9}{4y}$ $= \frac{3x}{2y}$	Since this is a division, we have to convert the fraction after the division sign to its reciprocal and then multiply. Always simplify where appropriate.
c. $\frac{y^2 - 3y - 10}{y^2 - 5y} \times \frac{2y^2 - 2y}{y^2 - y - 6}$ $= \frac{(y+2)(y-5)}{y(y-5)} \times \frac{2y(y-1)}{(y-3)(y+2)}$ $= \frac{2(y-1)}{(y-3)}$ $= \frac{2y-2}{y-3}$	Factorise all the numerators and denominators. Cancel like terms where possible. Multiply the numerators and denominators. Expand if required.
d. $\frac{x^2 - 1}{x^2 + 2x + 1} \div \frac{x^2 - 2x + 1}{x^2 + 3x + 2}$ $= \frac{(x-1)(x+1)}{(x+1)(x+1)} \div \frac{(x-1)(x-1)}{(x+2)(x+1)}$ $= \frac{(x-1)(x+1)}{(x+1)(x+1)} \times \frac{(x+2)(x+1)}{(x-1)(x-1)}$ $= \frac{x+2}{x-1}$	Factorise both the numerators and denominators. Take the reciprocal of the algebraic fraction after the division sign and multiply. Cancel like terms where possible. Multiply the numerators and denominators. Expand if required.

Exercise 3.5

Simply the following algebraic expressions.

a. $\dfrac{x^2+x}{x^2-2x-3}$

b. $\dfrac{x^2+3x-10}{x^2+6x+5}$

c. $\dfrac{x}{2}+\dfrac{y}{10}$

d. $\dfrac{x-3}{2}-\dfrac{x+3}{9}$

e. $\dfrac{2}{x-3}+\dfrac{x}{4}$

f. $\dfrac{x^2+5x-14}{x^2-4}\times\dfrac{x^2+4x+4}{x^2+8x+7}$

g. $\dfrac{x^2+6x}{x^2+4x-12}\div\dfrac{2x}{2x^2+4x-16}$

h. $\dfrac{x^2+4x+4}{4}\div\dfrac{x^2+3x+2}{2}\div\dfrac{x+2}{3}$

Answers

Exercise 3.1.1

a. 4 terms
b. 1 and -4
c. -4
d. -25

Exercise 3.1.2

a. b
b. $x^2 - 2x + 4$
c. $\frac{9x}{2} - 5$
d. $\frac{23t}{6}$
e. $-4x^2 - x^3$
f. $\frac{2y}{3}$
g. 10
h. $\frac{8a}{21b^2}$

Exercise 3.2

a. $2x + 8$
b. $4d - 12$
c. $-12 + 3r$
d. $6a + 5$
e. $-\frac{x}{3} + 2$
f. $-3y^2 + 6xy$
g. $2x^2 - 4xy$
h. $3a + 13$

Exercise 3.3

a. $2x^2 + 6x - 8$
b. $3k^2 + 10k - 8$
c. $n^2 - 49$
d. $4a^2 - 12a + 9$
e. $25 + 10r + r^2$
f. $9k^2 - 4$
g. $f - f^2 + 6$
h. $16y^2 - 1$
i. $3e^2 - 14e + 8$

Exercise 3.4

a. $4(a + 3)$
b. $6x(y - 3)$
c. $-25(2 + x)$
d. $(2a + 3)(2x - 1)$
e. $(3g - h)(2g + 1)$
f. $(2x + y)(2 + y)$
g. $(x - 10)(x + 14)$
h. $(x - 5)(x - 7)$
i. $(x - 2)(x - 11)$
j. $(x + 9)(x - 7)$
k. $2(x - 2)(x + 3)$
l. $-3(x - 4)(x - 2)$
m. $(x + 7)^2$
n. $(x - 11)^2$
o. $-(x - 6)^2$
p. $(x - 8)(x + 8)$
q. $(x + 12)(x - 12)$
r. $(4d - 1)(4d + 1)$

Exercise 3.5

a. $\frac{x}{x - 3}$
b. $\frac{x - 2}{x + 1}$
c. $\frac{5x + y}{10}$
d. $\frac{7x - 33}{18}$
e. $\frac{x^2 - 3x + 8}{4x - 12}$
f. $\frac{x + 2}{x + 1}$
g. $x + 4$
h. $\frac{3}{2x + 2}$

Chapter 4 – Solving linear equations, simultaneous equations and linear inequalities

4.1 Solving linear equations

Linear equations are equations where the unknown has the power of 1, e.g. $5x - 3 = 17$.

To solve a linear equation, we need to collect like terms and isolate the unknown on one side of the equation. One way we can do this is by adding numbers to both sides of the equation so that the unknown becomes isolated (on its own).

For example, in the equation above ($5x - 3 = 17$), we would first add 3 to both sides: $5x - 3 + 3 = 17 + 3$. Simplifying gives $5x = 20$. Dividing both sides by 5 and simplifying isolates the unknown, giving the solution: $x = 4$.

Hint: whatever operation you apply to one side of the equation must also be applied to the other side of the equation; that is, the equation must always be in balance.

Example

Solve the following linear equations.

a. $6x = 12$ **b.** $3x - 2 = 13$ **c.** $2x - 3 = 4x + 5$

d. $2(x + 3) = 8$ **e.** $3(x + 2) = 10$ **f.** $4(x + 1) = 5(x - 2)$

✓ *Solution*

Working	Explanation
a. $6x = 12$ $\frac{6x}{6} = \frac{12}{6}$ $x = 2$	The unknown is already on the left-hand side of the equation. Divide both sides by the coefficient of the unknown and simplify. (This step can be ignored once you are used to solving linear equations.) The value of the unknown is obtained.
b. $3x - 2 = 13$ $3x - 2 + 2 = 13 + 2$ $3x = 15$ $\frac{3x}{3} = \frac{15}{3}$ $x = 5$	First collect the constant terms. To do this, add 2 to both sides of the equation and simplify to isolate the unknown. Divide both sides by the coefficient of the unknown and simplify to obtain the value of the unknown.

c. $2x - 3 = 4x + 5$ $2x - 3 + 3 - 4x = 4x + 5 + 3 - 4x$ $-2x = 8$ $\frac{-2x}{-2} = \frac{8}{-2}$ $x = -4$	Isolate the unknown terms by adding 3 and subtracting $4x$ on both sides of the equation, then simplify it. Divide both sides by the coefficient of the unknown and simplify to obtain the value of the unknown.
d. $2(x + 3) = 8$	There are two ways of solving this linear equation.
Method 1 $2(x + 3) = 8$ $\frac{2(x + 3)}{2} = \frac{8}{2}$ $x + 3 = 4$ $x + 3 - 3 = 4 - 3$ $x = 1$	This method can be used when the coefficient of the algebraic expression is a factor of the constant on the right-hand side. Divide both sides by the coefficient and then isolate the unknown on the left-hand side to obtain the solution.
Method 2 $2(x + 3) = 8$ $2x + 6 = 8$ $2x + 6 - 6 = 8 - 6$ $2x = 2$ $x = 1$	Expand the bracketed expression according to the distributive law. Isolate the unknown on one side of the equation. Solve for the unknown.
e. $3(x + 2) = 10$ $3x + 6 = 10$ $3x = 4$ $x = \frac{4}{3}$	Expand the bracketed expression according to the distributive law. Isolate the unknown on one side of the equation. Solve for the unknown. **Note:** the unknown can be a fraction or a decimal. There is no need to convert the improper fraction to a mixed number.
f. $4(x + 1) = 5(x - 2)$ $4x + 4 = 5x - 10$ $-x = -14$ $x = 14$	Expand both bracketed expressions according to the distributive law. Isolate the unknown on one side of the equation. Solve for the unknown.

Exercise 4.1

Solve the following linear equations.

a. $5x = -100$
b. $-7x = 4$
c. $6x + 1 = 13$
d. $7 - 3x = 3$
e. $9x - 2 = 8x - 6$
f. $11x - 3 = 15x + 5$
g. $6(x + 2) = 36$
h. $7(x + 3) = 11$
i. $-3(x - 2) = -24$
j. $4(x + 3) = 8(x - 2)$
k. $2(x + 2) = 5(x - 4)$
l. $-2(x - 7) = 4(x + 2)$

4.2 Applying linear equations

Linear equations can be used to solve many problems in real life, such as determining the dimensions of a two-dimensional shape.

Writing algebraic expressions

You need to be able to interpret problems expressed in words and convert them into an algebraic expression. For example, if you were told that a number is 7 more than x, the algebraic expression is $7 + x$.

Note: you may need to define a variable if the variable is not stated.

Example

Write algebraic expressions corresponding to the following situations.

a. 6 less than y
b. 7 more than 3 times x
c. the difference between c and d is multiplied by 2
d. the product of 5 and the square of r
e. the sum of x and y is divided by 8

✓ *Solution*

Working	Explanation
a. $y - 6$	'Less than' means subtract (−).
b. $7 + 3x$	'Times' means multiply (×) and 'more than' means add (+).
c. $2(c - d)$	'Difference' means subtract (−) and this operation has to be performed before multiplication (×).
d. $5r^2$	'Square' means to multiply a number by itself ($r \times r$) and 'product' means multiply (×).
e. $\frac{x + y}{8}$	'Sum' means add (+). **Note:** division is written as a fraction in this case.

Writing linear equations and solving practical problems

Follow the steps below when interpreting and solving practical problems involving linear equations.

- Assign a pronumeral to the unknown quantity (unless the pronumeral has already been defined). Be specific – for example, 'let x = the number Ming is thinking of'.

- Translate the problem into a linear equation using the definition of the pronumeral.
- Solve the problem using the techniques you have learned.
- Clearly state the solution to the problem.

Example

By first defining a variable, derive a linear equation for the following situations and solve it for the unknown.

a. Ming is thinking of a number. When the sum of the number and 2 is multiplied by 6, the result is 24. What number is Ming thinking of?

b. A fence measuring 36 metres is to be built around a rectangular garden. The length of the garden is twice its width. Determine the length and width of the garden.

c. Anita is 18 years older than her nephew Mark. In 6 years her age will be 3 times Mark's age. How old are both of them?

✓ *Solution*

Working	Explanation
a. Let $x =$ the number Ming is thinking of	Define a pronumeral.
$x + 2$	Formulate an algebraic expression from the words used in the problem.
$6(x + 2)$	'Sum' means add (+).
	Multiply the sum by 6.
$6(x + 2) = 24$	Equate this to 24 to form a linear equation.
$x + 2 = 4$	Solve the linear equation.
$x = 2$	State the solution.
The number Ming is thinking of is 2.	
b. Let $w =$ the width of the rectangular garden	Define a pronumeral.
Length $= 2w$	State that the length is double the width.
Perimeter $= 2(2w + w)$	State the perimeter using the pronumeral.
$2(2w + w) = 36$	Equate the perimeter to 36 to form a linear equation.
$6w = 36$	
$w = 6$	Solve the equation.
The width of the garden is 6 m and the length of the garden is 12 m.	State the solutions for both length and width.

c. Let m = Mark's current age	Define a pronumeral.
Anita's current age $= m + 18$	State Anita's age using the pronumeral defined.
In 6 years: Mark's age $= m + 6$; Anita's $= m + 18 + 6 = m + 24$	Add 6 years to both Anita's and Mark's ages.
$m + 24 = 3(m + 6)$	Equate Anita's age to 3 times Mark's age to form a linear equation.
$m = 3$	Solve the equation.
Mark is 3 years old and Anita is 21 years old.	State the current ages of both Anita and Mark.

Exercise 4.2.1

Write algebraic expressions for the following situations.

a. 5 more than x

b. 3 less than 2 times y

c. 2 times the square of m divided by 5

d. 3 times 2 less than r

Exercise 4.2.2

For the following situations, define the variable, derive the appropriate linear equation and solve the equation for the unknown.

a. Twelve is subtracted from a certain number and the result is divided by 5. If the answer is 14, what is the number?

b. The sum of three consecutive even numbers is 72. What are the numbers?

c. Albert has scored 87, 72, 92, and 88 in his first four mathematics tests. After the fifth test, his average is 84. What is the score of his fifth test?

d. Adam is 20 years younger than Brian. In two years, Brian will be twice as old as Adam. How old are they now?

4.3 Solving simultaneous equations

Simultaneous equations are a set of two or more algebraic equations that have a common solution; that is, there are values of the unknowns that satisfy all the equations.

Simultaneous equations can be solved graphically or algebraically. To solve simultaneous equations graphically, the equations are plotted on the Cartesian plane and the solution is the point of intersection. To solve simultaneous equations algebraically, the equations need to be manipulated to enable them to be solved by substitution or elimination.

Example

Graph the simultaneous equations $y = x + 4$ and $y = -2x - 2$ and solve for both unknowns.

✓ *Solution*

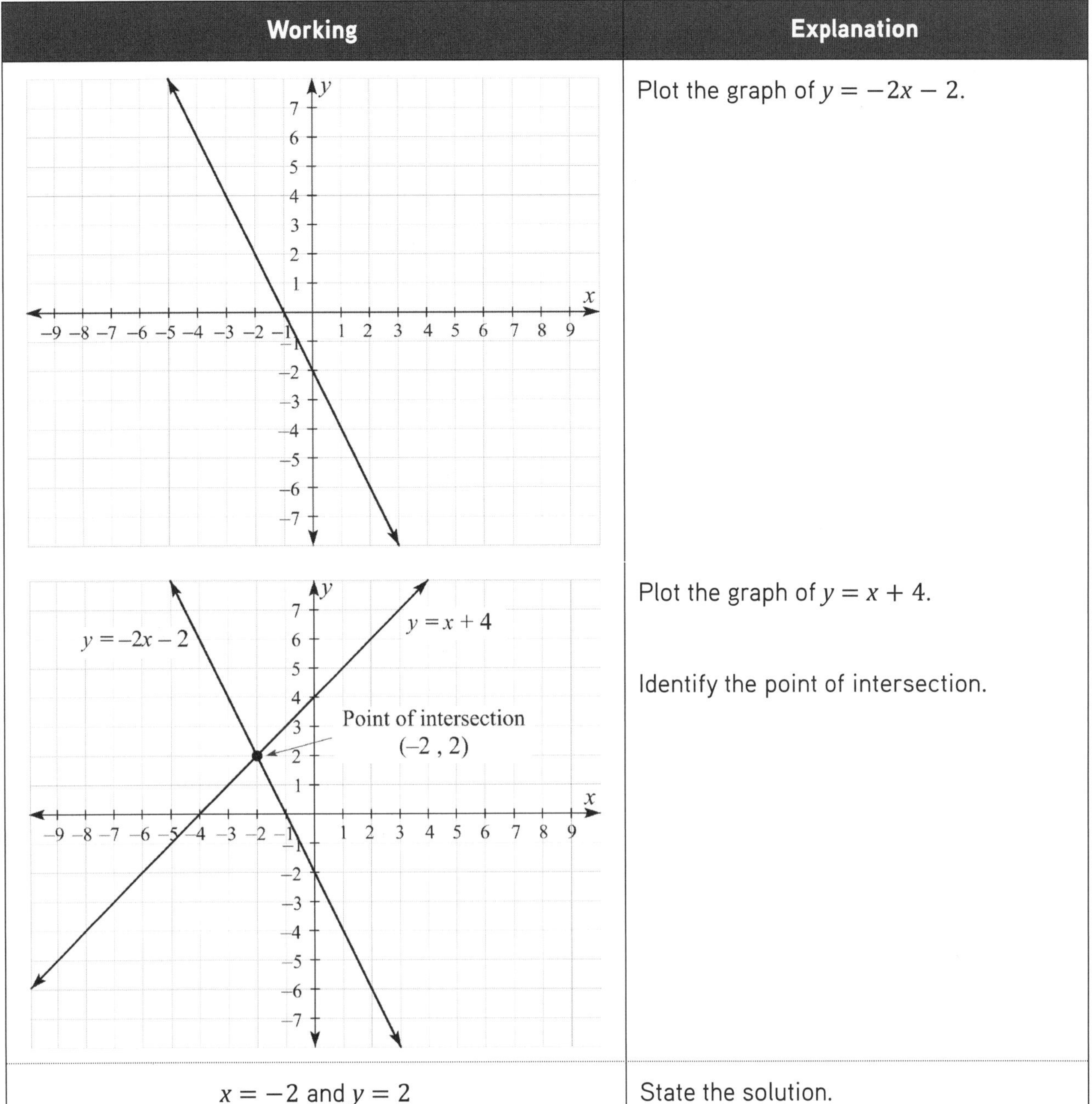

Working	Explanation
(graph)	Plot the graph of $y = -2x - 2$.
(graph)	Plot the graph of $y = x + 4$. Identify the point of intersection.
$x = -2$ and $y = 2$	State the solution.

Example

Solve the following simultaneous equations by the method of substitution.

a. $y = 3x - 2$ and $y = 2x + 1$

b. $9x = y + 95$ and $y + 4 = -4x$

✓ *Solution*

Working	Explanation
a. $y = 3x - 2$ [1] $y = 2x + 1$ [2]	Label the two equations.
$3x - 2 = 2x + 1$ $x = 3$	Substitute [1] into [2] and solve for x.
$y = 3(3) - 2 = 7$	Substitute the value of x into one of the equations to obtain the value of y.
The solution is $(3, 7)$.	State the solution.
b. $9x = y + 95$ [1] $y + 4 = -4x$ [2]	Label the two equations.
$y = -4x - 4$ [3]	Rearrange equation [2] to obtain equation [3].
$9x = -4x - 4 + 95$ $13x = 91$	Substitute equation [3] into equation [1] and solve for x.
$x = 7$ $y = -4(7) - 4 = -32$	Substitute the value of x into equation [3] to obtain the value of y.
The solution is $(7, -32)$.	State the solution.

Example

Solve the following simultaneous equations by the method of elimination.

a. $-y + x = 7$ and $5y + 3x = 13$

b. $5x - 2y = 17$ and $-y + 2x = 7$

✓ *Solution*

Working	Explanation
a. $-y + x = 7$ [1]	Label the two equations.
$5y + 3x = 13$ [2] $-5y + 5x = 35$ [3]	For the method of elimination to work, the unsigned coefficient of x (or y) for both equations must be the same. We can achieve that in this case by multiplying equation [1] by 5 to obtain equation [3].
[2] + [3] $-5y + 5x + 5y + 3x = 35 + 13$ $8x = 48$ $x = 6$	Since we have $5y$ in equation [2] and $-5y$ in equation [3], we add them together to eliminate the terms with y. This leaves us with an equation to solve for x.
$-y + 6 = 7$ $y = -1$	Substitute the value of x into one of the equations to obtain the value of y.
The solution is $(6, -1)$.	State the solution.

b. $5x - 2y = 17$ [1] $-y + 2x = 7$ [2] $-2y + 4x = 14$ [3]	Label the two equations. For the method of elimination to work, the unsigned coefficient of x (or y) for both equations must be the same. We can achieve that in this case by multiplying equation [2] by 2 to obtain equation [3].
[3] – [1] $-2y + 4x - (5x - 2y) = 14 - 17$ $-x = -3$ $x = 3$	Since we have $-2y$ in both equation [1] and equation [3], we subtract one from the other to eliminate the terms with y. This leaves us with an equation to solve for x.
$-y + 2(3) = 7$ $y = -1$	Substitute the value of x into one of the equations to obtain the value of y.
The solution is $(3, -1)$.	State the solution.

Note:

- It is good practice to check your answer once you have solved it. Substitute the values of x and y into both equations to make sure that the solution is correct.
- For the method of elimination, it does not matter which terms you choose to eliminate.
- Generally, the method of substitution is used when you can easily rearrange one of the equations in the form of $y = \ldots$ or $x = \ldots$.

Exercise 4.3.1

Graph and solve the following simultaneous equations.

a. $y = 2x + 5$ and $y = \frac{x}{2} + 2$

b. $y = -3x - 3$ and $y = 2x + 2$

Exercise 4.3.2

Solve the following simultaneous equations by the method of substitution.

a. $y = -2x + 29$ and $3x - 2y = 19$

b. $3y - x = 10$ and $y = -x + 6$

c. $7x + 4y = 25$ and $4y - 33 = x$

d. $2x + 3y = 11$ and $x = 10 - 3y$

Exercise 4.3.3

Solve the following simultaneous equations by the method of elimination.

a. $3x + 4y = 3$ and $2y + 3x = 9$

b. $5x + 3y = 27$ and $y + 2x = 10$

c. $7x - 12y = 39$ and $5x - 4y = 5$

d. $2y + 3x = 5$ and $-6y + 5x = 27$

4.4 Applying simultaneous equations

Follow the steps below when interpreting and solving practical problems involving simultaneous equations with two unknowns.

- Assign two pronumerals to the unknown quantities, unless the pronumerals have been defined.
- Translate the problem into two simultaneous equations using the pronumerals defined.
- Solve the problem using the techniques you have learned.
- Clearly state the solution to the problem.

Example

Jack and Jill each has a number of marbles. Jill has 20 marbles more than Jack and in total they have 180 marbles. How many marbles do each of them have?

✓ Solution

Working	Explanation
Let a = the number of marbles belonging to Jack	Define the variables.
b = the number of marbles belonging to Jill.	Interpret the question and formulate the equations.
$a + b = 180$ [1]	Equation [1] states the total number of marbles.
$a + 20 = b$ [2]	Equation [2] states that Jill (b) has 20 marbles more than Jack (a).
Substitute [2] into [1].	Solve using the method of substitution.
$a + (a + 20) = 180$ $2a = 160$ $a = 80$	
$b = 80 + 20 = 100$	Substitute $a = 80$ into equation [2].
Jack has 80 marbles and Jill has 100.	Answer the question.

Example

A farm has some sheep and some chickens. In total there are 150 heads and 500 legs. Determine the number of sheep and the number of chickens on the farm.

✓ Solution

Working	Explanation
Let s = the number of sheep c = the number of chickens.	Define the variables. Interpret the question and formulate the equations.
$s + c = 150$ [1] $2c + 4s = 500$ [2]	Equation [1] states the total number of animals. Equation [2] states the total number of legs (based on the fact that chickens have 2 legs and sheep have 4 legs).
$c = 150 - s$ [3]	Rearrange [1] to [3].
$2(150 - s) + 4s = 500$ $300 - 2s + 4s = 500$ $2s = 200$ $s = 100$ $100 + c = 150$ $c = 50$	Solve using the method of substitution. • Substitute [3] into [2]. • Substitute $s = 100$ into [1].
The farm has 50 chickens and 100 sheep.	Answer the question.

Example

Anita is 18 years older than Mark. In 6 years, Anita's age will be 3 times Mark's age. How old are both of them? (**Note:** this is the same example as in Section 4.2, but this time the problem will be solved using simultaneous equations.)

✓ Solution

Working	Explanation
Let a = Anita's current age m = Mark's current age.	Define the variables.
Now: $a = m + 18$ [1]	Interpret the question and formulate the equations.
In 6 years: $a + 6 = 3(m + 6)$ $a = 3m + 12$ [2]	Equation [1] states that Anita is 18 years older than Mark. Equation [2] states that in 6 years Anita's age will be three times Mark's age.
$3m + 12 = m + 18$ $2m = 6$ $m = 3$ $a = 3 + 18 = 21$	Solve using the method of substitution. • Substitute [2] into [1]. • Substitute $m = 3$ into [1].
Mark is 3 years old and Anita is 21 years old.	Answer the question.

Example

Ben went to a sports store and bought some items of clothing. He bought several T-shirts costing $10 each and a number of shorts costing $20 each. If he spent $120 in total and bought twice as many T-shirts as shorts, how many of each did he buy?

✓ ***Solution***

Working	Explanation
Let $t =$ the number of T-shirts $s =$ the number of shorts.	Define the variables.
$10t + 20s = 120 \quad [1]$ $2s = t \quad [2]$	Interpret the question and formulate the equations. Equation [1] states the total cost. Equation [2] states that the number of T-shirts was twice the number of shorts.
$10(2s) + 20s = 120$ $40s = 120$ $s = 3$ $t = 6$	Solve using the method of substitution. • Substitute [2] into [1]. • Substitute $s = 3$ into [2].
Ben bought 3 shorts and 6 T-shirts.	Answer the question.

Exercise 4.4.1

The Smiths and the Adams went to a local fair. The Smiths bought 4 children's tickets and 2 adult tickets for a total cost of $58. The Adams bought 7 children's tickets and 4 adult tickets for a total cost of $109. Determine the cost of each type of ticket.

Exercise 4.4.2

Alice sells two types of bowls at her market stall. The price of a pottery bowl is $7 and the price of a wooden bowl is $9. She sold 35 bowls for $277 last weekend. Determine the number of each type of bowl she sold.

Exercise 4.4.3

Rohan is currently 20 years younger than Becky. In 2 years, Becky will be twice as old as Rohan. How old are they now?

Exercise 4.4.4

The sum of two numbers is 14 and their difference is 2. Find the numbers.

4.5 Solving linear inequalities

A linear inequality is an expression that **compares** two values. Unlike equations, inequalities do not use the equals sign. This means that the solution is not a specific number, but a range of numbers.

The table below shows the types of comparisons that a linear inequality can state.

Symbol	Notation	Explanation
$<$	$x < 3$	x is **less than** 3 but does not include 3.
$>$	$x > -8$	x is **greater than** -8 but does not include -8.
$\leq$	$x \leq 4$	x is **less than or equal to** 4.
$\geq$	$x \geq -10$	x is **greater than or equal to** -10.
$\neq$	$x \neq 6$	x **does not equal** 6.

Set notation and the number line

We can write inequalities in set notation. For example, $x < 3$ can be written as:

$$\{x : x < 3\}$$

This can be plotted on the number line as shown below:

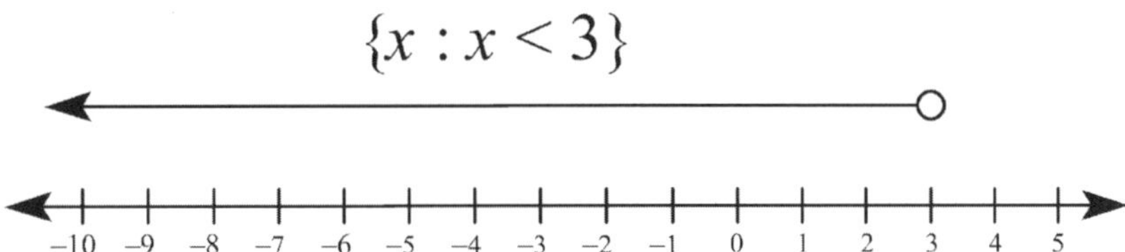

The figure below shows $\{x : x \geq -10\}$ plotted on the number line.

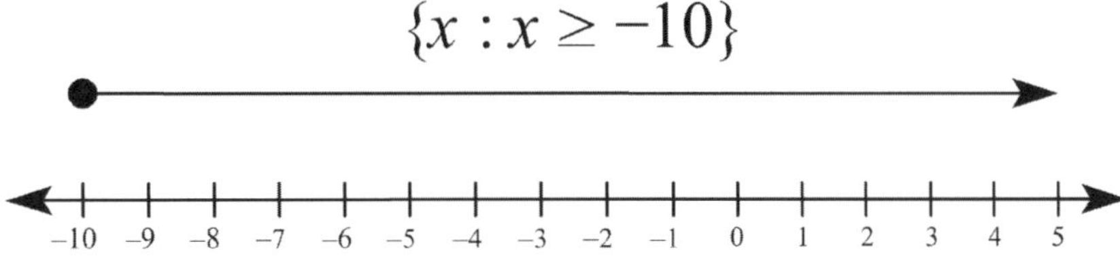

Note that the circles on inequalities plotted on the number line have special meanings.

○	An open circle means that the number **is not** included.
●	A filled circle means that the number **is** included.

Solving linear inequalities is similar to solving linear equations, except that you use the inequality symbols. The major difference is that when you multiply (or divide) both sides by a negative number, you have to invert the inequality symbol, so that $-x > 2$, for example, becomes $x < -2$.

Example

Solve the following inequalities.

a. $x + 3 < 4$ **b.** $3 - 2x \leq 4$ **c.** $-2(x + 1) > 4$ **d.** $2x + 3 \geq 3x - 4$

✓ ***Solution***

Working	Explanation
a. $x + 3 < 4$ $x + 3 - 3 < 4 - 3$ $x < 1$	Isolate the unknown on the left-hand side of the inequality by subtracting 3 from both sides.
b. $3 - 2x \leq 4$ $3 - 2x - 3 \leq 4 - 3$ $-2x \leq 1$ $x \geq -\frac{1}{2}$	Isolate the unknown on the left-hand side of the inequality by subtracting 3 from both sides. Divide both sides by -2 and invert the inequality sign from $\leq$ to $\geq$.
c. $-2(x + 1) > 4$ $-2x - 2 > 4$ $-2x - 2 + 2 > 4 + 2$ $-2x > 6$ $x < -3$	Expand the left-hand side according to the distributive law. Isolate the unknown on the left-hand side of the inequality by adding 2 to both sides. Divide both sides by -2 and invert the inequality sign from $>$ to $<$.
d. $2x + 3 \geq 3x - 4$ $2x - 3x \geq -4 - 3$ $-x \geq -7$ $x \leq 7$	Isolate the unknown on the left-hand side of the equation. Divide both sides by -1 and invert the inequality sign from $\geq$ to $\leq$.

Exercise 4.5

Solve the following inequalities.

a. $4x + 6 < 10$ **b.** $2(x + 4) > 5$ **c.** $3x - 7 \leq 8x + 8$

d. $4(x - 1) \leq 3(x + 2)$ **e.** $x \geq 5x - 20$

4.6 Applying linear inequalities

Follow the steps below when interpreting and solving practical problems involving linear inequalities.

- Assign a pronumeral to the unknown quantity, unless the pronumeral has already been defined.
- Translate the problem into a linear inequality using the definition of the pronumeral.
- Solve the problem by using the techniques you have learned.
- Clearly state the solution to the problem, which for linear inequalities will be a range.

Example

When an integer is multiplied by 3, the result is greater than 10. Determine the possible values of the integer.

✓ ***Solution***

Working	Explanation
Let $x =$ the integer.	Define a variable.
$3x > 10$ $x > \frac{10}{3}$	Set up an inequality and solve it.
The possible values are all integers greater than or equal to 4.	Since the question states that the number is an integer, the possible values of the number will have to be all integers greater than $\frac{10}{3}$.

Example

At the Royal Melbourne Show, Mandy went on a number of rides. The cost of each ride was \$14.50. She paid \$12.50 for lunch. In total she spent \$99. Determine the maximum number of rides taken by Mandy.

✓ ***Solution***

Working	Explanation
Let $r =$ the number of rides.	Define a variable.
$14.5r + 12.5 \leq 99$ $14.5r \leq 86.5$ $r \leq 5.97$	Set up an inequality and solve it.
The maximum number of rides taken by Mandy is 5.	The number of rides must be an integer, so the maximum will have to be 5. The closest integer is 6, but this is outside the allowable range (less than or equal to 5.97).

Example

A group of Year 9 students is selling calendars to raise money for a charity. They earn \$0.40 for each calendar they sell. Their goal is to earn more than \$327. Determine the minimum number of calendars they need to sell to achieve their goal.

✓ ***Solution***

Working	Explanation
Let $c =$ the number of calendars sold.	Define a variable.
$0.4c > 327$ $c > 817.5$	Set up an inequality and solve it.
The students must sell at least 818 calendars to achieve their goal of raising more than \$327.	The number of calendars has to be an integer, so the minimum number of calendars must be 818.

Exercise 4.6.1

When 12 is added to 3.5 times a real number, the result is greater than 8. Determine the possible values of the number (to 2 decimal places).

Exercise 4.6.2

Samira worked during the summer holiday and saved \$850 in her bank account. She now withdraws \$25 each week. How many weeks can Samira withdraw \$25 from her account before her account is below \$200?

Exercise 4.6.3

Mitch is planning to buy some games. They each cost \$19.50 and postage is \$12.50. If he only has \$100 to spend, what is the maximum number of games Mitch can buy?

Answers

Exercise 4.1

a. $x = -20$ b. $x = -\frac{4}{7}$ c. $x = 2$ d. $x = \frac{4}{3}$

e. $x = -4$ f. $x = -2$ g. $x = 4$ h. $x = -\frac{10}{7}$

i. $x = 10$ j. $x = 7$ k. $x = 8$ l. $x = 1$

Exercise 4.2.1

a. $5 + x$ b. $2y - 3$ c. $\frac{2m^2}{5}$ d. $3(r - 2)$

Exercise 4.2.2

a. Let x = the number. Then $\frac{x - 12}{5} = 14$ and the number is 82.

b. Let x = the first even number. Then $x + (x + 2) + (x + 4) = 72$ and $x = 22$. The three consecutive even numbers are 22, 24, 26.

c. Let s = the score of the fifth test. Then $\frac{87 + 72 + 92 + 88 + s}{5} = 84$ and Albert scored 81 in the fifth test.

d. Let b = Brian's current age. Then $b + 2 = 2(b - 18)$ and $b = 38$. Adam is 18 and Brian is 38.

Exercise 4.3.1

a.

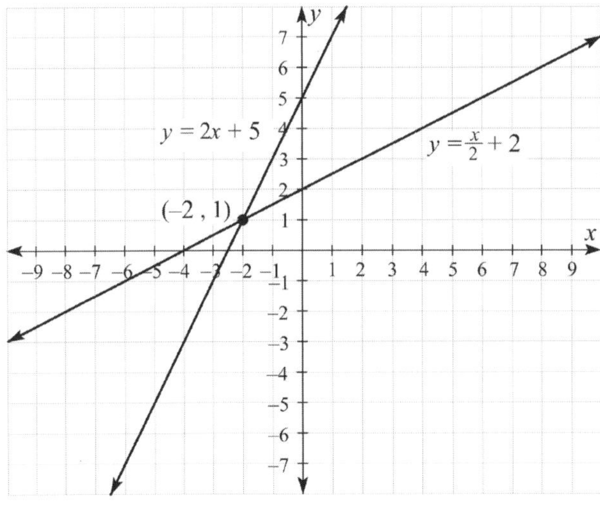

The solution is (−2, 1).

b.

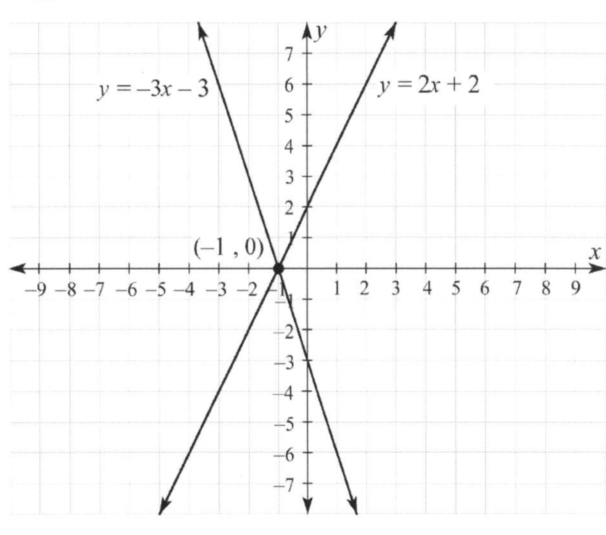

The solution is (−1, 0).

Exercise 4.3.2

a. (11, 7) b. (2, 4) c. (−1, 8) d. (1, 3)

Exercise 4.3.3

a. (5, −3) b. (3, 4) c. (−3, −5) d. (3, −2)

Exercise 4.4.1

The cost of an adult ticket is \$15 and the cost of a children's ticket is \$7.

Exercise 4.4.2

Alice sold 19 pottery bowls and 16 wooden bowls.

Exercise 4.4.3

Rohan is 18 and Becky is 38.

Exercise 4.4.4

6 and 8.

Exercise 4.5

a. $x < 4$ **b.** $x > -\frac{3}{2}$ **c.** $x \geq -3$ **d.** $x \leq 10$ **e.** $x \leq 5$

Exercise 4.6.1

If $x =$ the number, then $12 + 3.5x > 8$ and $x > -1.14$.

Exercise 4.6.2

If $w =$ the number of weeks Samira withdraws \$25, then if $850 - 25w < 200$, then $w > 26$.

Samira can withdraw \$25 for 26 weeks before her account is below \$200.

Exercise 4.6.3

If $g =$ the number of games Mitch can buy, then $19.5g + 12.5 < 100$, then $g < 4.4872$.

Mitch can buy a maximum of 4 games.

Chapter 5 – Index laws, scientific notation and surds

5.1 Index laws

Index laws are rules that enable us to simplify expressions that contain terms with indices.

For example, we can express 7 lots of 3 as $3 \times 3 \times 3 \times 3 \times 3 \times 3 \times 3 = 3^7$. Similarly, we can use pronumerals instead of numbers. If we have n lots of b, we can express it as b^n.

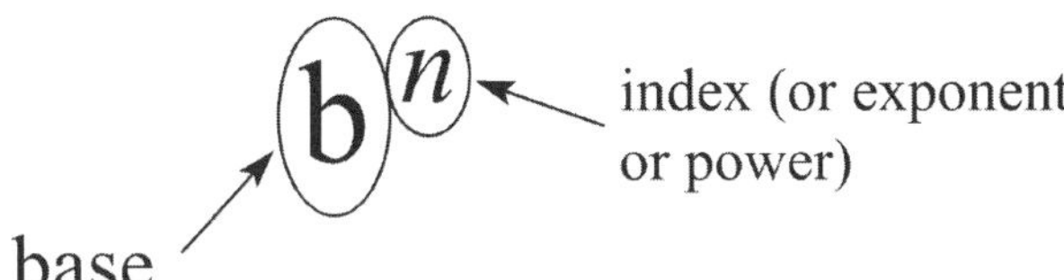

The following table explains several important index laws.

Index law	Explanation	Examples
$a^m \times a^n = a^{m+n}$	When multiplying terms with the same base, we add the indices.	$2^2 \times 2^3 = 2 \times 2 \times 2 \times 2 \times 2 = 2^5$ $2^2 \times 2^3 = 2^{2+3} = 2^5$ $a^3 \times a^4 = a^{3+4} = a^7$
$a^m \div a^n = a^{m-n}$ $(a \neq 0)$	When dividing terms with the same base, we subtract the second index from the first.	$2^6 \div 2^4 = \frac{2 \times 2 \times 2 \times 2 \times 2 \times 2}{2 \times 2 \times 2 \times 2}$ $2^6 \div 2^4 = 2^{6-4} = 2^2$ $a^7 \div a^2 = a^{7-2} = a^5$ **Note:** it is possible to have a negative index. For example: $2^4 \div 2^6 = \frac{2 \times 2 \times 2 \times 2}{2 \times 2 \times 2 \times 2 \times 2 \times 2} = 2^{-2}$ $a^2 \div a^7 = a^{2-7} = a^{-5}$
$(a^m)^n = a^{m \times n}$	When raising an index to another index, we multiply the indices.	$(2^2)^3 = (2 \times 2)^3$ $= (2 \times 2) \times (2 \times 2) \times (2 \times 2)$ $= 2^6$ $(2^2)^3 = 2^{2 \times 3} = 2^6$ $(a^5)^3 = a^{5 \times 3} = a^{15}$
$a^m \times b^m = (ab)^m$	When multiplying two variables with different bases but the same indices, we multiply the bases and raise the result to the same index.	$2^3 \times 5^3 = 2 \times 2 \times 2 \times 5 \times 5 \times 5$ $= (2 \times 5) \times (2 \times 5) \times (2 \times 5)$ $= 10 \times 10 \times 10$ $= 10^3$ $2^3 \times 5^3 = (2 \times 5)^3 = 10^3$ $a^4 \times b^4 = (ab)^4$

$a^m \div b^m = \left(\frac{a}{b}\right)^m$ $(b \neq 0)$	When dividing two variables with different bases but the same indices, we divide the bases and raise the result to the same index.	$6^3 \div 3^3 = \frac{6 \times 6 \times 6}{3 \times 3 \times 3}$ $= 2 \times 2 \times 2$ $= 2^3$ $6^3 \div 3^3 = \left(\frac{6}{3}\right)^3 = 2^3$ $a^4 \div b^4 = \left(\frac{a}{b}\right)^4$
$a^0 = 1$	A number or variable raised to the power of zero equals 1.	$2^0 = 1$ $b^0 = 1$ $4x^0 = 4 \times x^0 = 4$ $(4x)^0 = 4^0 \times x^0 = 1$
$a^{-m} = \left(\frac{1}{a}\right)^m = \frac{1}{a^m}$ $(a \neq 0)$	A number raised to a negative index can be rewritten as its reciprocal raised to the same but positive index.	$2^{-3} = \frac{1}{2} \times \frac{1}{2} \times \frac{1}{2} = \left(\frac{1}{2}\right)^3 = \frac{1}{2^3}$ $2^{-3} = \left(\frac{1}{2}\right)^3 = \frac{1}{2^3}$ $\left(\frac{a}{b}\right)^{-4} = \left(\frac{b}{a}\right)^4$

We can combine the index laws to simplify complex algebraic expressions.

Example

Simplify the following expressions and express the indices as positive numbers.

a. $\frac{25m^{12} \times 4n^7}{15m^2 \times 8n}$

b. $(-3)^0 + 6y^0$

c. $\frac{2^3x^3}{2^5y^4} \times \frac{y^0}{x}$

d. $\left(\frac{p}{2r}\right)^4 \times \frac{4p^0r}{3p^2}$

e. $\left(\frac{x}{2y}\right)^0 \div \frac{3^3(xy)^2}{18xy^5}$

✓ Solution

Working	Explanation
a. $\frac{25m^{12} \times 4n^7}{15m^2 \times 8n} = \left(\frac{25 \times 4}{15 \times 8}\right)\left(\frac{m^{12}n^7}{m^2n}\right)$ $= \frac{5}{6}m^{12-2}n^{7-1}$ $= \frac{5m^{10}n^6}{6}$	Group all the constants and the pronumerals. Simplify the constants and apply the index laws. Express the final expression as a fraction.
b. $(-3)^0 + 6y^0 = 1 + 6 \times 1$ $= 1 + 6$ $= 7$	The zero power applies to -3 and y but not to 6. Hence the expression can be simplified to 7.
c. $\frac{2^3x^3}{2^5y^4} \times \frac{y^0}{x} = 2^{3-5}x^{3-1}y^{0-4}$ $= 2^{-2}x^2y^{-4}$ $= \frac{x^2}{2^2y^4}$ $= \frac{x^2}{4y^4}$	Apply the index laws to simplify the expression. Convert the negative indices to positive indices. Evaluate the constant.
d. $\left(\frac{p}{2r}\right)^4 \times \frac{4p^0r}{3p^2} = \frac{p^4}{2^4r^4} \times \frac{4p^0r}{3p^2}$ $= \left(\frac{4}{2^4 \times 3}\right)p^{4-2}r^{1-4}$ $= \frac{1}{12}p^2r^{-3}$ $= \frac{p^2}{12r^3}$	Apply the index law to expand the first term. Group the constants and apply the index laws to group the pronumerals. Convert the negative index to a positive index.
e. $\left(\frac{x}{2y}\right)^0 \div \frac{3^3(xy)^2}{18xy^5} = 1 \times \frac{18xy^5}{3^3(xy)^2}$ $= \frac{18xy^5}{3^3x^2y^2}$ $= \frac{18}{27}x^{1-2}y^{5-2}$ $= \frac{2}{3}x^{-1}y^3$ $= \frac{2y^3}{3x}$	The first term is 1 since the entire term is raised to the power of zero. Convert the division to multiplication by taking the reciprocal of the second term. Apply the index laws to simplify the terms. Express the indices as positive numbers.

Exercise 5.1

Simplify the following expressions and express the indices as positive numbers.

a. $m^2 \times m^3 \div m^4$

b. $(a^2)^2 \div (3a)^2$

c. $\frac{-8a^6}{c^3}$

d. $(3r^{-10})^0 - 5(s^{20})^0$

e. $(x^2y^3)^6 \times \left(\frac{y}{x}\right)^8$

f. $4 \times z^{-2} \times y^3$

g. $-\frac{15x^3y^2}{3(xy)^3z^{-2}}$

h. $3x^2y^4 \times 4x^{-3}y^5$

i. $\left(\frac{x^2}{2y}\right)^2 \div \left(\frac{x^{-2}}{y}\right)^3$

j. $\left(\frac{m^{-3}n^{-2}}{p^{-2}q^0}\right)^{-1} \div \left(\frac{m^{-3}n^{-1}}{p^{-2}q^{-2}}\right)^{-2}$

5.2 Scientific notation

When we have a very large number (such as the geological age of the earth, which is about 4 600 000 000 years) or a very small number (such as the mass of a sugar molecule, which is about 0.00000000000000000000568 grams), it is easier to express the number using scientific notation (also known as standard notation). Instead of dealing with all the zeros, we represent the number in terms of the index of 10.

…	0.0001	0.001	0.01	0.1	1	10	100	1000	10 000	…
…	10^{-4}	10^{-3}	10^{-2}	10^{-1}	10^0	10^1	10^2	10^3	10^4	…

For example:

- 4 600 000 000 can be represented as $4.6 \times 1\,000\,000\,000$. Since we know that $1\,000\,000\,000 = 10^9$, we can write the full number as 4.6×10^9.
- Likewise, the mass in grams of a sugar molecule can be written as 5.68×10^{-21}.

For any number greater than 1, the index of 10 is a positive integer.

For any number less than 1 but greater than 0, the index of 10 is a negative integer.

Scientific notation is just a convenient way of representing a very large or very small number as the product of two parts: a simpler number multiplied by 10 raised to a power. Its general form is

$$a \times 10^n$$

where $1 < a < 10$ and n is either a positive or negative integer.

To convert from decimal to scientific notation

For numbers greater than 1, imagine a decimal point at the end of the number. Now count the number of times it would take to move the decimal point to the left until it is between the first and second digits. The number of times the decimal point is moved is the index of 10.

For example, consider the number 81 362 000 000.

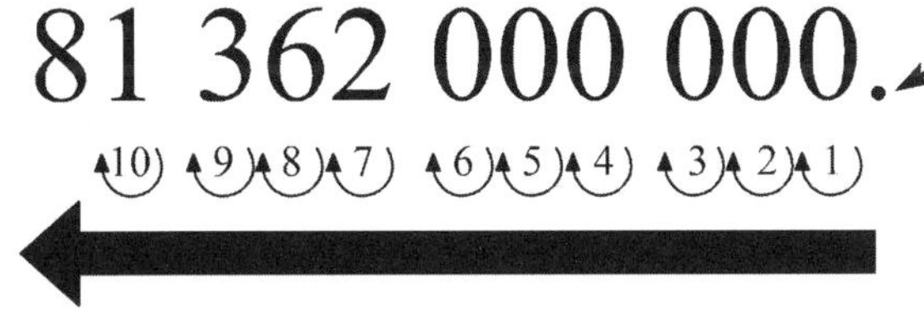

Imagine a decimal point at the end of the number.

Count the number of times the decimal point has to move to the left before it is between the first and second digits: 10.

Therefore 81 362 000 000 = 8.1362×10^{10}.

For numbers between 0 **and** 1, count the number of times the decimal point has to be moved to the right until it is on the right of the first non-zero digit. The number of times the decimal point is moved is the negative index of 10.

For example, consider the number 0.00000000008136.

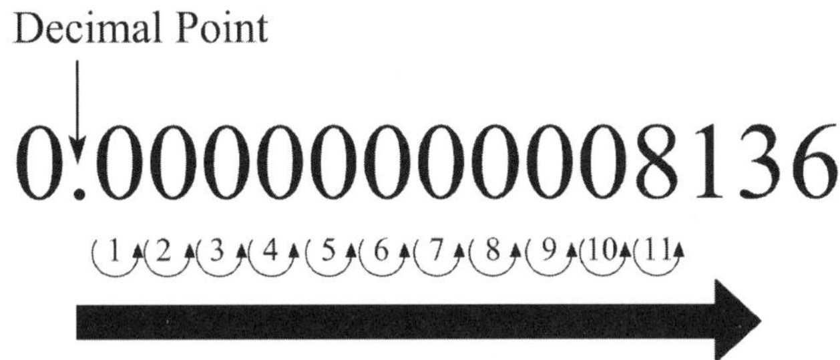

Count the number of times the decimal point has to move to the right before it is in front of the first non-zero digit: 11.

Therefore 0.00000000008136 = 8.136×10^{-11}.

To convert from scientific notation to decimal

For positive powers of 10, move the decimal point to the right the same number of times as the power and add zeros when you go beyond the digits.

For example, consider the number 2.234×10^{7}.

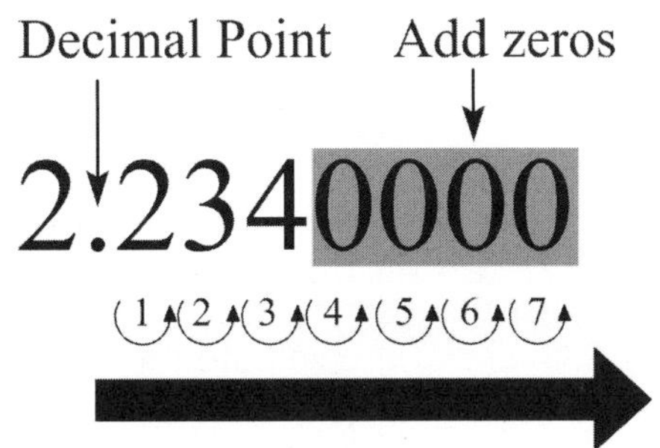

Move the decimal point to the right the number of times indicated by the power (7), adding zeros where necessary.

Therefore 2.234×10^{7} = 22 340 000.

For negative powers of 10, move the decimal point to the left the same number of times as the power and add zeros when you go beyond the digits.

For example, consider the number 2.234×10^{-5}.

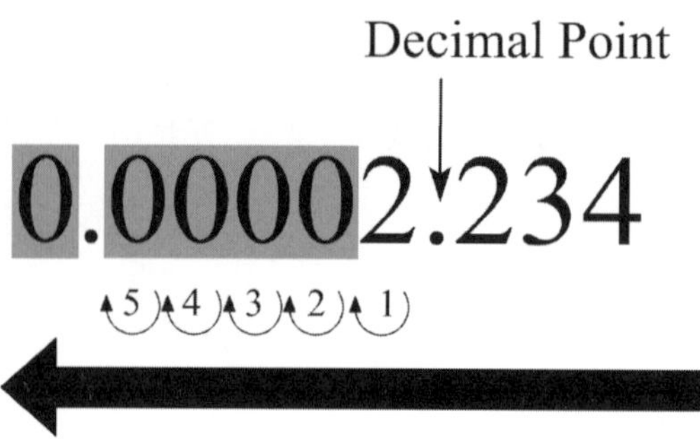

Therefore $2.234 \times 10^{-5} = 0.00002234$.

When working with scientific notation, the index laws apply. This enables us to simplify expressions written in scientific notation.

Example

Simplify the following expressions.

a. $(3 \times 10^4) \times (2.5 \times 10^5)$

b. $(5 \times 10^5)^2$

c. $(9 \times 10^7) \div (3 \times 10^{-5})$

d. $(2 \times 10^6)^{-3}$

✓ *Solution*

Working	Explanation
a. $(3 \times 10^4) \times (2.5 \times 10^5)$ $= 3 \times 2.5 \times 10^{4+5}$ $= 7.5 \times 10^9$	Multiply the two numbers and apply the index laws to determine the power of 10.
b. $(5 \times 10^5)^2 = 5^2 \times 10^{5\times2}$ $= 25 \times 10^{10}$ $= 2.5 \times 10^{11}$	Apply the index laws to determine the power of 5 and the power of 10. Evaluate the square of 5. Note that 25×10^{10} is not scientific notation. Convert it to scientific notation.

c. $(9 \times 10^7) \div (3 \times 10^{-5}) = \frac{9 \times 10^7}{3 \times 10^{-5}}$ $= \frac{9}{3} \times 10^{7-(-5)}$ $= 3 \times 10^{12}$	Rewrite the expression as a fraction. Apply the index laws to simplify the power of 10 and divide 9 by 3.
d. $(2 \times 10^6)^{-3} = 2^{-3} \times 10^{6\times(-3)}$ $= \frac{1}{2^3} \times 10^{-18}$ $= 0.125 \times 10^{-18}$ $= 1.25 \times 10^{-19}$	Apply the index laws to determine the power of 2 and the power of 10. Convert the fraction to a decimal. Rewrite the answer in scientific notation.

Note: you have to be careful not to introduce inaccuracy when using scientific notation. For example, suppose you measure a distance as 17845 m and write it in scientific notation, rounding to 2 decimal places. The distance would be represented as 1.78×10^4 m. On the other hand, if we expressed it in kilometres and rounded to two decimal places it would be 17.85 km. Note the discrepancy – some of the accuracy can be lost when using scientific notation.

Exercise 5.2.1

Rewrite the following numbers in scientific notation.

a. 23 570 000 **b.** 510 000
c. 8 250 000 000 000 **d.** 0.0033
e. 0.000000781 **f.** 0.0000000020394

Exercise 5.2.2

Simplify the following expressions and give your answers in scientific notation.

a. $(4 \times 10^{-6}) \times (8 \times 10^{12})$ **b.** $(2 \times 10^{-3})^4$
c. $(1 \times 10^4) \div (5 \times 10^6)$ **d.** $(5 \times 10^3)^{-2}$

5.3 Surds

Surds are a type of irrational number. An irrational number is a number that cannot be formed by dividing two integers.

Surds are expressed using the radical sign: $\sqrt{}$. A surd can be a square root, cube root or any other root, but this chapter will concentrate solely on square roots.

$\sqrt{2} = 1.414213562...$
$\sqrt{20} = 4.472135955...$

Surds (Exact value) Decimals (Approximate value)

There are rules for arithmetic operations involving surds. These rules can be used to simplify surds.

Simplifying single surds

The two rules below can help us simplify a single surd.

$$\sqrt{a} \times \sqrt{b} = \sqrt{ab} \qquad\qquad \sqrt{\frac{a}{b}} = \frac{\sqrt{a}}{\sqrt{b}}$$

Both rules require that $a > 0$ and $b > 0$.

Note that $\sqrt{a} \times \sqrt{a} = \sqrt{a^2} = a$

Surds of the form $\sqrt{\frac{a}{b}}$ can be rationalised (that is, the denominator can be converted into a rational number), as shown below.

$$\sqrt{\frac{a}{b}} = \frac{\sqrt{a}}{\sqrt{b}} \times \frac{\sqrt{b}}{\sqrt{b}} = \frac{\sqrt{ab}}{b}$$

Example

Simplify the following surds.

a. $\sqrt{20}$ b. $\sqrt{98}$ c. $\sqrt{324}$

d. $\sqrt{\frac{63}{25}}$ e. $\sqrt{\frac{80}{7}}$ f. $\frac{\sqrt{70}}{\sqrt{14}}$

✓ Solution

Working	Explanation
a. $\sqrt{20} = \sqrt{4 \times 5}$ $= \sqrt{4} \times \sqrt{5}$ $= 2\sqrt{5}$	First look for the factors of 20. They are 1×20, 2×10 and 4×5. There are no square numbers in 1×20 or 2×10 – that is, factors whose square root is a whole number – so these factors can be ignored. The factors 4×5 do contain a square number (4), since the square root of 4 is a whole number (2). Hence $\sqrt{20} = 2\sqrt{5}$.
b. $\sqrt{98} = \sqrt{2 \times 49}$ $= \sqrt{2} \times \sqrt{49}$ $= 7\sqrt{2}$	Determine the factors of 98 that are square numbers. There is only one: 49. Simplify the surd by taking out the square root of 49 (7).
c. $\sqrt{324} = \sqrt{4 \times 81}$ $= \sqrt{4} \times \sqrt{81}$ $= 2 \times 9$ $= 18$	Sometimes a number is not an obvious square number. Once you can find the factors of 324, it is obvious that it can be simplified to 18.

d. $\sqrt{\frac{63}{25}} = \sqrt{\frac{9 \times 7}{25}}$ $= \frac{\sqrt{9} \times \sqrt{7}}{\sqrt{25}}$ $= \frac{3\sqrt{7}}{5}$	The procedure for division is similar to that for multiplication: look for factors of the given numbers that are square numbers. Calculate the square root of the square numbers and simplify the expression.
e. $\sqrt{\frac{80}{7}} = \frac{\sqrt{80}}{\sqrt{7}}$ $= \frac{\sqrt{16 \times 5}}{\sqrt{7}}$ $= \frac{4\sqrt{5}}{\sqrt{7}}$ $= \frac{4\sqrt{5}}{\sqrt{7}} \times \frac{\sqrt{7}}{\sqrt{7}}$ $= \frac{4\sqrt{5 \times 7}}{7}$ $= \frac{4\sqrt{35}}{7}$	Determine the factors of 80 that contain a square number (16 and 5). There are no factors of 7 that include a square number. Rationalise the surd by multiplying the numerator and the denominator by $\sqrt{7}$. The denominator is now a rational number: 7. Multiply the two surds in the numerator to form a single surd.
f. $\frac{\sqrt{70}}{\sqrt{14}} = \frac{\sqrt{10} \times \sqrt{7}}{\sqrt{2} \times \sqrt{7}}$ $= \frac{\sqrt{10}}{\sqrt{2}}$ $= \sqrt{\frac{10}{2}}$ $= \sqrt{5}$	You can also simplify by finding factors that are not square numbers. In this case, 7 is a common factor of the numerator and denominator, so you can simplify the surd to $\sqrt{5}$.
or $\frac{\sqrt{70}}{\sqrt{14}} = \sqrt{\frac{70}{14}}$ $= \sqrt{5}$	or Rewrite the surd as a fraction under the one radical sign and simplify $\frac{70}{14}$ to 5.

Adding and subtracting surds

Just as we can add and subtract 'like terms' in algebra, we can add and subtract 'like surds'.

For example: we can add $13\sqrt{2}$ to $4\sqrt{2}$ since both terms share the same surd: $\sqrt{2}$. For the same reason, you can also subtract one surd from another. However, we cannot add $3\sqrt{2}$ to $3\sqrt{3}$ since these terms do not share the same surd.

Example

Evaluate the following expressions.

a. $4\sqrt{2}+4\sqrt{3}-8\sqrt{2}+5\sqrt{3}$

b. $\sqrt{32}-7\sqrt{2}+2\sqrt{8}$

✓ ***Solution***

Working	Explanation
a. $4\sqrt{2}+4\sqrt{3}-8\sqrt{2}+5\sqrt{3}$ $=9\sqrt{3}-4\sqrt{2}$	Add and subtract like surds.
b. $\sqrt{32}-7\sqrt{2}+2\sqrt{8}$ $=\sqrt{16\times 2}-7\sqrt{2}+2\sqrt{4\times 2}$ $=4\sqrt{2}-7\sqrt{2}+2\times 2\sqrt{2}$ $=4\sqrt{2}-7\sqrt{2}+4\sqrt{2}$ $=\sqrt{2}$	Simplify all the surds until they are like surds. (Note that $2\sqrt{4\times 2}=2\times 2\sqrt{2}$). Once the surds are all like surds, you can add and subtract them.

Multiplying and dividing surds

The two rules below can help when multiplying and dividing surds.

$$a\sqrt{b}\times c\sqrt{d}=ac\sqrt{bd}$$

$$a\sqrt{b}\div c\sqrt{d}=\frac{a}{c}\sqrt{\frac{b}{d}}$$

Once you have multiplied or divided the surds, you must always rationalise the final surd when appropriate.

Example

Evaluate the following expressions.

a. $4\sqrt{3}\times 5\sqrt{6}$

b. $(3\sqrt{7})^2$

c. $25\sqrt{56}\div 15\sqrt{8}$

d. $\frac{24\sqrt{20}}{8\sqrt{12}}$

✓ ***Solution***

Working	Explanation
a. $4\sqrt{3} \times 5\sqrt{6} = 4 \times 5 \times \sqrt{3 \times 6}$ $= 20\sqrt{18}$ $= 20\sqrt{9 \times 2}$ $= 60\sqrt{2}$	Multiply the non-surds and the surds to obtain a single surd. Simplify $\sqrt{18}$ to $\sqrt{9 \times 2} = 3\sqrt{2}$. Multiply 20 by the square root of 9 (3) to obtain 60.
b. $(3\sqrt{7})^2 = 3\sqrt{7} \times 3\sqrt{7}$ $= 9 \times 7$ $= 63$	Expand the expression and multiply the factors.
c. $25\sqrt{56} \div 15\sqrt{8} = \frac{25\sqrt{56}}{15\sqrt{8}}$ $= \frac{25}{15}\sqrt{\frac{56}{8}}$ $= \frac{5\sqrt{7}}{3}$	Rewrite the expression as a fraction. Rewrite the surds as a fraction under a single radical sign. Simplify the non-surd fraction and the fraction under the radical sign.
d. $\frac{24\sqrt{20}}{8\sqrt{12}} = 3\sqrt{\frac{5}{3}}$ $= \frac{3\sqrt{5}}{\sqrt{3}} \times \frac{\sqrt{3}}{\sqrt{3}}$ $= \frac{3\sqrt{15}}{3}$ $= \sqrt{15}$	Simplify both fractions. Rationalise the surd. Simplify the fractions by cancelling.

Exercise 5.3.1

Simplify the following surds.

a. $\sqrt{300}$

b. $\sqrt{\frac{225}{3}}$

c. $3\sqrt{20}$

d. $\frac{3\sqrt{18}}{\sqrt{12}}$

Exercise 5.3.2

Evaluate the following expressions.

a. $3\sqrt{15} + 3\sqrt{7} - 5\sqrt{7} + \sqrt{15}$

b. $3\sqrt{75} - 4\sqrt{72} + 2\sqrt{3} + 18\sqrt{2}$

c. $15\sqrt{6} \times 2\sqrt{3}$

d. $3\sqrt{3} \times 2\sqrt{10} \times 2\sqrt{2}$

e. $4\sqrt{15} \div 8\sqrt{5}$

f. $\frac{(2\sqrt{3})^2 \times \sqrt{10}}{3\sqrt{15}}$

Answers

Exercise 5.1

a. m b. $\frac{a^2}{9}$ c. $\frac{-8a^6}{c^3}$ d. -4 e. x^4y^{26}

f. $\frac{4y^3}{z^2}$ g. $\frac{5z^2}{y}$ h. $\frac{12y^9}{x}$ i. $\frac{x^{10}y}{4}$ j. $\frac{p^2q^4}{m^3}$

Exercise 5.2.1

a. 2.357×10^7 b. 5.1×10^5 c. 8.25×10^{12}

d. 3.3×10^{-3} e. 7.81×10^{-7} f. 2.0394×10^{-9}

Exercise 5.2.2

a. 3.2×10^7 b. 1.6×10^{-11}

c. 2×10^{-3} d. 4×10^{-8}

Exercise 5.3.1

a. $10\sqrt{3}$ b. $5\sqrt{3}$ c. $6\sqrt{5}$ d. $\frac{3\sqrt{6}}{2}$

Exercise 5.3.2

a. $4\sqrt{15} - 2\sqrt{7}$ b. $17\sqrt{3} - 6\sqrt{2}$ c. $90\sqrt{2}$

d. $24\sqrt{15}$ e. $\frac{\sqrt{3}}{2}$ f. $\frac{4\sqrt{6}}{3}$

Chapter 6 – Measurement

6.1 Units of measurement

In Australia, we use the International System of Units (SI units) for measurement. The SI unit for length is metres (m). We also use centimetres (cm), millimetres (mm) and kilometres (km). The relationships between these units are as follows.

$$1 \text{ kilometre} = 1000 \text{ metres}$$

$$1 \text{ metre} = 100 \text{ centimetres} = 1000 \text{ millimetres}$$

The following diagram may help when converting between these units.

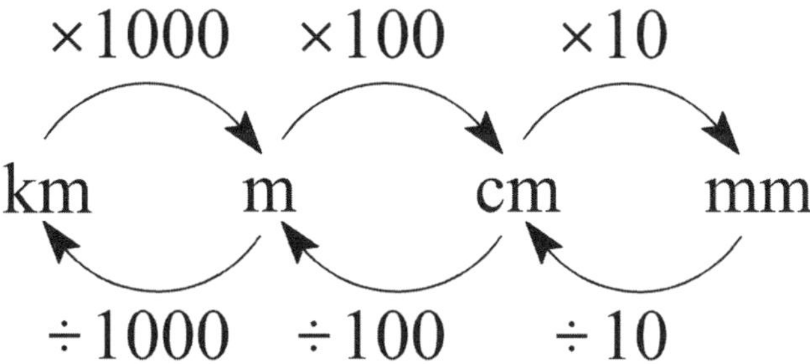

The units for area are square metres (m^2), square centimetres (cm^2), square millimetres (mm^2) and square kilometres (km^2). The relationships between these units are as follows.

$$1 \text{ km}^2 = 1000 \text{ m} \times 1000 \text{ m} = 1\,000\,000 \text{ m}^2$$

$$1 \text{ m}^2 = 1000 \text{ mm} \times 1000 \text{ mm} = 1\,000\,000 \text{ mm}^2$$

$$1 \text{ m}^2 = 100 \text{ cm} \times 100 \text{ cm} = 10\,000 \text{ cm}^2$$

$$1 \text{ cm}^2 = 10 \text{ mm} \times 10 \text{ mm} = 100 \text{ mm}^2$$

The following diagram may help when converting between these units.

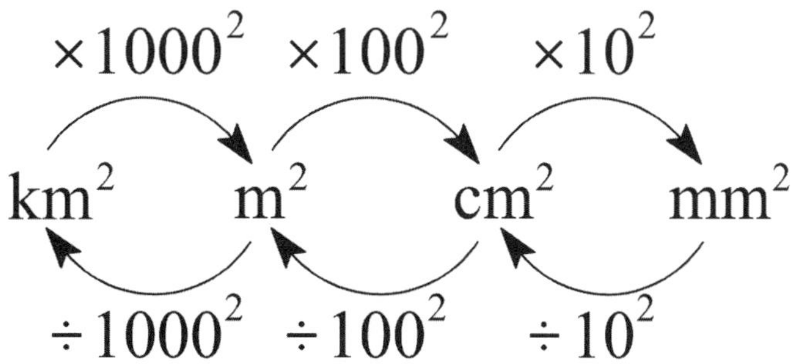

The measurements for volume are cubic metres (m^3), cubic centimetres (cm^3), cubic millimetres (mm^3), and cubic kilometres (km^3). The relationships between these units are as follows.

$$1\text{ km}^3 = 1000\text{ m} \times 1000\text{ m} \times 1000\text{ m} = 1\,000\,000\,000\text{ m}^3$$

$$1\text{ m}^3 = 100\text{ cm} \times 100\text{ cm} \times 100\text{ cm} = 1\,000\,000\text{ cm}^3$$

$$1\text{ m}^3 = 1000\text{ mm} \times 1000\text{ mm} \times 1000\text{ mm} = 1\,000\,000\,000\text{ mm}^3$$

The following diagram may help when converting between these units.

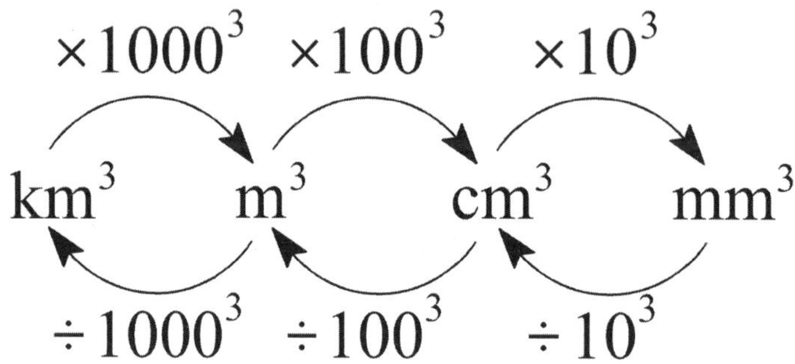

Example

Convert the following measurements into the units shown in brackets.

a. 9.6 km (m)
b. 45 cm (m)
c. 12.3 cm^2 (m^2)
d. 0.56 cm^2 (mm^2)
e. 2.01 cm^3 (mm^3)
f. 5800 cm^3 (m^3)

✓ Solution

Working	Explanation
a. $9.6 \times 1000 = 9600$ m	1 km = 1000 m, therefore we multiply by 1000.
b. $45 \div 100 = 0.45$ m	1 m = 100 cm, therefore we divide by 100.
c. $12.3 \div 10\,000 = 0.00123$ m^2	1 m^2 = 100 cm × 100 cm, therefore we divide by 10 000.
d. $0.56 \times 100 = 56$ mm^2	1 cm^2 = 10 mm × 10 mm, therefore we multiply by 100.
e. $2.01 \times 1000 = 2010$ mm^3	1 cm^3 = 10 mm × 10 mm × 10 mm, therefore we multiply by 1000.
f. $5800 \div 1\,000\,000 = 0.0058$ m^3	1 m^3 = 100 cm × 100 cm × 100 cm, therefore we divide by 1 000 000.

Exercise 6.1

Convert the following measurements into the units shown in brackets.

a. 18 235 m (km) **b.** 3.65 m (mm) **c.** 6.78 m^2 (cm^2)

d. 2300 mm^2 (cm^2) **e.** 102 mm^3 (cm^3) **f.** 0.678 m^3 (cm^3)

6.2 Area and perimeter of basic two-dimensional shapes

The formulas for the perimeter and area of basic two-dimensional shapes are shown below. We will apply these formulas in the next section of this chapter.

Shape	Diagram	Formula	
		Perimeter	Area
Square	a	$4a$	a^2
Rectangle	a, b	$2(a + b)$	ab
Triangle	c, h, a, b	$a + b + c$	$\frac{1}{2}bh$
Parallelogram	h, a, b	$2(a + b)$	bh

Trapezium	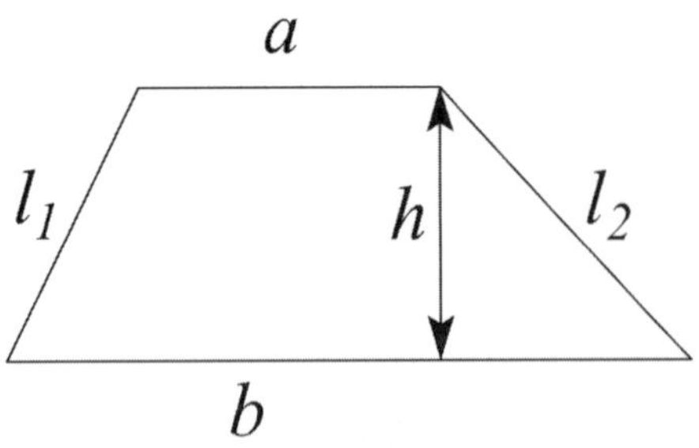	$a + b + l_1 + l_2$	$\frac{1}{2}(a + b)h$
Rhombus	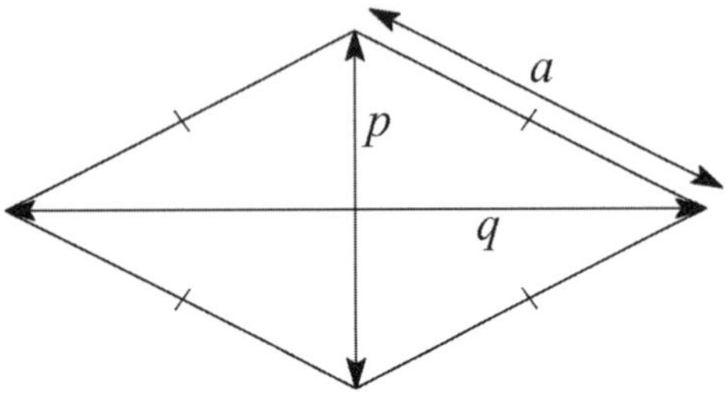	$4a$	$\frac{1}{2}pq$
Kite	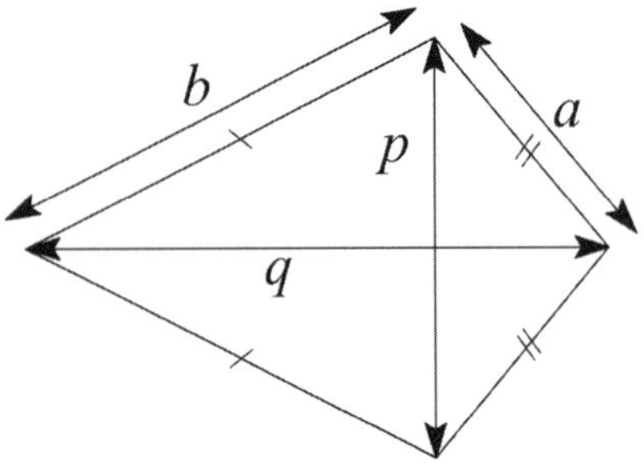	$2(a + b)$	$\frac{1}{2}pq$
Circle	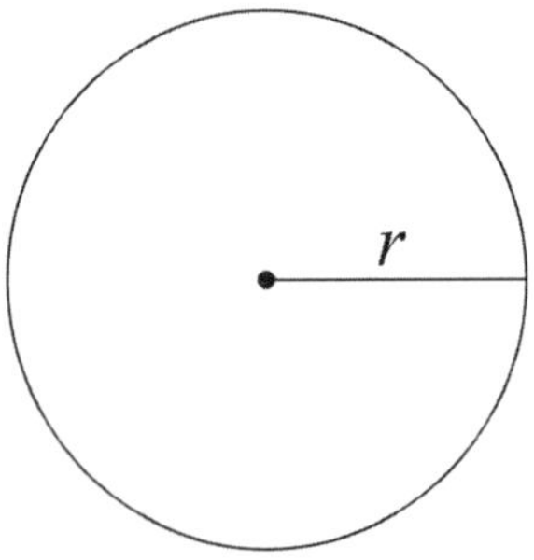	$2\pi r$ **Note:** the term circumference is used instead of the term perimeter when discussing a circle.	πr^2
Sector	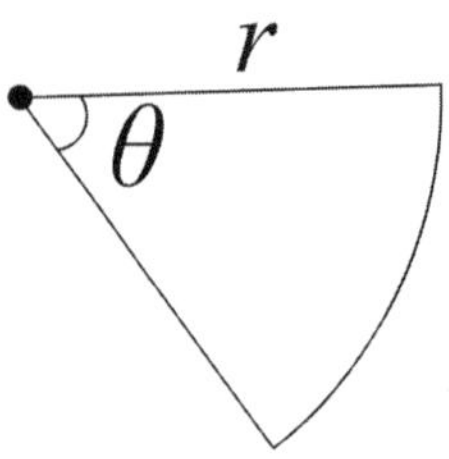	$\frac{\theta}{180}\pi r + 2r$ **Note:** a sector is a wedge-shaped part of a circle bounded by the centre of the circle and two points on the circle's circumference.	$\frac{\theta}{360}\pi r^2$

6.3 Area and perimeter of two-dimensional composite shapes

A composite shape is one made up of two or more basic shapes. The area of a composite shape can usually be obtained by adding the areas of the basic shapes that comprise it. (Sometimes the area of a composite shape can be calculated by subtracting the area of a basic shape that is 'missing'.)

Example

Calculate the perimeter and area of the following composite shapes.

a.

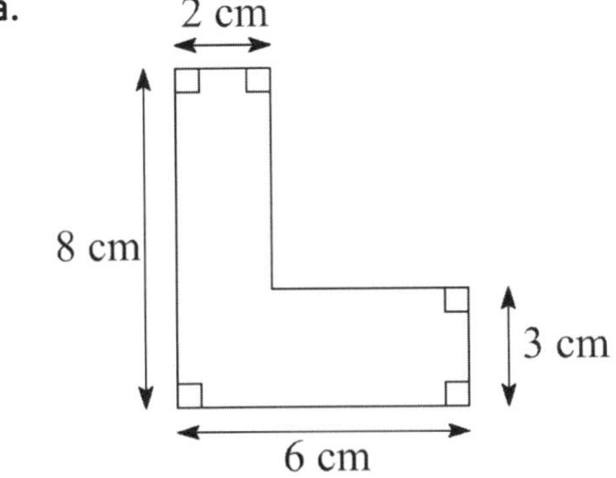

b.

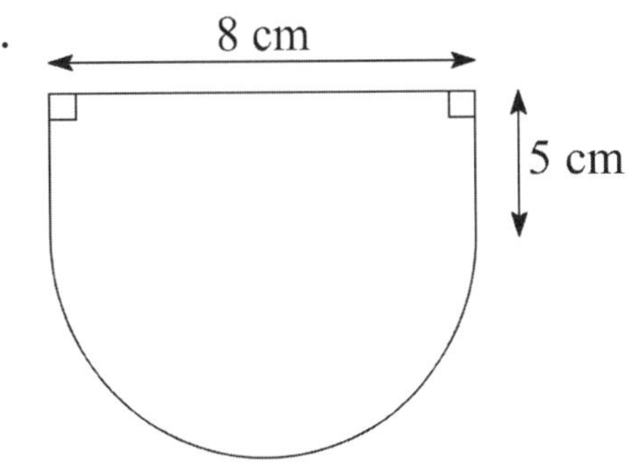

✓ *Solution*

Working	Explanation
a. 2 cm; 8 cm; A; $6-2=4$ cm; B; 3 cm; 6 cm	This is a composite shape made up of two rectangles.
Area $A = 2 \times 8 = 16$ Area $B = 3 \times 4 = 12$	Calculate the area of each rectangle.
Total area $= 16 + 12 = 28$ cm^2	Add the two areas to determine the total area of the composite shape.
Perimeter $= 2 + 8 + 6 + 3 + 4 + (8 - 3)$ $= 28$ cm	Find the perimeter by adding the length of each side of the composite shape.

b. 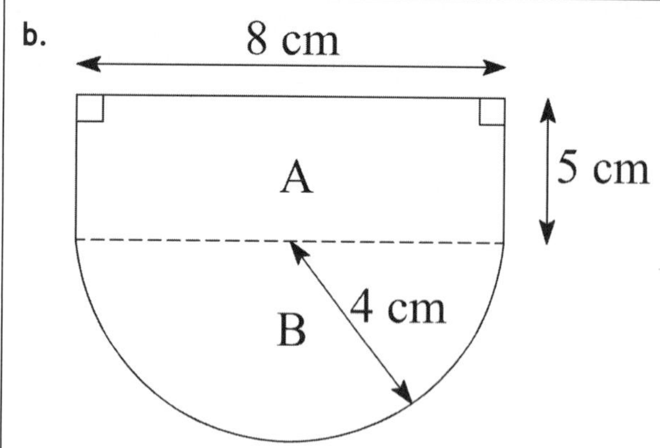	This is a composite shape made up of a rectangle and a semicircle (half a circle). Calculate the area of the rectangle and the area of the semicircle. The area of the composite shape is the sum of the area of the rectangle and the area of the semicircle.
Area $A = 5 \times 8 = 40$ Area $B = \frac{1}{2}\pi(4^2) = 8\pi = 25.132741$ Total area $= 65.132741 = 65.13$ cm^2	**Note:** when you are calculating the area of a circle (or part of a circle), an answer with π is the exact value. When giving the answer as a decimal, always give the answer to 2 decimal places unless the question says otherwise.
$A = 5 + 5 + 8 = 18$ $B = \frac{1}{2}(2\pi 4) = 4\pi = 12.56637$ Total perimeter $= 30.56637 = 30.57$ cm	Calculate the perimeter of the rectangle: A. (Remember not to add the 8 cm side in the centre of the composite shape.) Calculate the perimeter of the semicircle: B. (Remember not to add the 8 cm side that forms the base of the semicircle.) Add the perimeters of the rectangle and semicircle to determine the perimeter of the entire shape.

Example

Calculate the area of the shaded region.

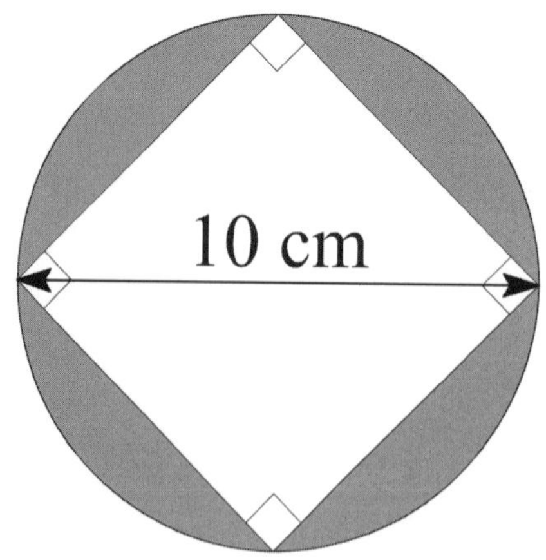

✓ ***Solution***

Working	Explanation
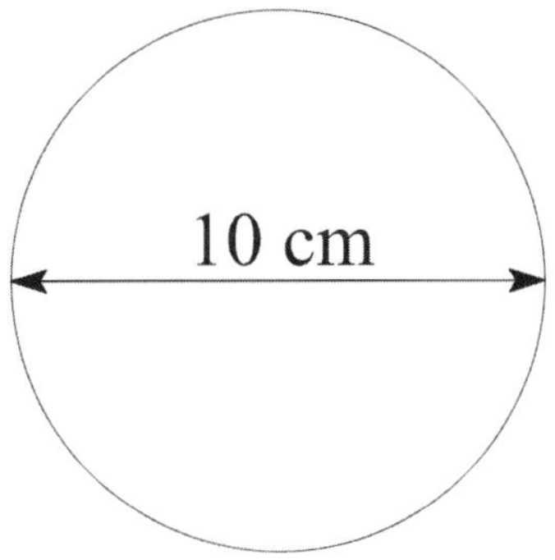 10 cm	The composite shape is made up of a circle surrounding a rhombus (which in this case is also a square).
Area of circle $= 25\pi = 78.53982$	Calculate the area of the circle.
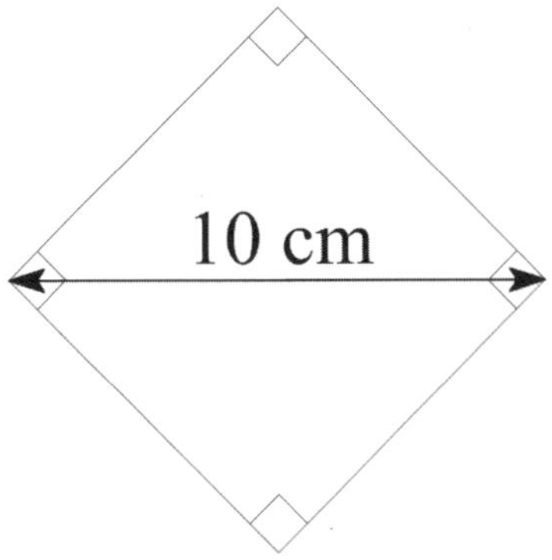 10 cm	
Area of rhombus $= \frac{1}{2}(10)(10) = 50$	Calculate the area of the rhombus.
Area of shaded region $= 78.53982 - 50 = 28.54\text{ cm}^2$	Subtract the area of the rhombus from the area of the circle to determine the area of the shaded region.

Note:

- Always state the units at the end of your answer.
- Give your answers to 2 decimal places, unless the answer is a whole number or the question says otherwise.

Exercise 6.3.1

Calculate the perimeters and areas of the following composite shapes.

a.

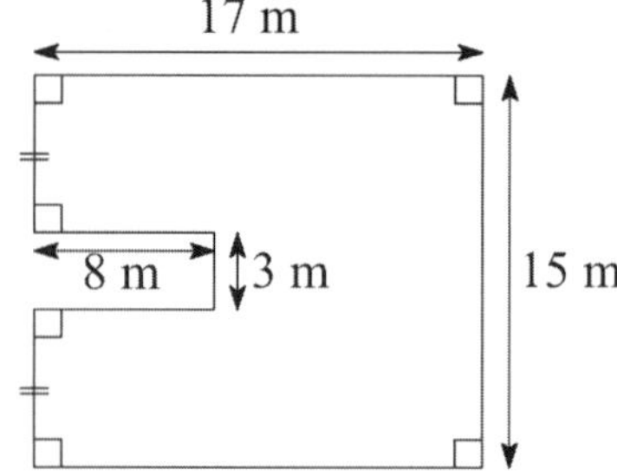

b.

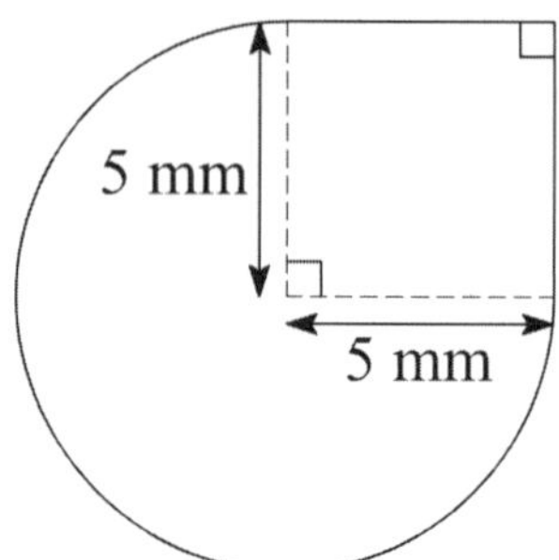

c.

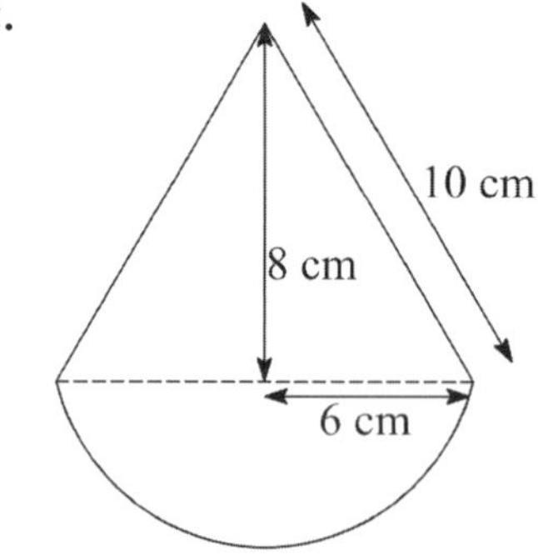

Exercise 6.3.2

Calculate the areas of the shaded regions in the shapes below.

a.

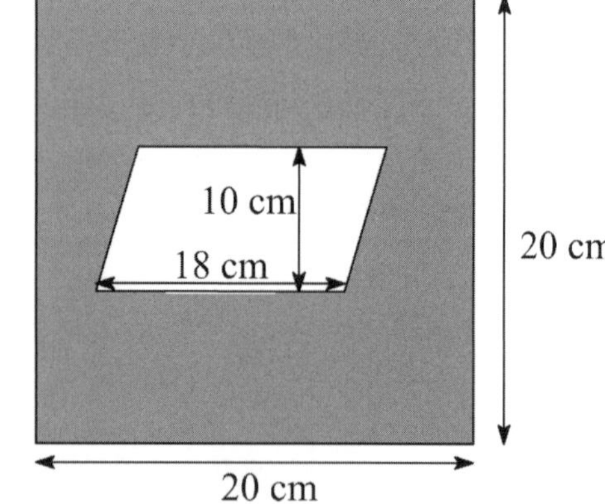

b.

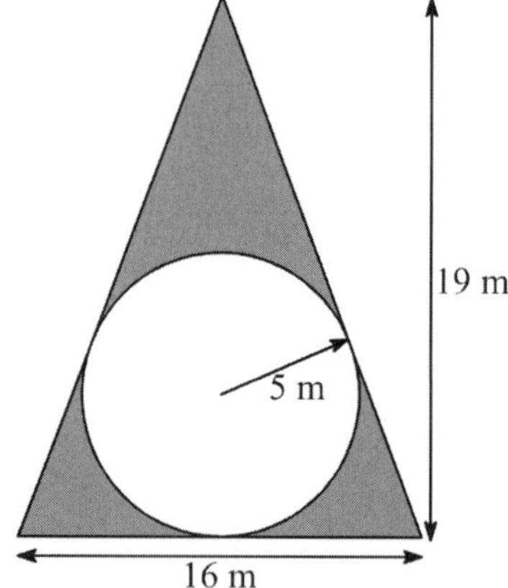

6.4 Total surface area of a three-dimensional object

For a three-dimensional object, the total surface area (TSA) is the sum of the areas of each of the shapes that make up the surface of the object. To help you see the shapes of the surfaces that make up a three-dimensional object, draw a net of the object. You can then use the area formula for each shape to calculate the TSA.

Note: in geometry, a three-dimensional object is also called a 'solid'.

The following are the nets of some common three-dimensional objects.

Three-dimensional object	Net of the object	Two-dimensional shapes
Rectangular prism 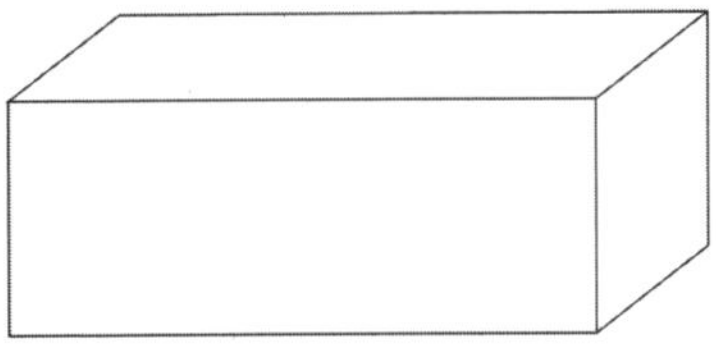	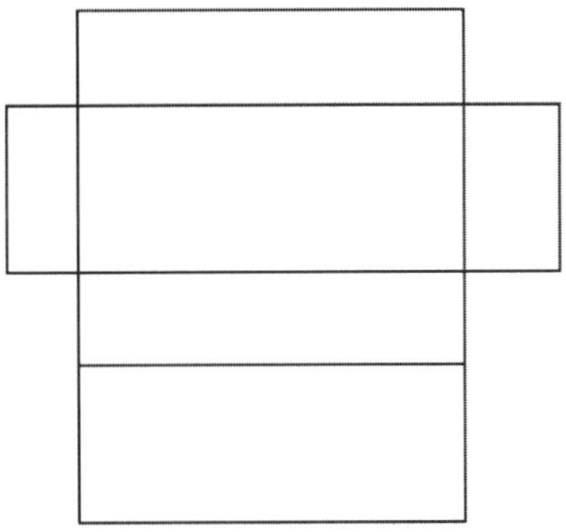	A rectangular prism has 6 surfaces, each one a rectangle.
Triangular prism 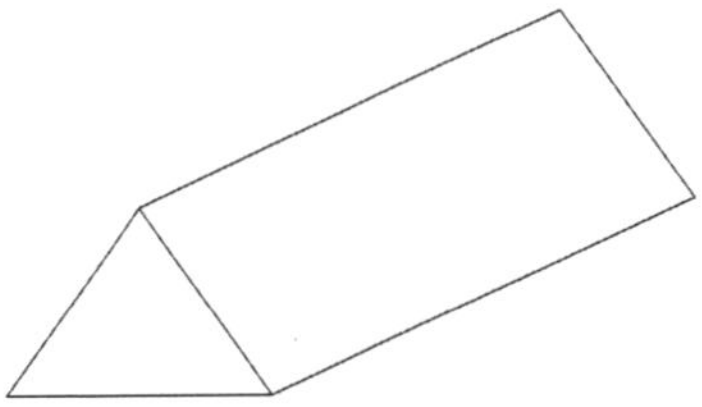	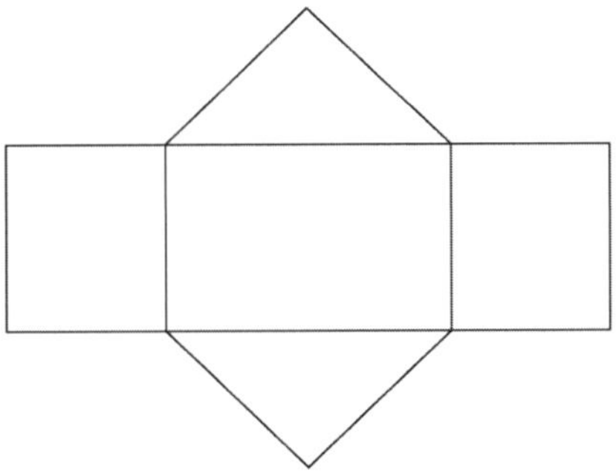	A triangular prism has 5 surfaces: 2 triangles and 3 rectangles.
Pyramid 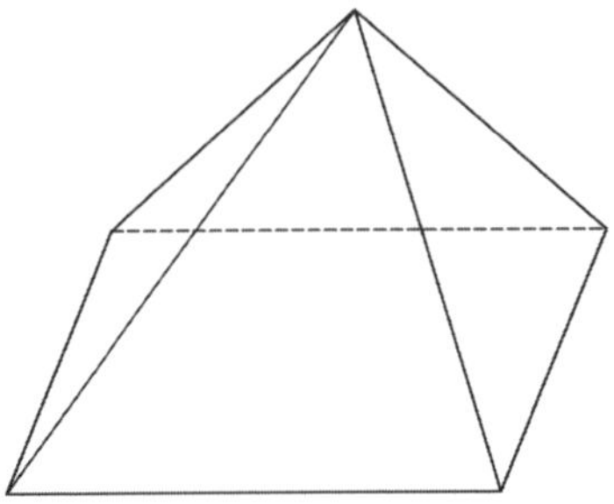	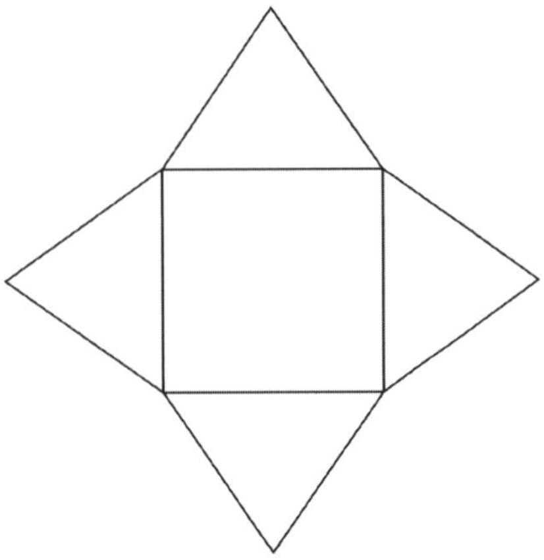	A pyramid has 5 surfaces: 4 triangles and 1 square.
Cylinder 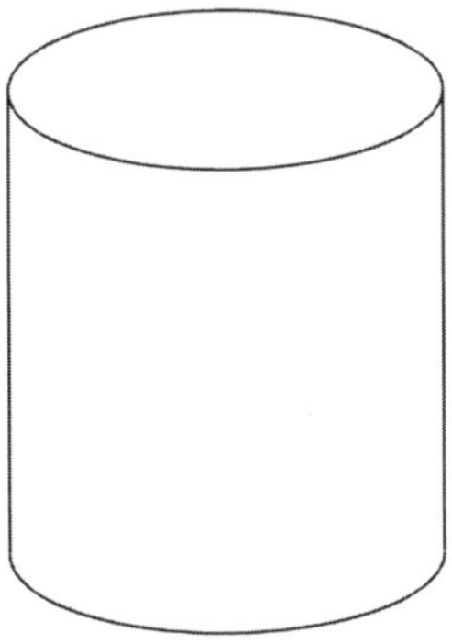	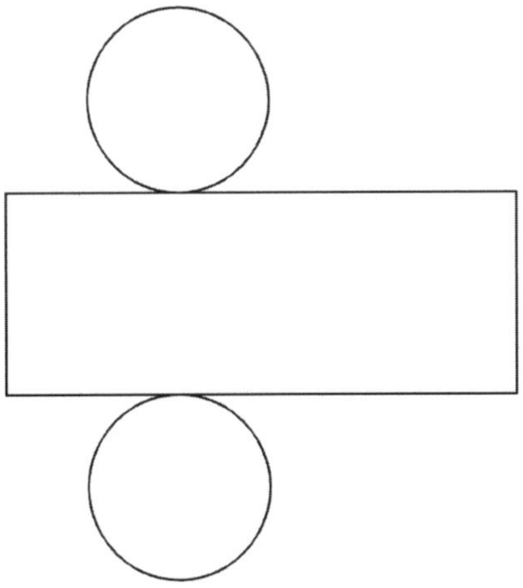	A cylinder has 3 surfaces: 2 circles and 1 rectangle. **Note:** the width of the rectangle is the height of the cylinder and the length of the rectangle is the circumference of the circle.

Example

Determine the total surface area (TSA) of the following three-dimensional objects.

a.

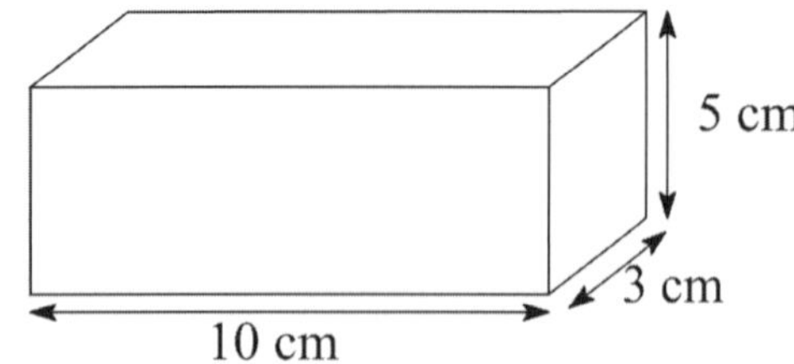

b.

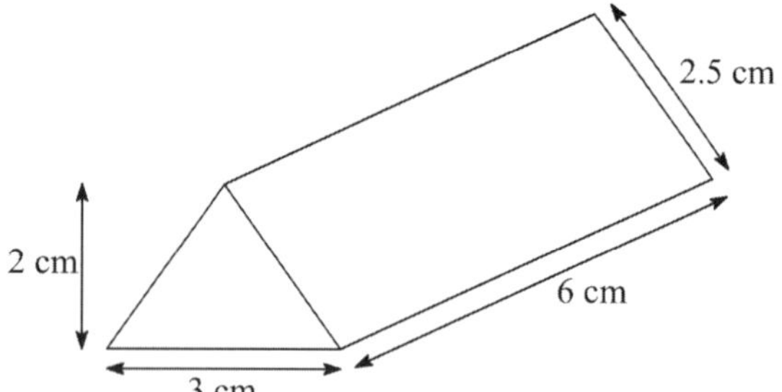

c.

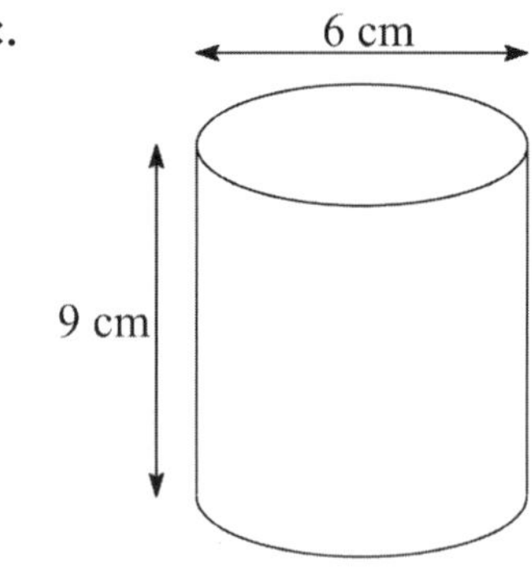

✓ *Solution*

Working	Explanation
a. (net: 10 cm; 3 cm; A; C; B; C; 5 cm; 3 cm; A; B; 5 cm)	Draw the net of a rectangular prism. (You can skip this step if you can visualise the net.) Label shapes of identical dimensions and work out the dimensions of each two-dimensional shape.
Area $A = 10 \times 3 = 30$ Area $B = 10 \times 5 = 50$ Area $C = 5 \times 3 = 15$	Calculate the area of each shape.
$\text{TSA} = 2 \times 30 + 2 \times 50 + 2 \times 15 = 190 \text{ cm}^2$	Add the areas to determine the TSA of the rectangular prism.

b. 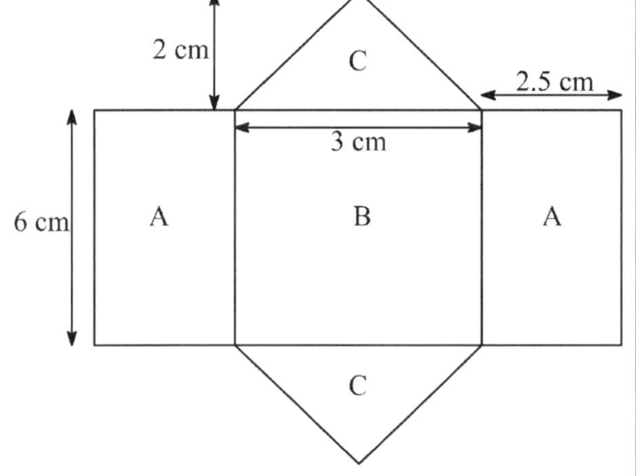	Draw the net of the triangular prism and work out the dimensions of each two-dimensional shape. Label shapes of identical dimensions.
Area $A = 6 \times 2.5 = 15$ Area $B = 6 \times 3 = 18$ Area $C = 0.5(3 \times 2) = 3$	Calculate the area of each shape.
$\text{TSA} = 2 \times 15 + 18 + 2 \times 3 = 54\text{ cm}^2$	Add the areas to determine the TSA of the triangular prism.
c. 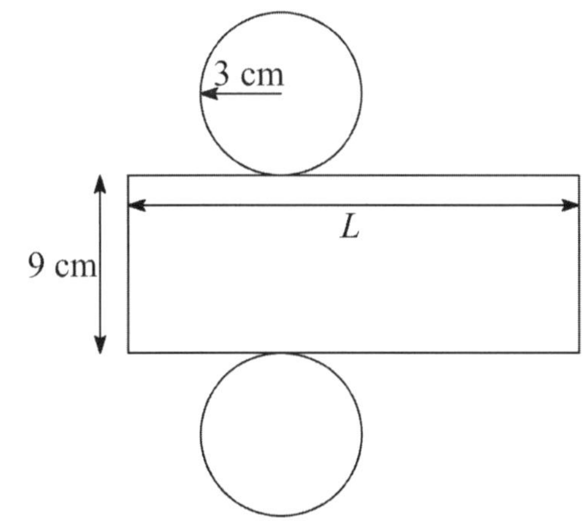	Draw the net of a cylinder and work out the dimensions of each two-dimensional shape. **Note:** the original diagram provides the diameter of a circle (the top of the cylinder). You need the radius for your calculations, which is half the diameter. Determine the length of the rectangle (i.e. the body of the cylinder). This is the circumference of a circle.
$L = 2\pi(3) = 6\pi$ Area of the circle $= \pi 3^2 = 9\pi = 28.27433$ Area of the body $= 6\pi \times 9 = 54\pi = 169.64600$	Calculate the area of both shapes.
$\text{TSA} = 2 \times 28.27433 + 169.64600$ $= 226.19\text{ cm}^2$	Add the areas to determine the TSA of the cylinder.

Exercise 6.4

Determine the total surface area (TSA) of the following objects.

a. A square-based pyramid

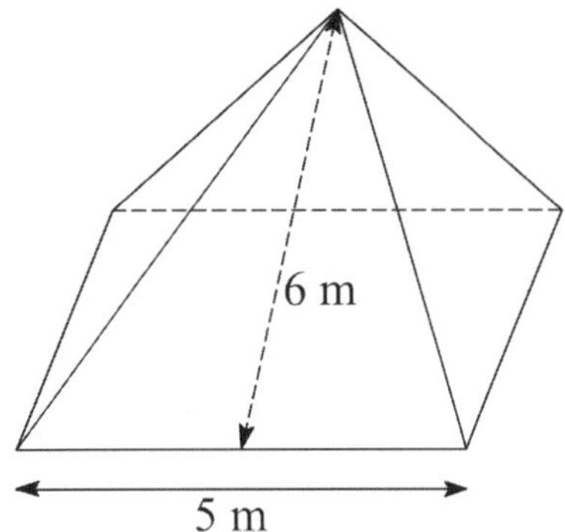

b. A triangular prism

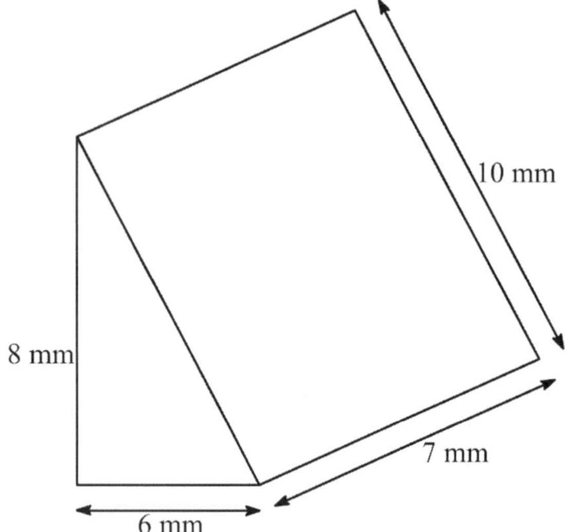

c. The outside surface of an open pipe

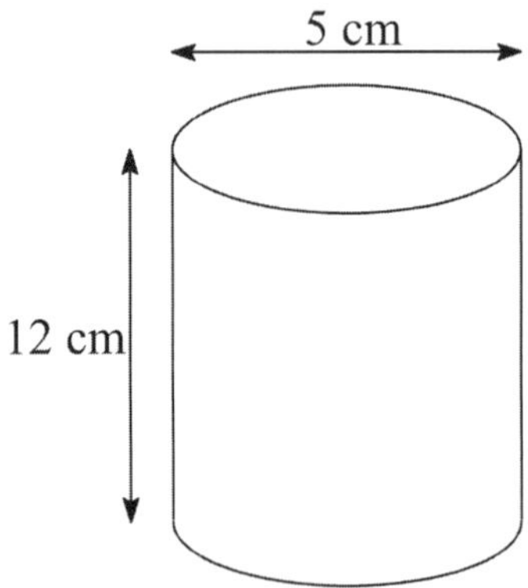

6.5 Volume of a right prism and a cylinder

A right prism is an object with two parallel bases of the same shape and several rectangular faces joining the bases. The bases and the rectangular faces meet at an angle of 90°.

(**Note:** a pyramid is not a right prism because it has no parallel faces.)

The volume of a right prism is given by the formula

volume = base area × height

The following three diagrams are examples of right prisms. The first is called a rectangular prism and the second is called a triangular prism. As the third diagram indicates, the two bases of a right prism can be any shape, as long as they are identical and parallel.

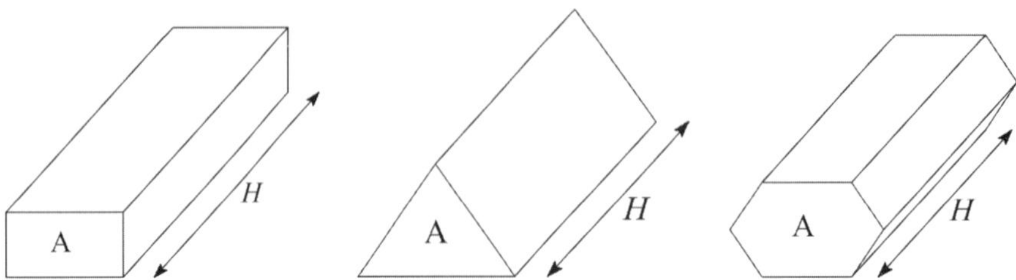

In each case, the volume of the right prism is the base area (A) multiplied by the height (H). You can determine the base area using the area formula for the type of shape that the base is.

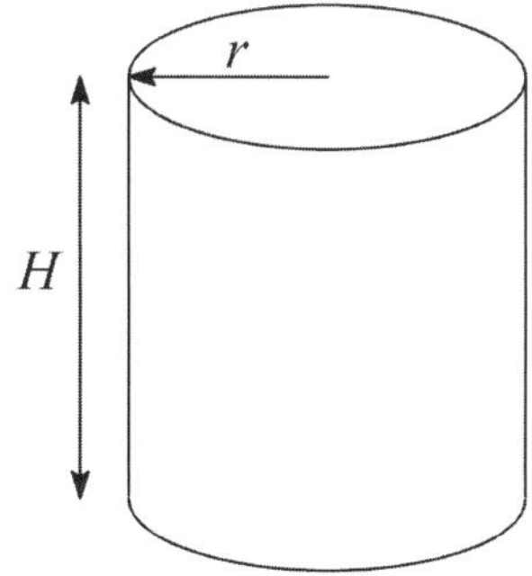

Although a cylinder is not a right prism (as it has no rectangular faces), the formula for the volume of a cylinder is the same: $A \times H$. Since the base area for a cylinder is the area of a circle, the volume of a cylinder is given by

$$\textbf{\textit{volume}} = \pi r^2 H$$

6.6 Volume of a composite solid

A composite solid is a solid made by combining two or more other solids. (Recall that a solid is a three-dimensional object.)

To calculate the volume of a composite solid, separate it into the different solids that comprise it, and then calculate the volume of each solid. Finally, add together the volumes of each component solid to determine the volume of the composite solid.

Example

Determine the volume of the following three-dimensional objects.

a. An L-shaped right prism

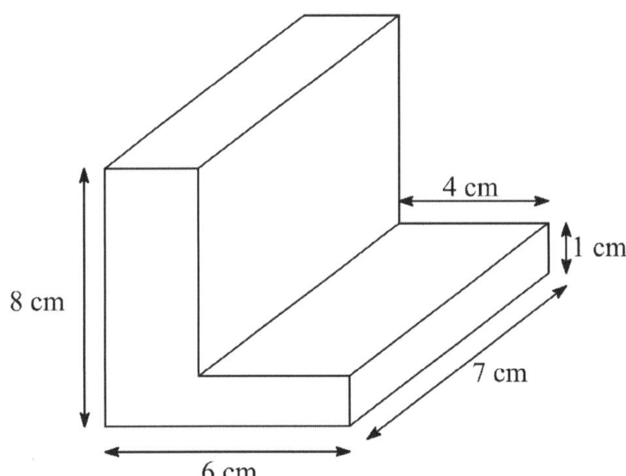

b. A rectangular prism with a round hole drilled through it

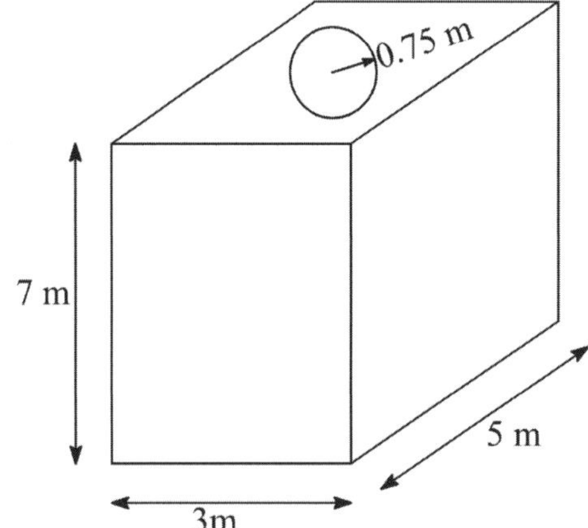

✓ *Solution*

Working	Explanation
a. 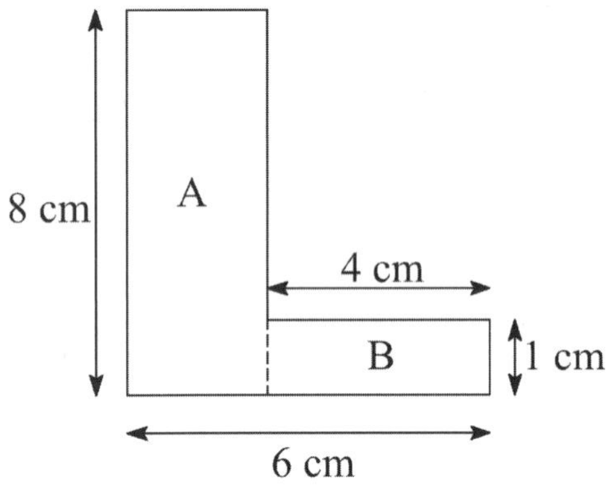 8 cm, A, 4 cm, B, 1 cm, 6 cm	Determine the area of the L-shaped base of the prism.
Area $A = 2 \times 8 = 16$ Area $B = 4 \times 1 = 4$ Total base area $= 20$ cm^2 Volume $= 20 \times 7 = 140$ cm^3	Multiply the area by the height to obtain the volume of the object.
b. 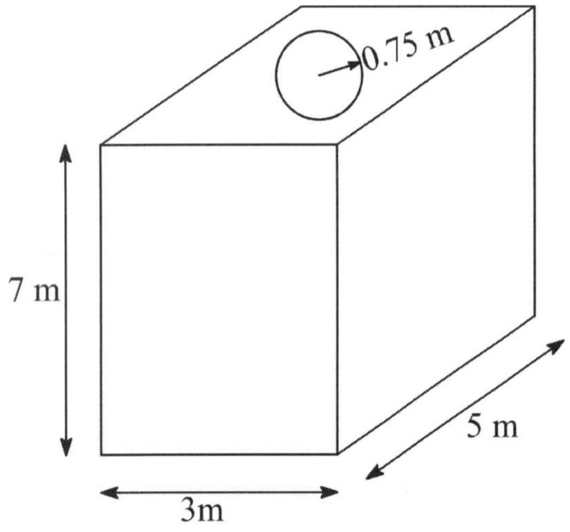 0.75 m, 7 m, 5 m, 3m	
Volume of the rectangular prism $= 3 \times 5 \times 7$ $= 105$ m^3	Determine the volume of the rectangular prism if there is no hole drilled through it.
Volume of hole/cylinder $= \pi \times 0.75 \times 0.75 \times 7$ $= 12.37002$ m^3	Determine the volume of the hole (which is cylindrical in shape).
Volume of solid $= 105 - 12.37002$ $= 92.63$ m^3	Subtract the volume of the hole from the volume of the rectangular prism.

Exercise 6.6

Determine the volume of:

a. the rectangular prism with a cylinder on top, as shown below

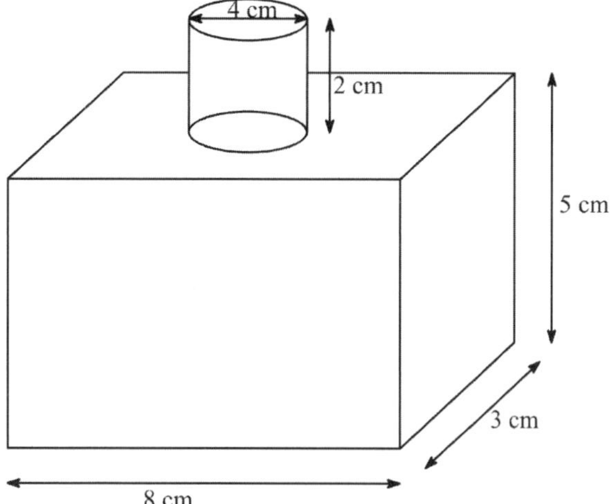

b. the cylinder with two square holes passing right through it, as shown below.

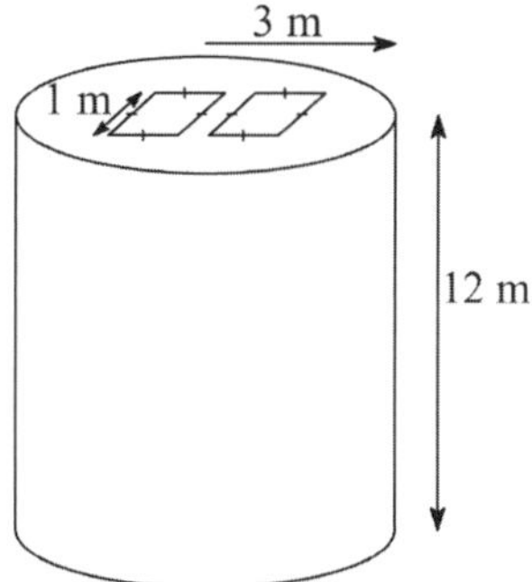

6.7 Volume versus capacity

It is important to recognise the difference between the volume of a solid and the capacity of an object of the same size.

- **Volume** is the amount of space the object occupies.
- **Capacity** is the amount of something (e.g. water) that the object can hold.

Volume is usually measured in cubic metres (m^3), cubic centimetres (cm^3) or a similar unit. Capacity is usually measured in litres (L), kilolitres or a similar unit.

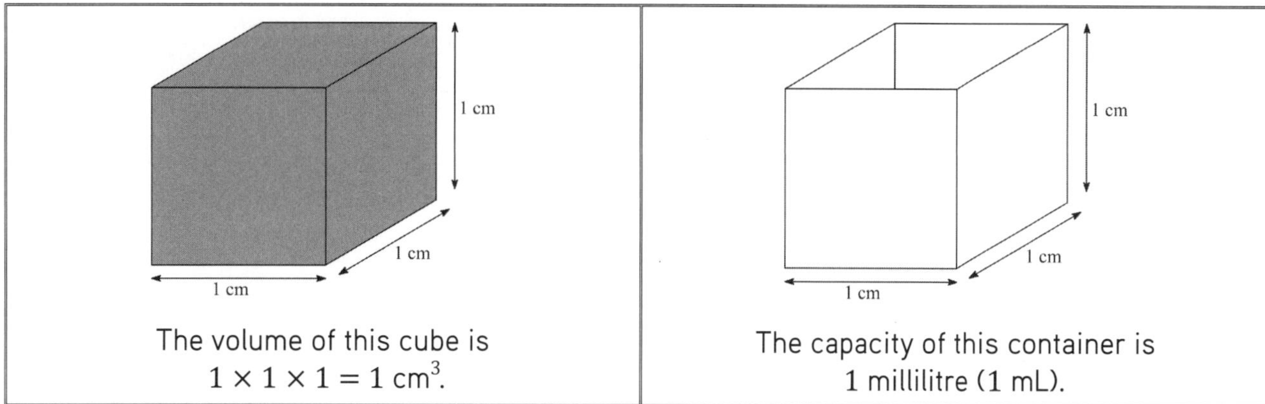

The volume of this cube is $1 \times 1 \times 1 = 1$ cm^3.	The capacity of this container is 1 millilitre (1 mL).

By comparing these two objects, we can see that 1 cubic centimetre (cm^3) = 1 millilitre (mL). Further, since 1000 mL = 1 litre (L), 1 L = 1000 cm^3.

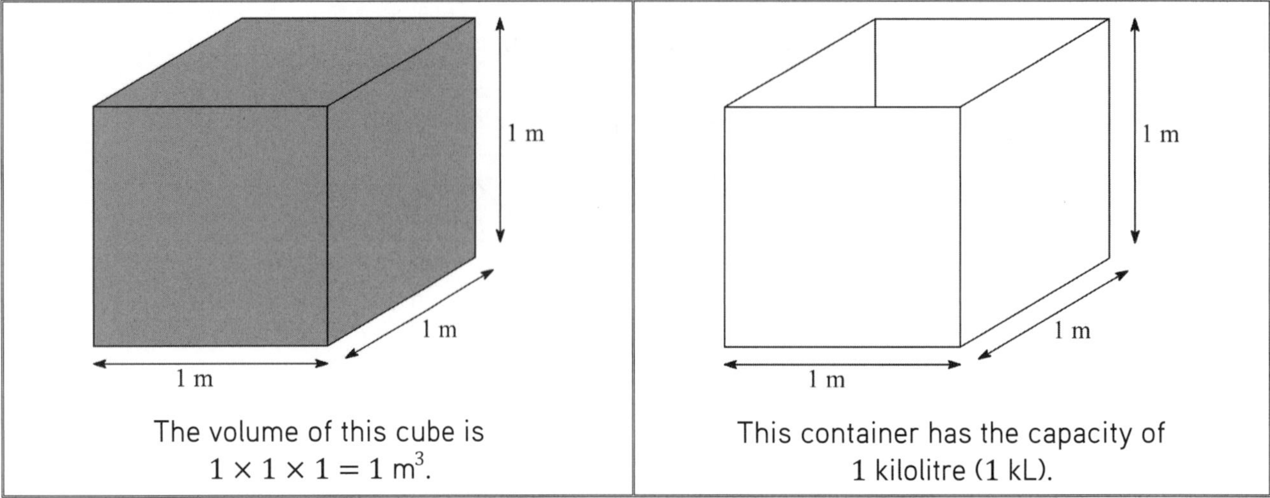

The volume of this cube is $1 \times 1 \times 1 = 1\ m^3$.	This container has the capacity of 1 kilolitre (1 kL).

By comparing these two objects, we can see that 1 cubic metre (m^3) = 1 kilolitre (kL).

Example

Convert the following measurements into the units shown in brackets.

a. 18.2 m^3 (L)

b. 385 cm^3 (L)

c. 24 800 L (m^3)

d. 102 L (cm^3)

✓ *Solution*

Working	Explanation
a. 18.2 m^3 = 18.2 kL = 18 200 L	Since 1 m^3 = 1 kL and 1 kL = 1000 L, multiply 18.2 by 1000 to convert it from m^3 to L.
b. 385 cm^3 = 385 mL = 0.385 L	Since 1 cm^3 = 1 mL and 1000 mL = 1 L, divide 385 by 1000 to convert it from cm^3 to L.
c. 24 800 L = 24.8 kL = 24.8 m^3	Since 1 kL = 1000 L, divide 24 800 by 1000 to convert it from L to kL and then to m^3, since 1 kL = 1 m^3.
d. 102 L = 102 000 mL = 102 000 cm^3	Since 1 L = 1000 mL, multiply 102 by 1000 to convert it from L to mL and then to cm^3, since 1 mL = 1 cm^3.

Exercise 6.7

Convert the following measurements into the units shown in brackets

a. $28\ 000$ cm^3 (kL)

b. 32.45 m^3 (L)

c. 98.6 L (cm^3)

d. 634.25 L (m^3)

6.8 Practical applications

We will now look at some practical applications of calculating measurements.

Example

Mark wants to paint a wall in his living room. The width of the wall is 2.95 m and the height is 3.10 m. The room has a square window, with each side measuring 850 mm.

a. Determine the total area Mark needs to paint.

b. Mark wants to paint the wall with two coats of paint. He knows that 85 mL of paint is required for 1 m^2 of wall. Determine the amount of paint required to paint the entire wall.

✓ Solution

Working	Explanation
a. Area of the wall $= 2.95 \times 3.10 = 9.145$ m^2 The length of the window is 850 mm $= 0.85$ m. Area of the window $= 0.85^2 = 0.7225$ m^2	Determine the area of the wall. Convert the length of the sides of the window to metres and calculate the area of the window.
Area of the wall to be painted $= 9.145 - 0.7225$ $= 8.4225$ $= 8.42$ m^2	Subtract the area of the window from the area of the wall to obtain the area to be painted.
b. Amount of paint required $= 85 \times 8.4225 \times 2$ $= 1431.83$ mL	Multiply the area by the amount of paint required per square metre, and then double the answer to obtain the amount of paint required for two coats. **Note:** for accuracy, the area used in the calculation has more than 2 decimal places.

Example

A fishpond is to be built in a garden. The dimensions of the garden and the fishpond are shown in the diagram to the right.

a. Determine the area of the garden after the fishpond is built.

b. The depth of the fishpond is 1.5 m. Determine the volume of soil that needs to be excavated to build the fishpond.

c. After the fishpond is built, its capacity is found to be 90% of its volume (due to the thickness of the concrete base and sides). Determine the amount of water required to fill the fishpond, to the nearest litre.

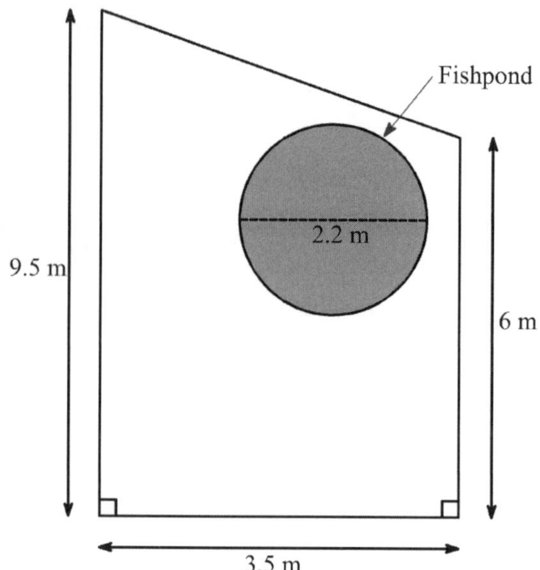

✓ *Solution*

Working	Explanation
a. Area of the garden $= \frac{1}{2}(6 + 9.5)(3.5)$ $= 27.125\ \text{m}^2$ Area of the fishpond $= \pi\left(\frac{2.2}{2}\right)^2$ $= 3.801\ \text{m}^2$ Area of the remaining garden $= 23.32\ \text{m}^2$	Determine the area of the garden and the fishpond. Subtract the area of the fishpond from the area of the garden.
b. Volume of soil to be excavated $= 3.801 \times 1.5$ $= 5.70\ \text{m}^3$	Use the volume formula for a cylinder.
c. $5.7015 \times 0.9 = 5.13135$ kL $= 5131$ L	Convert m^3 to kL ($1\ \text{m}^3 = 1$ kL) and then convert the capacity to L. For accuracy, the value used for the volume has 4 decimal places. The final value is then rounded to the nearest litre as required by the question.

Exercise 6.8

The side-view design for a skateboard ramp shows a semicircle cut from a rectangle. The dimensions are shown in the diagram below.

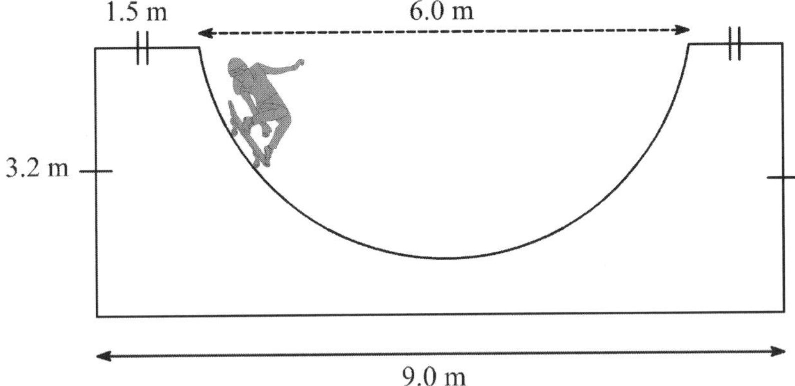

a. Determine the perimeter of the side view of the ramp, to 1 decimal place.

b. Determine the area of the side view of the ramp, to 2 decimal places.

c. The skateboard ramp will be 4.5 m long and made of concrete. Determine the amount of concrete required to build this skateboard ramp, to the nearest 1000 L.

6.9 Errors in measurement

It is important to realise that there are inherent errors in all measurements, and therefore measurements are actually estimates.

For example, suppose we drive from Melbourne to Bendigo and notice that the odometer records the distance travelled as 151 km. However, this is equivalent to any distance between 150 500 m and 151 400 m when converted to kilometres and rounded to zero decimal places. Relying on the odometer has introduced a **measurement error**.

When considering measurement errors, we need to distinguish between absolute error and percentage error.

Absolute error is the absolute difference between the actual value and the measured value.

Percentage error is the absolute error expressed as a percentage of the actual value.

Suppose that the actual distance between Melbourne and Bendigo is 151 230 m, but we say that the distance is 151 km (or 151 000 m).

$$\text{Absolute error} = 151\,230 - 151\,000 = 230\text{ m}$$

$$\text{Percentage error} = \frac{230}{151\,230} \times 100\% = 0.15\%$$

Note that absolute error is always positive, as we are only determining the magnitude of the difference between the measured and actual value.

For another example, suppose that the actual diameter of a bolt is 1.5 cm but we measure it as 1.7 cm.

$$\text{Absolute error} = 1.5 - 1.7 = 0.2 \text{ cm}$$

$$\text{Percentage error} = \frac{0.2}{1.5} \times 100\% = 13.33\%$$

Even though the absolute error is only 0.2 cm, the percentage error is 13.33%. This percentage error is quite large. Compare it with the Melbourne–Bendigo example considered earlier, where the percentage error was only 0.15%, even though the absolute error is much larger by comparison. This shows that it is important to think about context when stating an error.

You will often see a measurement quoted as $a \pm b$. This means that the upper bound of the measurement is $a + b$ and the lower bound of the measurement is $a - b$. In this case, the absolute error is b.

Example

Calculate the absolute and percentage errors in the following examples.

a. actual weight: 1220 g

measured weight: 1.2 kg

b. actual distance: 450 m

measured distance: 45 300 cm

✓ *Solution*

Working	Explanation
a. Absolute error $= 1220 - 1200 = 20$ g Percentage error $= \frac{20}{1220} \times 100\% = 1.64\%$	Convert the measured quantity to the same unit as the actual quantity. Calculate the actual and percentage error.
b. Absolute error $= 45\ 000 - 45\ 300 = 300$ cm Percentage error $= \frac{300}{45\ 000} \times 100\% = 0.67\%$	Remember that the absolute error is always a positive value. When calculating it, it doesn't matter whether you subtract the actual value from the measured value, or the measured value from the actual value.

Example

State the upper and lower bounds of the following measurements.

a. 250 ± 20 g

b. 340 ± 34 m

✓ ***Solution***

Working	Explanation
a. Upper bound $= 270$ g Lower bound $= 230$ g	Determine the upper bound by adding the second number to the first number. Determine the lower bound by subtracting the second number from the first number.
b. Upper bound $= 374$ m Lower bound $= 306$ m	

Exercise 6.9.1

Calculate the absolute and percentage errors in the following examples.

a. actual distance: 8.2 mm
measured distance: 1.0 cm

b. actual weight: 6.35 kg
measured weight: 6400 g

Exercise 6.9.2

State the upper and lower bounds of the following quantities.

a. 20 ± 0.5 km

b. 80 ± 8 cm^2

Exercise 6.9.3

A manufacturer of a chocolate bar states that the mass of a bar is 150 g. The manufacturer also states that the percentage error for each bar is $\pm 2\%$ of the stated measurement. What is the upper bound and lower bound of the mass of a bar?

Answers

Exercise 6.1

a. 18.235 km
b. 3650 mm
c. 67 800 cm^2
d. 23 cm^2
e. 0.102 cm^3
f. 678 000 cm^3

Exercise 6.3.1

a. 80 m , 231 m^2
b. 33.56 mm , 83.90 mm^2
c. 38.85 cm , 104.55 cm^2

Exercise 6.3.2

a. 220 cm^2
b. 73.46 m^2

Exercise 6.4

a. 85 m^2
b. 216 mm^2
c. 188.50 cm^2

Exercise 6.6

a. 145.13 cm^2
b. 315.29 m^2

Exercise 6.7

a. 0.028 kL
b. 32 450 L
c. 98 600 cm^3
d. 0.63425 m^3

Exercise 6.8

a. 27.8 m
b. 14.66 m^2
c. 66 000 L

Exercise 6.9.1

a. Absolute error = 1.8 mm
   Percentage error = 21.95%
b. Absolute error = 50 g
   Percentage error = 0.79%

Exercise 6.9.2

a. Upper bound = 20.5 km
   Lower bound = 19.5 km
b. Upper bound = 88 cm^2
   Lower bound = 72 cm^2

Exercise 6.9.3

Upper bound = 153 g

Lower bound = 147 g

Chapter 7 – Pythagoras' theorem and trigonometry

7.1 Pythagoras' theorem

Pythagoras' theorem states that for any right-angled triangle, the square of the length of the hypotenuse is the sum of the squares of the lengths of the other two sides of the triangle. The hypotenuse is the longest side of the triangle and is always opposite the right angle.

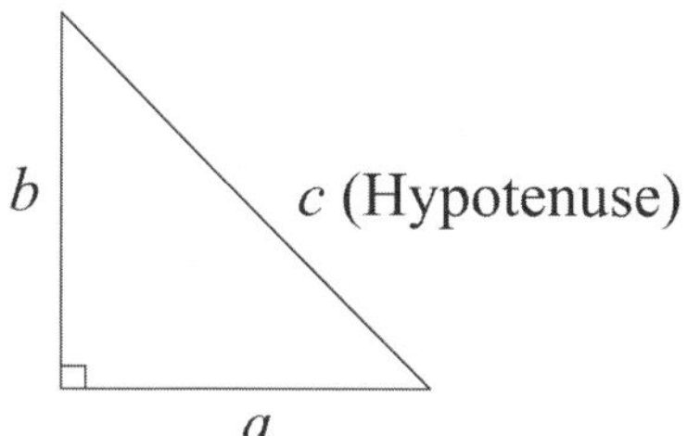

Pythagoras' theorem

$$c^2 = a^2 + b^2$$

Any triangle that satisfies Pythagoras' theorem is a right-angled triangle.

If the lengths of any two sides of a right-angled triangle are given, we can calculate the length of the third side using Pythagoras' theorem.

Unknown side	How to use Pythagoras' theorem
Hypotenuse	Since $c^2 = a^2 + b^2$ Therefore $c = \sqrt{a^2 + b^2}$
A side other than the hypotenuse	Since $c^2 = a^2 + b^2$ Therefore $a^2 = c^2 - b^2$ $a = \sqrt{c^2 - b^2}$

Example

Determine the length of the unknown side (x) in each of the following right-angled triangles. All dimensions are in cm.

a.

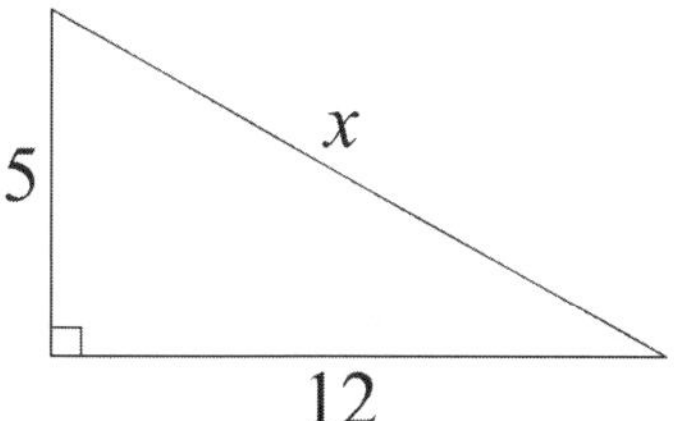

b.

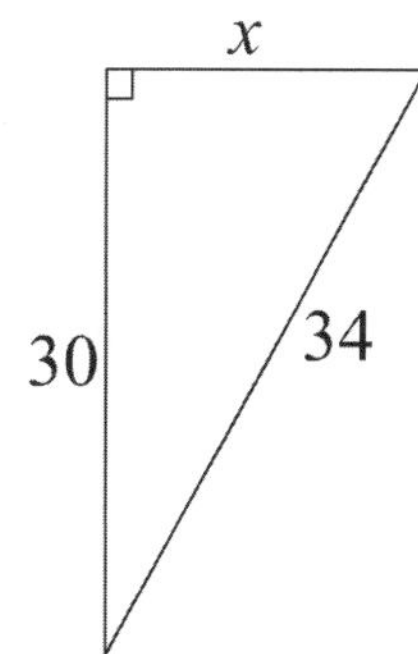

c.

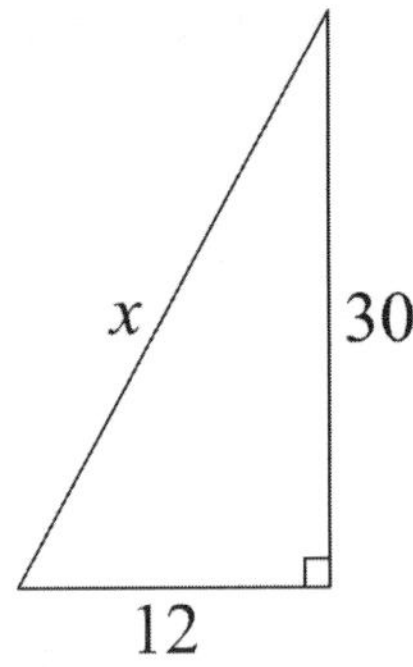

d.

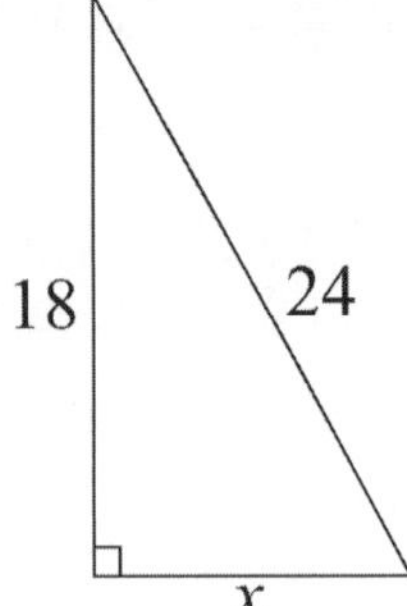

✓ Solution

Working	Explanation
a. $x^2 = 12^2 + 5^2$ $x = \sqrt{144 + 25}$ $x = \sqrt{169}$ $x = 13$ cm	Substitute the known values into Pythagoras' theorem and solve for the unknown value. **Note:** unless you are asked to give the answer in decimal form, you may give it as an exact value (i.e. as a surd).
b. $x^2 = 34^2 - 30^2$ $x = \sqrt{34^2 - 30^2}$ $x = \sqrt{256}$ $x = 16$ cm	
c. $x^2 = 12^2 + 30^2$ $x = \sqrt{1044}$ $x = 6\sqrt{29}$ cm $x = 32.31$ cm	
d. $x^2 = 24^2 - 18^2$ $x = \sqrt{252}$ $x = 6\sqrt{7}$ cm $x = 15.87$ cm	

Example

Determine if each set of values below could be the sides of a right-angled triangle.

a. 24, 32, 40

b. 16, 15, 28

✓ ***Solution***

Working	Explanation
a. Hypotenuse $= 40$ $40^2 = 1600$ $24^2 + 32^2 = 1600$ $1600 = 1600$ This is a right-angled triangle.	Identify the hypotenuse. It will be the greatest of the three values. Determine the square of the hypotenuse. Determine the square of each of the other two values and add the two squares. Only if the square of the hypotenuse is equal to the sum of the squares of the other two sides is the triangle a right-angled triangle. (Alternatively, you can determine the square root of the sum of the squares of the two shorter sides. If this is the same as the hypotenuse, then the triangle is a right-angled triangle.)
b. Hypotenuse $= 28$ $28^2 = 784$ $15^2 + 16^2 = 481$ $784 \neq 481$ This is not a right-angled triangle.	

Exercise 7.1.1

Determine the lengths of the unknown side (x) in the following right-angled triangles. All dimensions are in cm.

a.

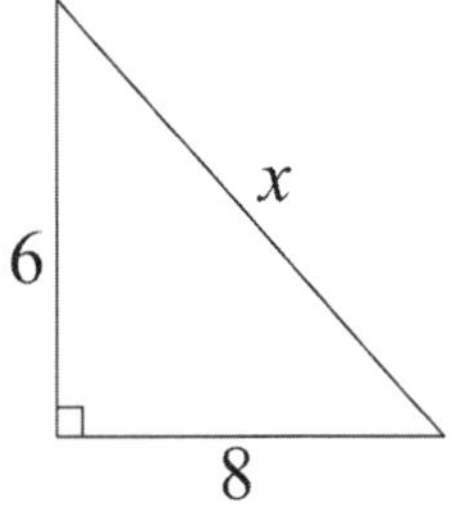

b.

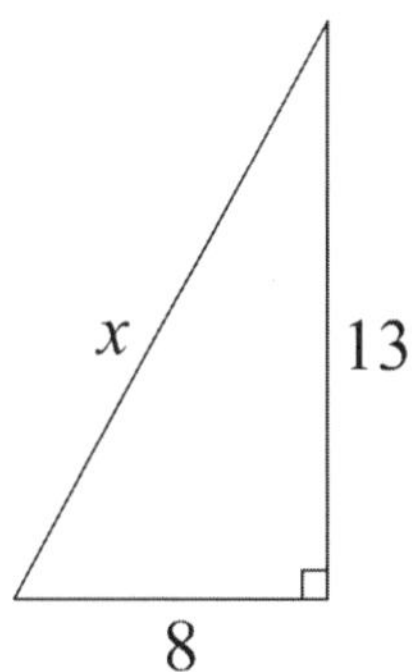

c.

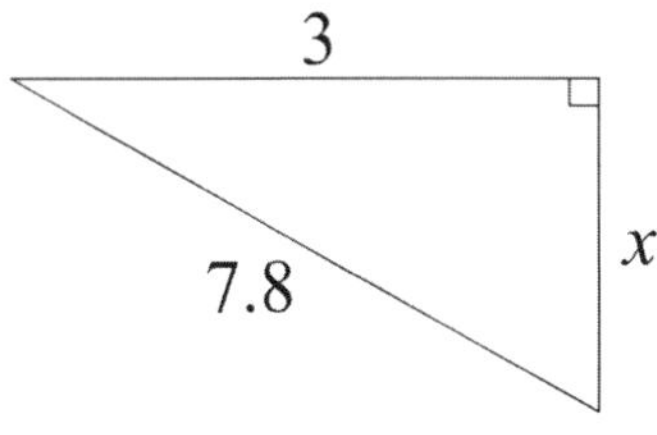

d.

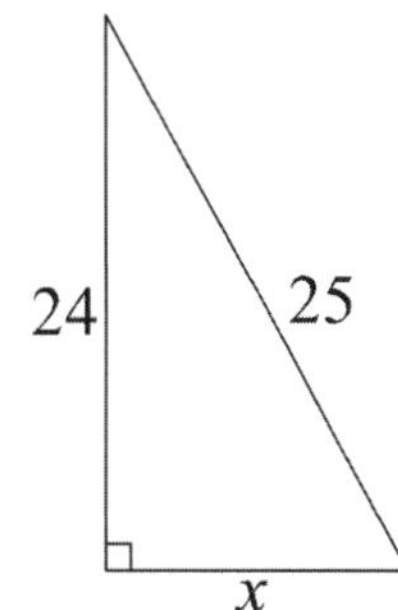

Exercise 7.1.2

For each of the following, determine if the set of three side lengths given can form a right-angled triangle.

a. 16, 63, 65

b. 5, 12, 15

7.2 Applying Pythagoras' theorem

There are many ways in which Pythagoras' theorem can be applied in real life – for example, in navigation and in designing a building. In this section, we will investigate some of these applications.

Hint: when solving problems using Pythagoras' theorem, it can be helpful to draw a right-angled triangle to represent the particular situation.

Example

A 9.5 m ladder leans against a wall of a building with its foot on the ground 4.7 m away from the wall. Determine how far up the wall the ladder reaches, to 2 decimal places.

✓ *Solution*

Working	Explanation
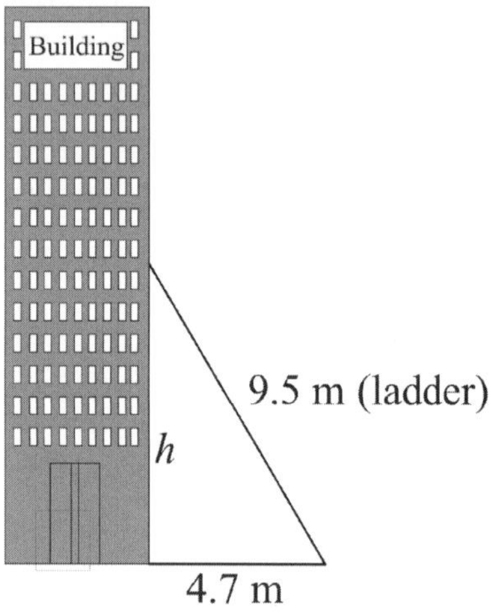 Building 9.5 m (ladder) h 4.7 m	Draw a diagram of the situation, giving the unknown value a pronumeral (h in this example). You can assume that the angle between the building and the ground is a right angle; therefore, the ladder forms the hypotenuse of a right-angled triangle.
$h = \sqrt{9.5^2 - 4.7^2} = 8.26$ The ladder reaches 8.26 m up the wall.	Using Pythagoras' theorem, determine how far up the wall the ladder reaches.

Example

Mary wants to get a computer monitor for her desk, which has enough space for a 45 cm monitor (measured diagonally). She has found a monitor that is 40 cm wide and 25 cm high. Will the monitor fit on her desk?

✓ *Solution*

Working	Explanation
Computer Monitor x 25 cm 40 cm	Draw the situation given. Note that the size of a screen is always given as the length of the diagonal. The screen is a rectangle and hence we can use Pythagoras' theorem to determine the length of the diagonal.
$x = \sqrt{40^2 + 25^2} = 47.17$ cm The size of the monitor is 47.17 cm, which is 2.17 cm larger than the space available. Hence the monitor will not fit.	Since the screen size is 47.17 cm, which is greater than the space available, the monitor will not fit.

Example

Bob is meeting his friend Katie at the cinema. He has two ways of getting there. He can follow the roads leading to the cinema by first heading south for 3 km and then heading west for 7 km. Alternatively, he can cut through a park and walk in a straight line to the cinema. How much shorter will the distance be if Bob cuts through the park?

✓ *Solution*

Working	Explanation
d km (park) 3 km (south) 7 km (west)	Draw the situation given. Note that walking south and then west indicates that Bob turns towards the cinema at a right angle.
Distance travelled by walking along the roads = 10 km	Calculate the distance travelled by walking along both roads.
$d = \sqrt{3^2 + 7^2} = 7.62$	Using Pythagoras' theorem, calculate the distance travelled by walking through the park.
The distance travelled by walking through the park is 2.38 km shorter than the distance along the two roads.	State the conclusion.

Example

The diagram on the right shows a rectangular box. Determine the values of x and y, to 2 decimal places.

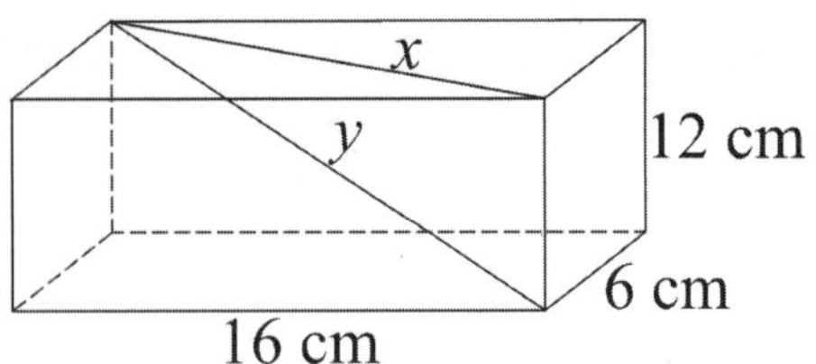

✓ Solution

Working	Explanation
Determine x. 16 cm, 6 cm, x $x = \sqrt{16^2 + 6^2} = 17.09$ cm	You need to recognise that: • there are two right-angled triangles to be considered, one involving x and the other involving both x and y • x must be determined before y can be determined. Draw the right-angled triangle that only involves x and use Pythagoras' theorem to determine x to 2 decimal places.
Determine y. x, 12 cm, y $y = \sqrt{x^2 + 12^2} = 20.88$ cm	Draw the other right-angled triangle, which involves both x and y. Use Pythagoras' theorem to determine y to 2 decimal places. **Note:** • We use x instead of 17.09 cm. The reason is that we should always use the actual number: 17.08800749. (17.09 cm is just an approximation.) • The longest object you could place in this box would be 20.88 cm long (i.e. the diagonal y).

Exercise 7.2.1

A square tile has a diagonal of 15.2 cm. Determine the perimeter of the tile to the nearest cm.

Exercise 7.2.2

A wooden rectangular frame measures 12.5 cm by 24.5 cm. To strengthen the frame, a piece of wood has been fixed to it diagonally. Determine the length of the piece of wood to 2 decimal places.

Exercise 7.2.3

Amy has a rectangular box measuring 3 cm (depth) by 8 cm (width) by 35 cm (length). Determine the longest object, to the nearest cm, that she can keep in the box.

Exercise 7.2.4

Hilary rode her bicycle in a straight line from her house to Grace's house, which is 16.8 km away. She could not use the same route on the way back because of a fallen tree. Instead, she travelled north for 8.7 km and then east to her house. Determine how much further she had to travel on her way back. Give your answer to 1 decimal place.

7.3 Trigonometry

Trigonometry is the study of the relationships between the sides and the acute angles of a right-angled triangle. These relationships can be used to determine an unknown angle or side of a right-angled triangle. For Year 9, we concentrate on just three trigonometric relationships.

If we assign one of the acute angles in a right-angled triangle as the reference angle (θ), we can give the sides of the triangle a standard name that is relative to θ. As shown in the diagram below, the side next to θ is named 'adjacent' and the side opposite θ is named 'opposite'. The longest side is always named 'hypotenuse'.

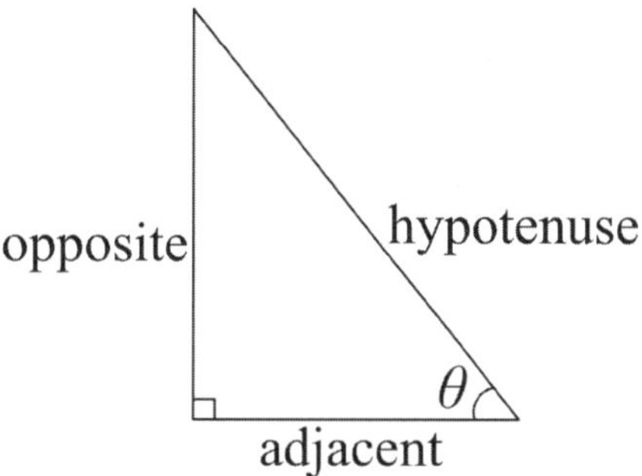

Note: the adjacent side is sometimes called the **base** of the triangle and the opposite side is sometimes called the **altitude**.

The three trigonometric relationships are ratios, and they relate the reference angle (θ) to the sides as follows.

$$\textbf{sine}\,\theta = \frac{\textit{opposite}}{\textit{hypotenuse}} \qquad \textbf{cosine}\,\theta = \frac{\textit{adjacent}}{\textit{hypotenuse}} \qquad \textbf{tangent}\,\theta = \frac{\textit{opposite}}{\textit{adjacent}}$$

It may help you to remember the trigonometric ratios if you memorise **SOH CAH TOA**. This stands for **sine opposite hypotenuse**, **cosine adjacent hypotenuse** and **tangent opposite adjacent**.

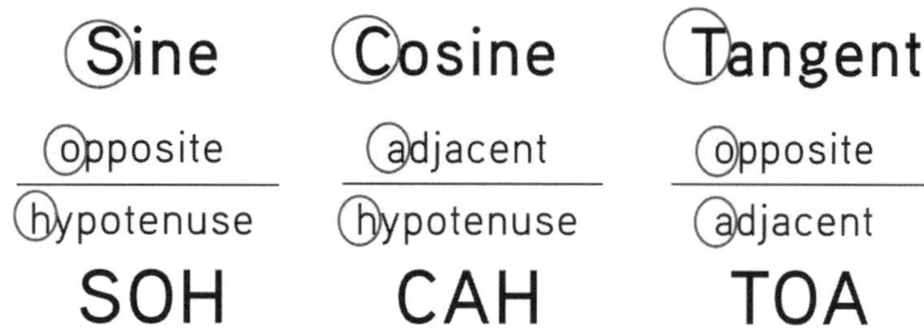

The trigonometric ratios are usually shortened to sin, cos and tan in an equation.

Consider the right-angled triangle below.

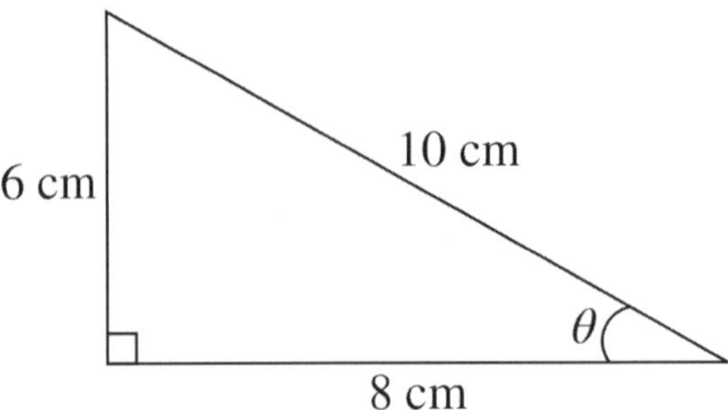

The trigonometric ratios for the angle marked θ are

$\sin\theta = \frac{6}{10} = \frac{3}{5}$ $\cos\theta = \frac{8}{10} = \frac{4}{5}$ $\tan\theta = \frac{6}{8} = \frac{3}{4}$

The ratios can be expressed as simplified fractions or as decimals. There are no units for trigonometric ratios. If the side lengths are given in decimals, give your answers in decimals.

Note that in the example above, the original and simplified ratios refer to two right-angled triangles. The lengths of the sides of the triangle matching the simplified ratio are half those of the sides of the triangle matching the original ratio. Compare the triangle above with the following triangle.

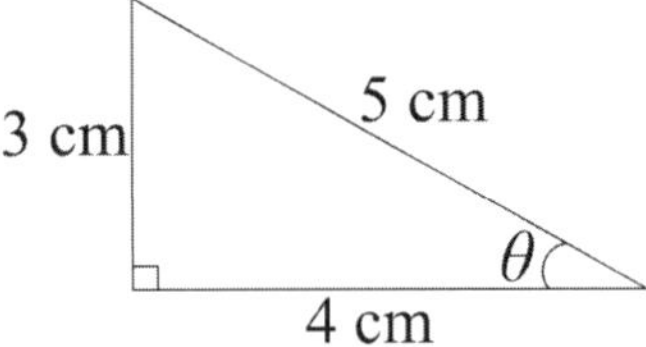

These right-angled triangles are **similar triangles** (discussed in detail in Chapter 9). We can therefore conclude that for any given angle, the sine ratio is always the same, the cosine ratio is always the same and the tangent ratio is always the same.

You can also use your calculator to determine the trigonometric ratios of an angle. Make sure that you set the mode of your calculator to DEGREE.

Example

a. Refer to the triangle on the right. Determine the trigonometric ratios for the angle θ to 4 decimal places.

b. Use your calculator to determine the trigonometric ratios for 27°, to 4 decimal places.

c. Given that $\tan\theta = \frac{5}{12}$, determine $\sin\theta$ and $\cos\theta$.

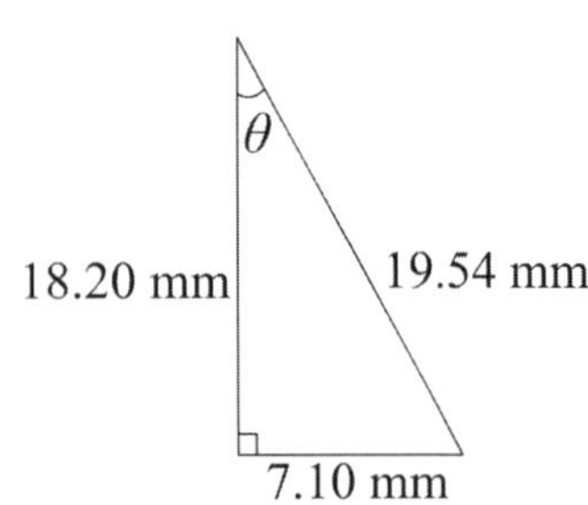

✓ ***Solution***

Working	Explanation
a. $\sin\theta = \frac{7.10}{19.54} = 0.3634$ $\cos\theta = \frac{18.20}{19.54} = 0.9314$ $\tan\theta = \frac{7.10}{18.20} = 0.3901$	Identify the sides that are adjacent and opposite to the reference angle. Calculate the trigonometric ratios.
b. $\sin 27° = 0.4540$ $\cos 27° = 0.8910$ $\tan 27° = 0.5095$	Use the sin, cos and tan functions on your calculator to determine the ratios to 4 decimal places.
c. $h = \sqrt{12^2 + 5^2} = 13$ $\sin\theta = \frac{5}{13}$ $\cos\theta = \frac{12}{13}$	Sketch a triangle from the information given. Use Pythagoras' theorem to determine the length of the hypotenuse. Use the information given and the length of the hypotenuse to state $\sin\theta$ and $\cos\theta$ as ratios of the sides of the triangle.

Note that the trigonometric ratios of sin and cos will not be greater than 1. This is because the hypotenuse (which is the denominator) is always longer than the sides adjacent to or opposite the reference angle. However, tan can be greater than 1 because the opposite side can be longer than the adjacent side.

Exercise 7.3.1

Determine the trigonometric ratios for the angles marked θ in the following right-angled triangles. Give your answers to 4 decimal places.

a.

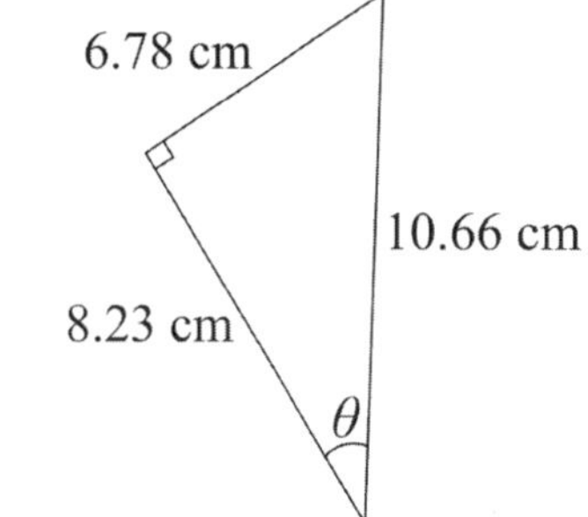

b.

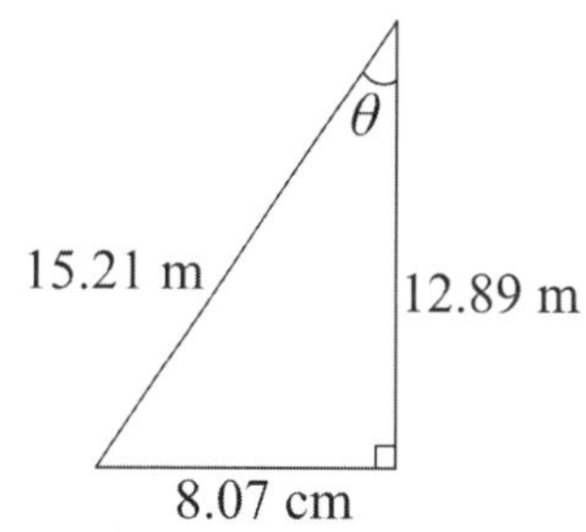

Exercise 7.3.2

Use your calculator to determine the trigonometric ratios of the following angles.

a. 22.5° b. 45° c. 82° d. 65°

Exercise 7.3.3

Given that $\sin\theta = \frac{24}{25}$, determine $\tan\theta$ and $\cos\theta$.

7.4 Determining the sides of a right-angled triangle

If you know the length of one side of a right-angled triangle and one angle, you can use trigonometry to determine the length of the other sides.

Example

Determine the lengths of the unknown sides (labelled x and y) in each of the following right-angled triangles.

a.

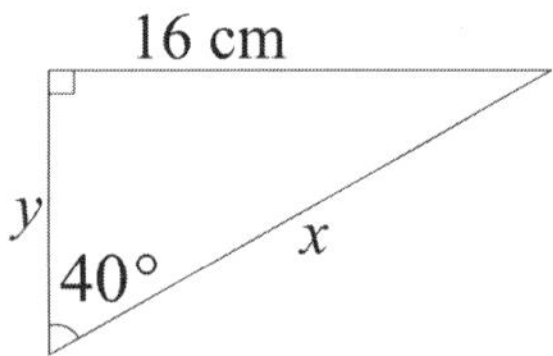

b.

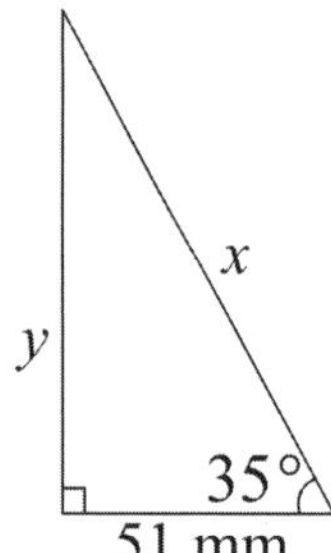

c.

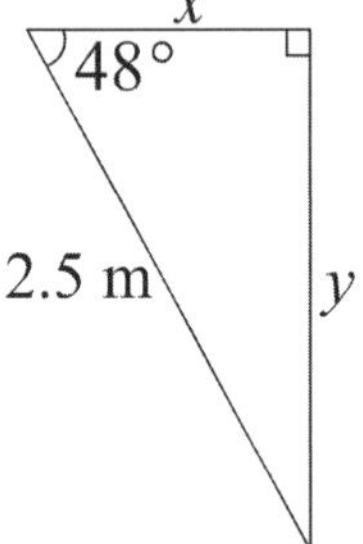

✓ ***Solution***

Working	Explanation
a. Determine x $\sin 40° = \frac{16}{x}$ $x = \frac{16}{\sin 40°}$ $x = 24.89$ cm	Identify the adjacent, opposite and hypotenuse of the triangle with respect to the known angle. In this case, x is the hypotenuse and y is the adjacent. To determine x (the hypotenuse), use sin (since the opposite is known).
Determine y $\tan 40° = \frac{16}{y}$ $y = \frac{16}{\tan 40°}$ $y = 19.07$ cm	To determine y (the adjacent), use tan (since the opposite is known). **Note:** you could also use x to determine y using cos once you have determined the value of x. However, for accuracy, you should use the whole number given in the question if possible.
b. Determine x $\cos 35° = \frac{51}{x}$ $x = \frac{51}{\cos 35°}$ $x = 62.26$ mm Determine y $\tan 35° = \frac{y}{51}$ $y = 51 \tan 35°$ $y = 35.71$ mm	Identify the adjacent, opposite and hypotenuse of the triangle with respect to the known angle. In this case, x is the hypotenuse and y is the opposite. To determine x (the hypotenuse), use cos (since the adjacent is known). To determine y (the opposite), use tan (since the adjacent is known). **Note**: You could also use x to determine y using sin once you have determined the value of x. However, for accuracy, you should use the whole number given in the question.
c. Determine x $\cos 48° = \frac{x}{2.5}$ $x = 2.5 \cos 48°$ $x = 1.67$ m Determine y $\sin 48° = \frac{y}{2.5}$ $y = 2.5 \sin 48°$ $y = 1.86$ m	Identify the adjacent, opposite and hypotenuse of the triangle with respect to the known angle. In this case, x is the adjacent and y is the opposite. To determine x (the adjacent), use cos (since the hypotenuse is known). To determine y (the opposite), use sin (since the hypotenuse is known). **Note**: You could also use x to determine y using tan once you have determined the value of x. However, for accuracy, you should use the whole number given in the question.

Summary

- Use **sin** = $\frac{O}{H}$ if you have to find the opposite side and know the hypotenuse (and vice versa).
- Use **cos** = $\frac{A}{H}$ if you have to find the adjacent side and know the hypotenuse (and vice versa).
- Use **tan** = $\frac{O}{A}$ if you know either the opposite side or the adjacent side and have to determine the other side.

Exercise 7.4

Determine the lengths of the unknown sides (labelled x and y) in the following triangles.

a.

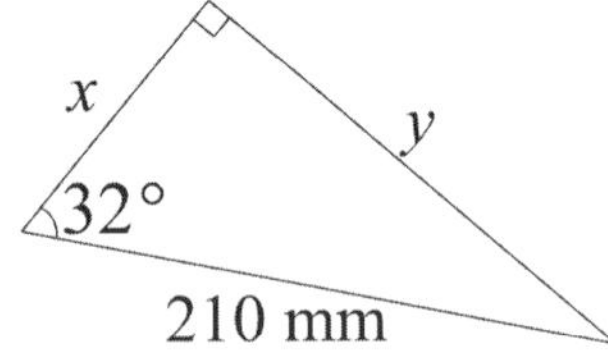

b.

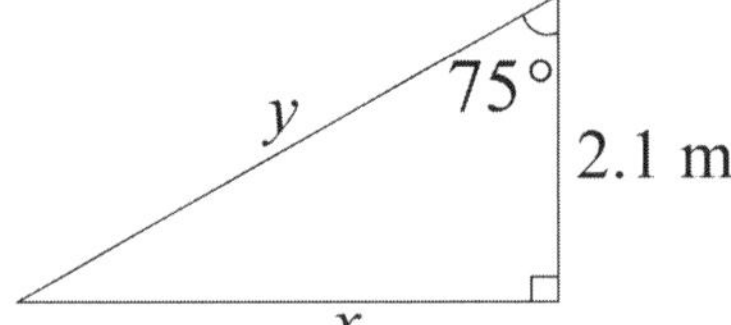

c.

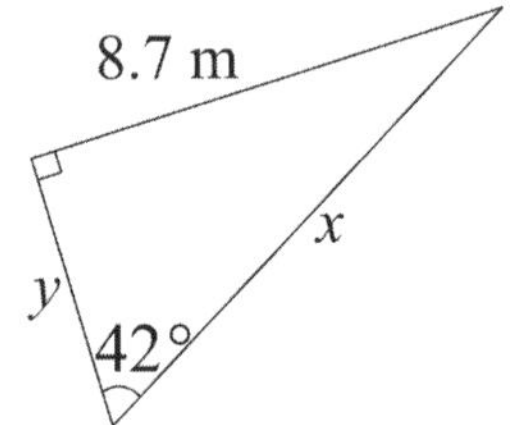

7.5 Determining the angles in a right-angled triangle

In order to find the angle from a given ratio (written as either a fraction or a decimal), you need to use the inverse function on a calculator.

Suppose we know that $\sin\theta = 0.56$. The angle θ is found by calculating inverse sin 0.56, which is written as $\sin^{-1}0.56$. Using a calculator shows that θ is 34.06°.

Similarly, if we know that $\cos\theta = 0.28$, the angle θ is found by calculating inverse cos 0.28, which is written as $\cos^{-1}0.28$. Using a calculator shows that θ is 73.74°.

Likewise, if we know that $\tan\theta = \frac{28}{32}$, then θ is equal to $\tan^{-1}\frac{28}{32}$. A calculator will show that θ is 41.19°.

Example

Determine the unknown angle (labelled θ) in the following right-angled triangles.

a.

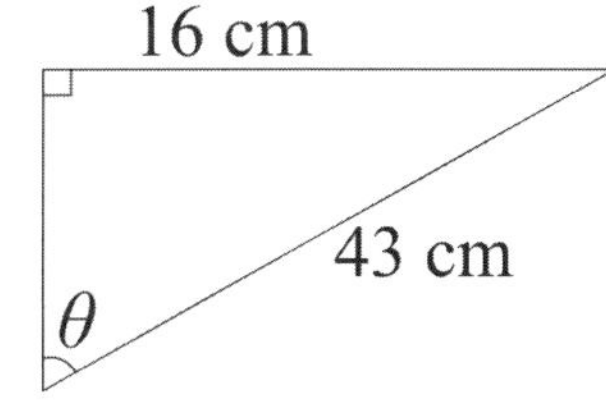

b.

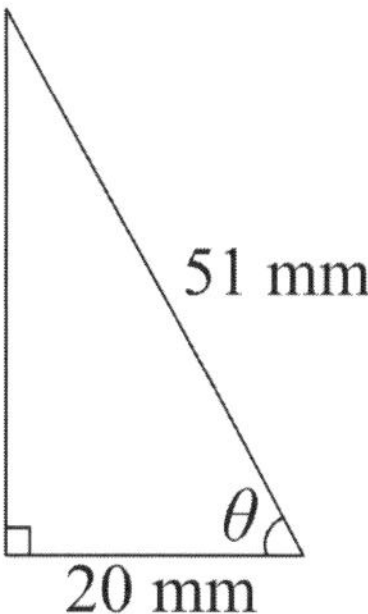

c.

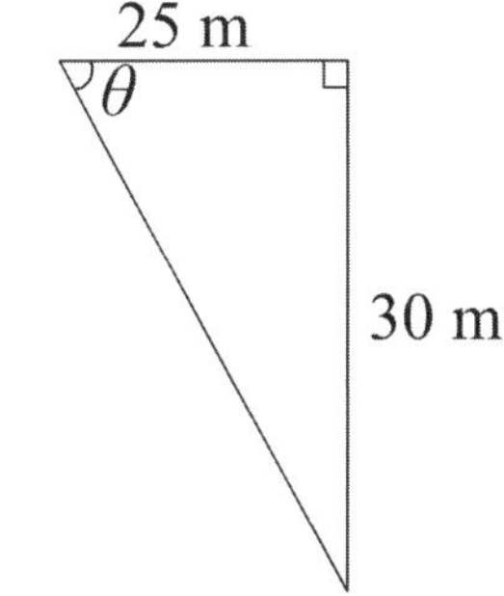

✓ ***Solution***

Working	Explanation
a. $\sin\theta = \frac{16}{43}$ $\theta = \sin^{-1}\frac{16}{43}$ $\theta = 21.84°$	Identify the adjacent, opposite and hypotenuse of the triangle with respect to the unknown angle, θ. In this case, 16 is the opposite side and 43 is the hypotenuse. Since the opposite and hypotenuse are known, inverse sin is used to determine θ.
b. $\cos\theta = \frac{20}{51}$ $\theta = \cos^{-1}\frac{20}{51}$ $\theta = 66.91°$	Identify the adjacent, opposite and hypotenuse of the triangle with respect to the unknown angle, θ. In this case, 20 is the adjacent side and 51 is the hypotenuse. Since the adjacent and hypotenuse are known, inverse cos is used to determine θ.
c. $\tan\theta = \frac{30}{25}$ $\theta = \tan^{-1}\frac{30}{25}$ $\theta = 50.19°$	Identify the adjacent, opposite and hypotenuse of the triangle with respect to the unknown angle, θ. In this case, 25 is the adjacent side and 30 is the opposite side. Since the adjacent and opposite are known, inverse tan is used to determine θ.

Note: once you know one of the acute angles of a right-angled triangle, you can calculate the other acute angle. The two acute angles add up to 90°. This is because the sum of the internal angles of a triangle is 180°, and the right angle is 90°. Therefore once θ is known, the other acute angle is $90° - \theta$.

Exercise 7.5

Determine the unknown angle (θ) and the unknown side (d) in the following right-angled triangles.

a.

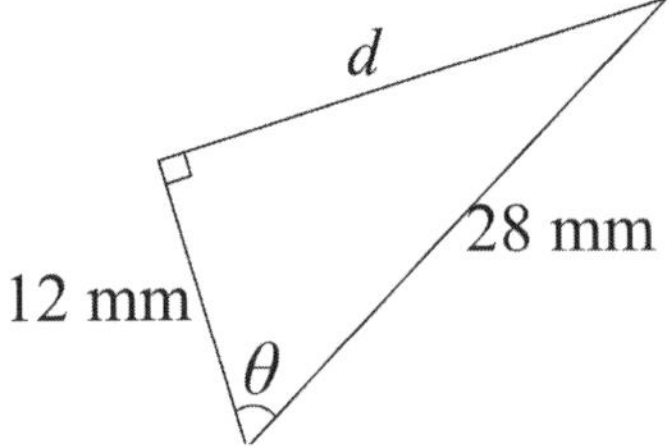

b.

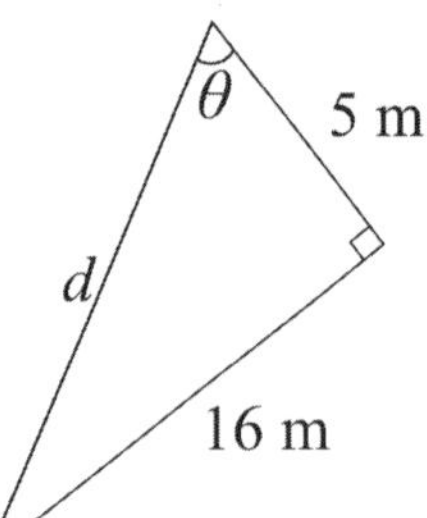

c.

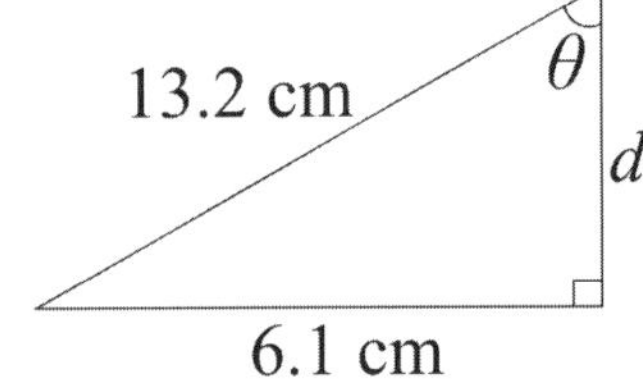

7.6 Applying trigonometry

Trigonometry has many applications in real life. We will investigate the use of trigonometry in determining measurements, as well as angles of elevation and depression.

Note: when you have intermediate steps in a calculation, always use all the decimal places when calculating the steps that follow. This is to ensure the accuracy of the final result.

Measurements

We can use trigonometry to determine unknown lengths and angles, which can then be used to calculate other values (such as areas and volumes).

Example

a. Consider the diagram on the right. Triangles ABC and BED are both right-angled triangles. Given that $AB = 24$ cm, $AC = 7$ cm, $\angle BDE = 25°$ and $BE = EC$, determine the length of BD to 2 decimal places.

b. Determine $\angle BCA$ to the nearest degree.

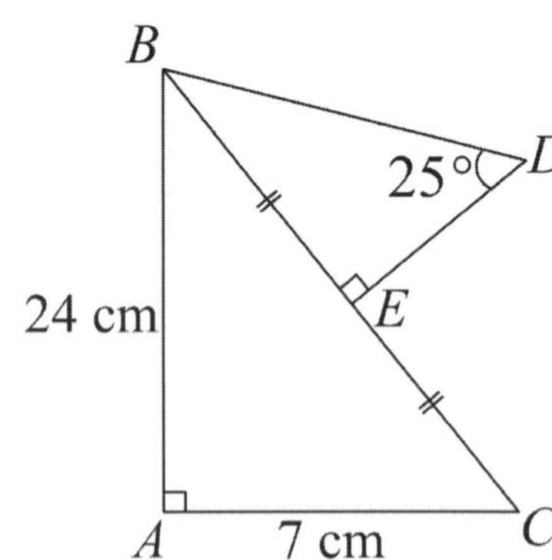

✓ ***Solution***

Working	Explanation
a. $BC = \sqrt{7^2 + 24^2} = 25$ cm $BE = 12.5$ cm $\sin 25° = \frac{BE}{BD}$ $BD = \frac{12.5}{\sin 25°}$ $BD = 29.58$ cm	Use Pythagoras' theorem to determine the length of BC. Since $BE = EC$, divide BC by 2 to determine the length of BE. BE is the opposite with respect to $\angle BDE$, and BD is the hypotenuse. Therefore BD can be determined using sin.
b. $\tan \angle BCA = \frac{24}{7}$ $\angle BCA = \tan^{-1}\frac{24}{7}$ $\angle BCA = 73.74°$ $\angle BCA = 74°$ (to the nearest degree)	AC is the adjacent and BA is the opposite with respect to $\angle BCA$, and lengths for both these sides are given. Therefore we can use inverse tan to determine $\angle BCA$.

The following two examples refer to the diagrams below.

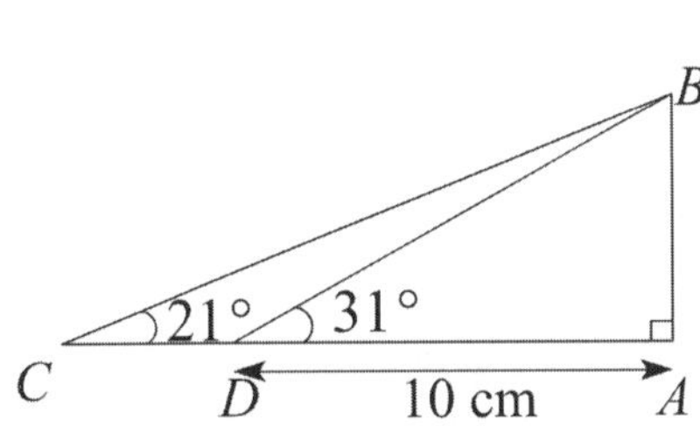

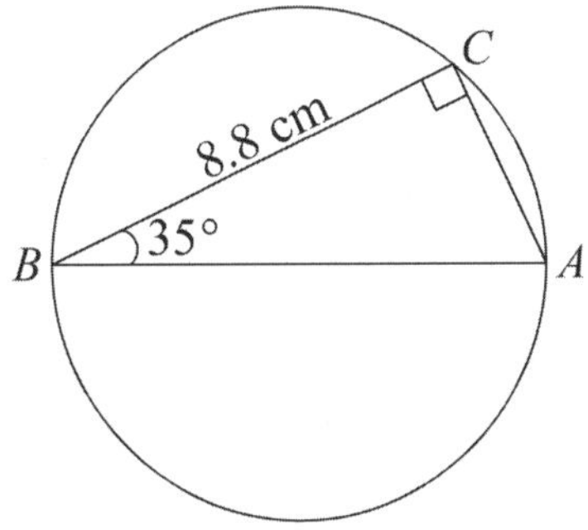

Example

Determine the area of the triangle BDC pictured above on the left. Give your answer to 2 decimal places.

✓ Solution

Working	Explanation
$\tan 31° = \frac{AB}{10}$ $AB = 10\tan 31°$ $AB = 6.01$ cm	The area of a triangle is $\frac{1}{2}$ × base × height. Hence to find the area of BDC, we need to find the length of CD (base) and the length of AB (height). Since ABD is a right-angled triangle, AB can be determined from the angle (31°) and the length of AD.
$\tan 21° = \frac{AB}{AC}$ $AC = \frac{AB}{\tan 21°}$ $AC = 15.65$ cm	Since ABC is also a right-angled triangle, AC can be determined from the angle (21°) and the length of AB.
$CD = 15.65 - 10 = 5.65$ cm	The length of CD is $AC - AD$.
Area of $BDC = \frac{1}{2} \times CD \times AB$ $= 16.98$ cm^2	Now use the area formula – with CD as the base and AB as the height – to determine the area of BDC.

Example

Consider the diagram of the circle shown on the previous page. Determine the area of the circle to 2 decimal places given that BC is 8.8 cm long. (AB is the diameter of the circle).

✓ Solution

Working	Explanation
$\cos 35° = \frac{8.8}{AB}$ $AB = 10.74$ cm	Use trigonometry to determine the diameter of the circle: AB.
Area of the circle $= \pi\left(\frac{10.74}{2}\right)^2$ $= 90.64$ cm^2	Use the area formula to determine the area of the circle. You need to halve the diameter to get the radius.

Angles of elevation and depression

Angles of elevation and depression are the angles measured between a horizontal line and the line of sight.

- If the line of sight is upwards relative to the horizontal line, the angle is the angle of **elevation**.
- If the line of sight is downwards relative to the horizontal line, the angle is the angle of **depression**.

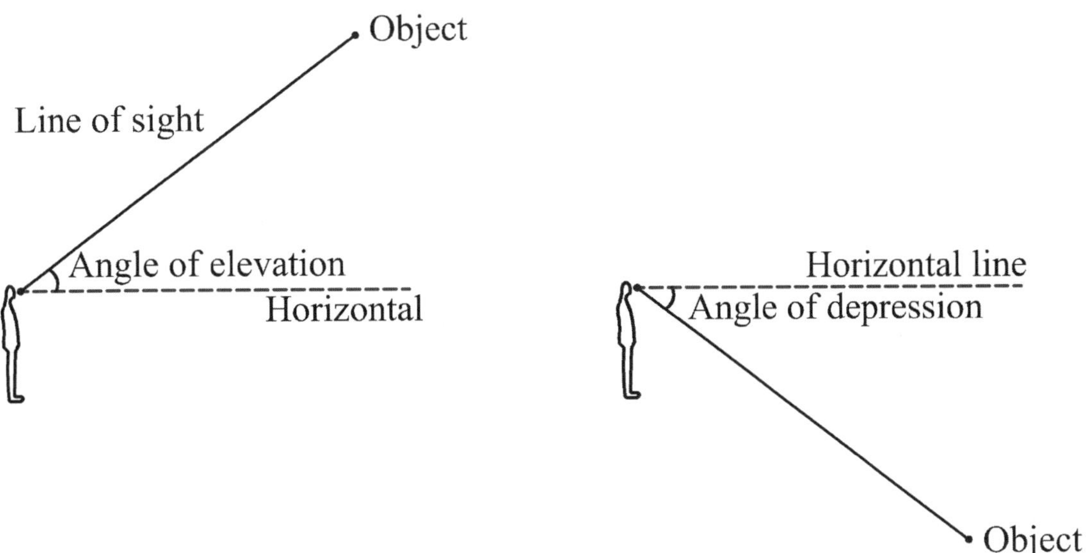

Example

Tom is 1.8 m tall and is standing 30 m away from a building. He is looking at the top of the building and the angle of elevation is 48°. Determine the height of the building to the nearest metre.

✓ ***Solution***

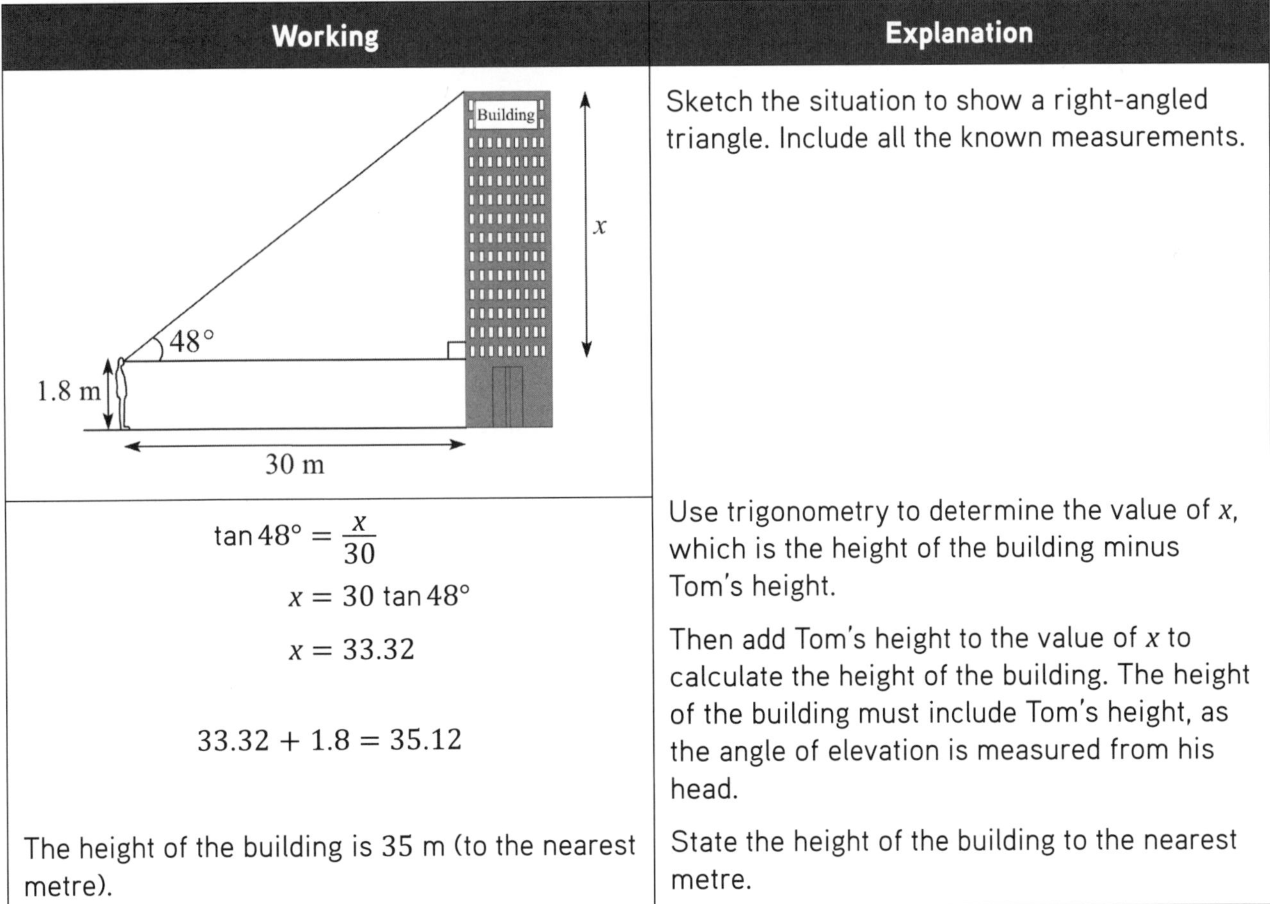

Working	Explanation
(diagram above)	Sketch the situation to show a right-angled triangle. Include all the known measurements.
$\tan 48° = \frac{x}{30}$ $x = 30 \tan 48°$ $x = 33.32$ $33.32 + 1.8 = 35.12$	Use trigonometry to determine the value of x, which is the height of the building minus Tom's height. Then add Tom's height to the value of x to calculate the height of the building. The height of the building must include Tom's height, as the angle of elevation is measured from his head.
The height of the building is 35 m (to the nearest metre).	State the height of the building to the nearest metre.

Example

From the top of a cliff 120 m above sea level, the angle of depression to a ship sailing below is 20°. Determine how far away the ship is from the base of the cliff. Give your answer to the nearest metre.

✓ *Solution*

Working	Explanation
20°, θ, 120 m, d m	Sketch the situation to show a right-angled triangle. Include all the known measurements.
$\theta = 90° - 20° = 70°$	Determine the angle θ.
$\tan 70° = \frac{d}{120}$ $d = 120 \tan 70°$ $d = 329.7$	Use trigonometry to determine the distance of the ship from the base of the cliff.
The ship is 330 m from the base of the cliff.	State the distance to the nearest metre.

Exercise 7.6.1

Consider the diagram below, which is composed of three right-angled triangles. Determine the value of x, to the nearest cm.

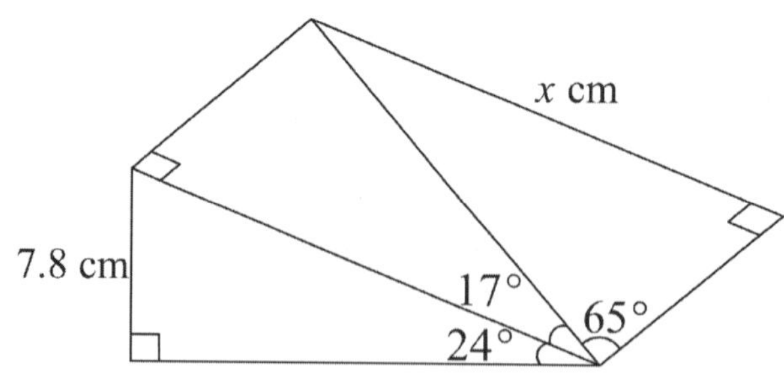

Exercise 7.6.2

In the diagram below, AB is the diameter of a circle. Given that the radius of the circle is 4.5 cm, determine the area of the triangle ABC to 2 decimal places.

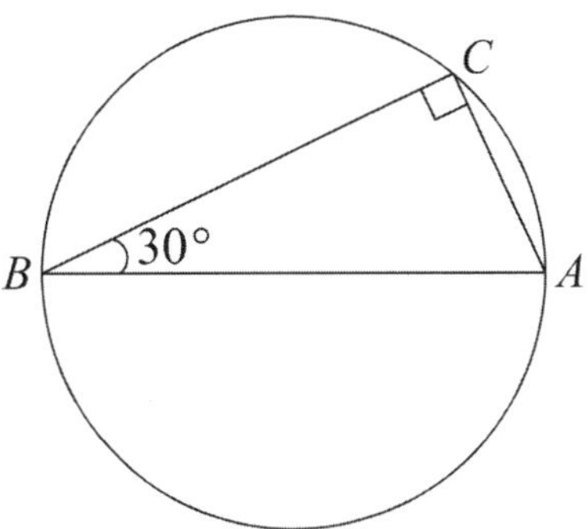

Exercise 7.6.3

Consider the diagram below. Determine the area of the circle to 2 decimal places.

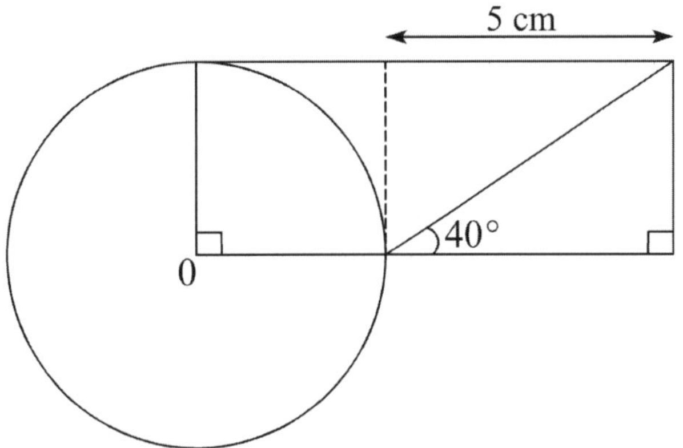

Exercise 7.6.4

A movie director wants to shoot a scene where the main character, Jasper, fires a grappling hook from the edge of the top of one building to the edge of the top of another building. The heights of the two buildings are 37 m and 54 m respectively and they are 10 m apart.

a. Sketch a diagram representing this situation.

b. Determine the angle of elevation created by the rope when it connects the buildings.

Exercise 7.6.5

Wendy was watching her friends Ben, Carrie and David bungee jump from a point 50 m away on a horizontal platform, as shown in the diagram below on the right.

a. Ben jumped first and his jump depth was 70 m. Determine the angle of depression from Wendy to Ben at the depth of 70 m.

b. Carrie jumped next and Wendy measured the maximum angle of depression to be 68°. Determine Carrie's jump depth.

c. Being a daredevil, David jumped to the river 195 m below the platform. Determine the angle of elevation from David to Wendy when his head touched the river.

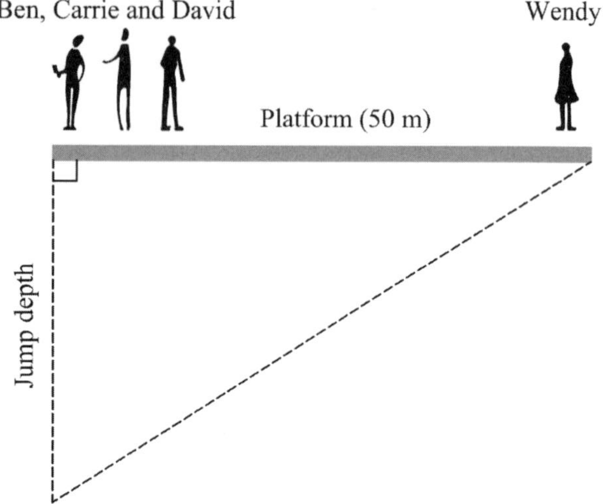

Answers

Exercise 7.1.1

a. 10 cm b. $\sqrt{233}$ cm or 15.26 cm c. 7.20 cm d. 7 cm

Exercise 7.1.2

a. Right-angled triangle b. Not a right-angled triangle

Exercise 7.2.1

43 cm

Exercise 7.2.2

27.50 cm

Exercise 7.2.3

36 cm

Exercise 7.2.4

6.3 km

Exercise 7.3.1

a. $\sin\theta = 0.6360$ $\cos\theta = 0.7720$ $\tan\theta = 0.8238$

b. $\sin\theta = 0.5306$ $\cos\theta = 0.8475$ $\tan\theta = 0.6261$

Exercise 7.3.2

a. $\sin 22.5° = 0.3827$ $\cos 22.5° = 0.9239$ $\tan 22.5° = 0.4142$

b. $\sin 45° = 0.7071$ $\cos 45° = 0.7071$ $\tan 45° = 1.0000$

c. $\sin 82° = 0.9903$ $\cos 82° = 0.1392$ $\tan 82° = 7.1154$

d. $\sin 65° = 0.9063$ $\cos 65° = 0.4226$ $\tan 65° = 2.1445$

Exercise 7.3.3

$\tan\theta = \frac{24}{7}$ $\cos\theta = \frac{7}{25}$

Exercise 7.4

a. $x = 178.09$ mm

$y = 111.28$ mm

b. $x = 7.84$ m

$y = 8.11$ m

c. $x = 13.00$ m

$y = 9.66$ m

Exercise 7.5

a. $\theta = 64.62°$

$d = 25.30$ mm

b. $\theta = 72.65°$

$d = 16.76$ m

c. $\theta = 27.52°$

$d = 11.71$ cm

Exercise 7.6.1

$x = 18.17$ cm

Exercise 7.6.2

17.54 cm^2

Exercise 7.6.3

55.30 cm^2

Exercise 7.6.4

a.

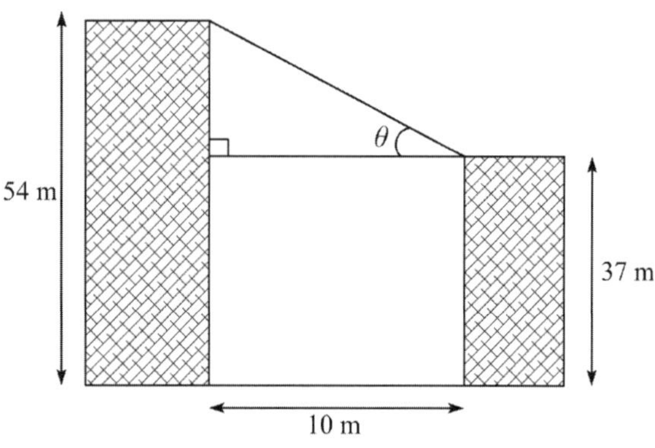

b. The angle of elevation, θ, is 59.53°.

Exercise 7.6.5

a. 54.46°

b. 123.75 m

c. 75.62°

Chapter 8 – Similarity, scale factor and enlargement

8.1 Similarity

Two figures are said to be **similar** if the following conditions are met.

- Condition 1: Each pair of corresponding (matching) sides is in the same ratio as the other pairs of corresponding sides.
- Condition 2: All pairs of corresponding (matching) angles are equal.

Consider the following rectangles: X, Y and Z.

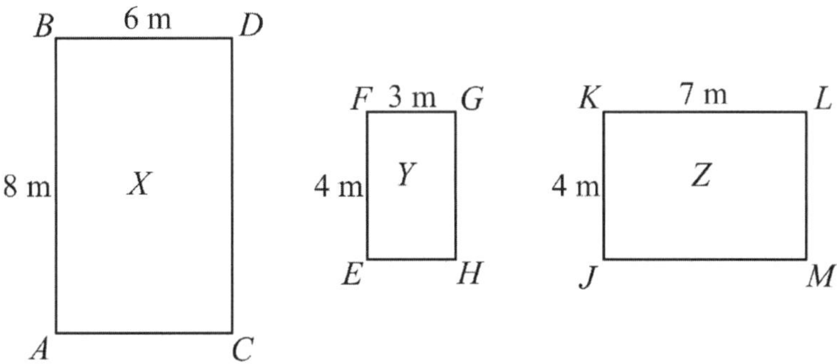

Although all three shapes are rectangles, only two are similar.

Condition 2 is met for all rectangles, as the corresponding angles are equal (90°).

For condition 1 to be met, all corresponding sides must have the same ratio.

Consider X $(ABCD)$ and Y $(EFGH)$. The corresponding pairs are sides AB and EF, BD and FG, DC and GH, and CA and HE. The ratios between these sides are

$$\frac{AB}{EF} = \frac{BD}{FG} = \frac{DC}{GH} = \frac{CA}{HE} = 2$$

So condition 1 is also met for rectangles X and Y: all ratios are equal. Hence X and Y are similar rectangles.

Now consider rectangles Y $(EFGH)$ and Z $(JKLM)$. Again condition 2 is met, as all angles are equal (90°). Now consider the ratios of corresponding sides. Note that

$$\frac{EF}{JK} = \frac{GH}{LM} = 1$$

So some ratios are equal. However

$$\frac{FG}{KL} = \frac{HE}{MJ} = \frac{3}{7} \neq 1$$

As the ratios of the pairs of corresponding sides are not equal, condition 1 is not met. Therefore, rectangles Y and Z are not similar.

By similar reasoning you can tell that rectangles X and Z are not similar. In this case, no ratios are equal. Hence, only X and Y are similar.

Example

Determine whether the following two figures are similar.

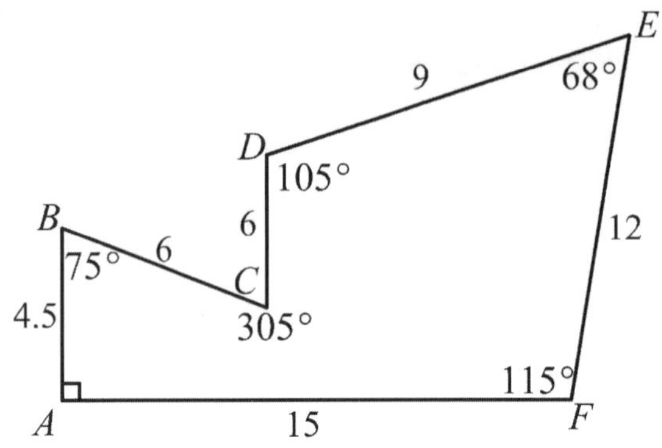

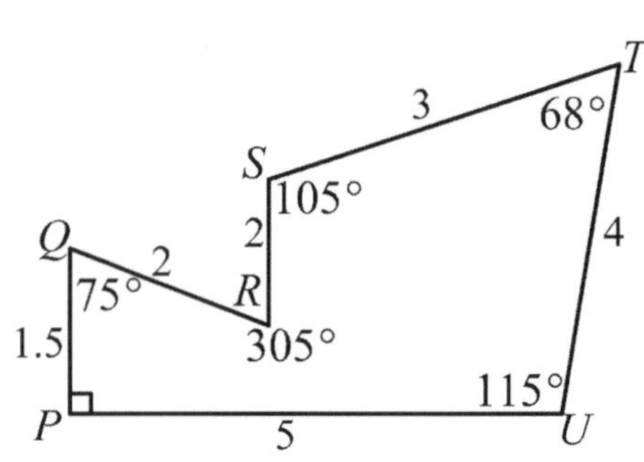

✓ ***Solution***

Working	Explanation
$\frac{AB}{PQ} = \frac{BC}{QR} = \frac{CD}{RS} = \frac{DE}{ST} = \frac{EF}{TU} = \frac{FA}{UP} = 3$	Check that all the ratios of the corresponding sides are equal.
All corresponding sides have the same ratio: 3.	
Hence condition 1 is met.	Check that all corresponding angles are equal.
$\angle ABC = \angle PQR = 75°$ $\angle BCD = \angle QRS = 55°$ $\angle CDE = \angle RST = 105°$ $\angle DEF = \angle STU = 68°$ $\angle EFA = \angle TUO = 115°$ $\angle FAB = \angle UPQ = 90°$	
All corresponding angles are the same. Hence condition 2 is also met.	
Therefore the figures are similar.	State your conclusion.

Example

Determine which of the following parallelograms are similar.

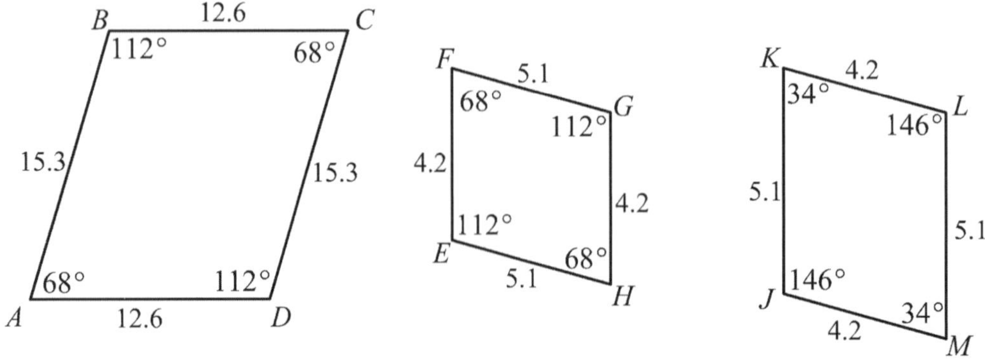

✓ Solution

Working	Explanation
ABCD and *HEFG* $\frac{HE}{AB} = \frac{EF}{BC} = \frac{FG}{CD} = \frac{GH}{DA} = \frac{1}{3}$ $\angle HEF = \angle ABC = 112°$ $\angle EFG = \angle BCD = 68°$ $\angle FGH = \angle CDA = 112°$ $\angle DAB = \angle GHE = 68°$ *ABCD* and *HEFG* are similar.	Each pair of parallelograms needs to be checked. Start by comparing the corresponding ratios and angles of *ABCD* and *HEFG*. Since corresponding sides have the same ratio and all corresponding angles are equal – thus satisfying both conditions of similarity – *ABCD* and *HEFG* are similar.
ABCD and *JKLM* Not similar	There is no need to check the sides and angles as it is clear just by looking at these pairs of parallelograms that there are no corresponding angles that are equal. Since condition 2 of similarity has not been met, the parallelograms are not similar.
EFGH and *JKLM* Not similar	

Exercise 8.1.1

Peter said that all squares are similar. Do you think this statement is true? Justify your answer by referring to the following two squares.

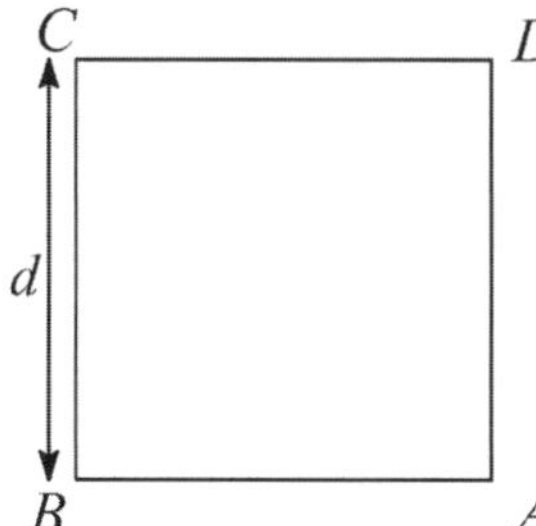

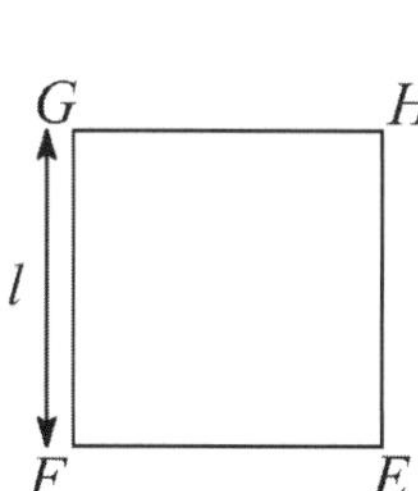

Exercise 8.1.2

Determine which two of the following five-sided polygons (pentagons) are similar.

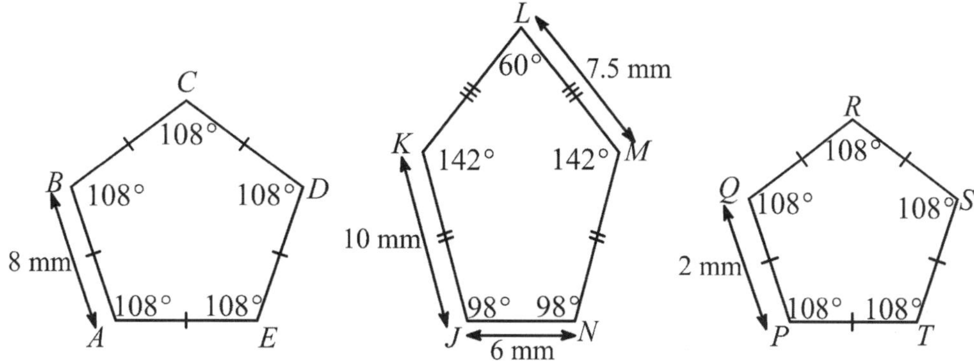

8.2 Scale factor

The ratio of similar figures is the **scale factor** required to enlarge one figure to create another similar figure. Consider the following two similar rectangles.

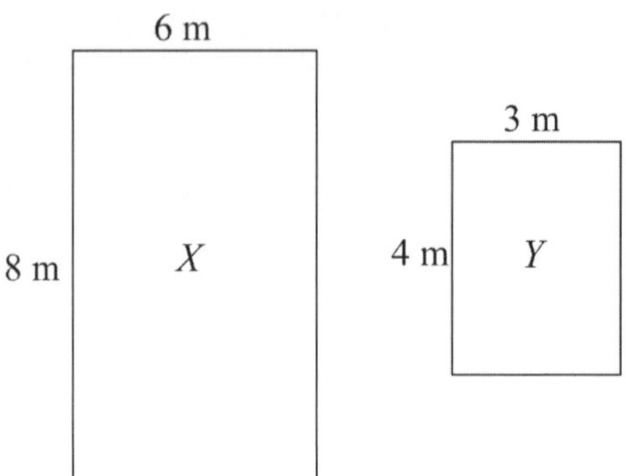

We can say that rectangle X is an enlargement of rectangle Y by a scale factor of 2. We can also say that rectangle Y is an enlargement of rectangle X by a scale factor of $\frac{1}{2}$.

Enlargement (also known as **dilation**) is a scaled up (or scaled down) version of a figure in which the transformed figure (also known as the **model**) is in proportion to the original figure.

If we know that two figures are similar, we can define the scale factor as:

$$k = \frac{l_m}{l_o}$$

where k = the scale factor
l_m = the length of the model
l_o = the length of the original.

If the scale factor is greater than 1, the model is larger than the original. If the scale factor is less than 1, the model is smaller than the original. If the scale factor is 1, then the model has exactly the same dimensions as the original.

A scale factor can also be written as $l_m : l_o$. This is the form commonly seen on maps. For example, 1:500 000 means that 1 cm measured on the map is equivalent to 500 000 cm (i.e. 5 000 m or 5 km).

Note: you must take the units into account. When you are determining the scale factor, the units must always be the same.

Example

Determine the scale factor for the following similar figures.

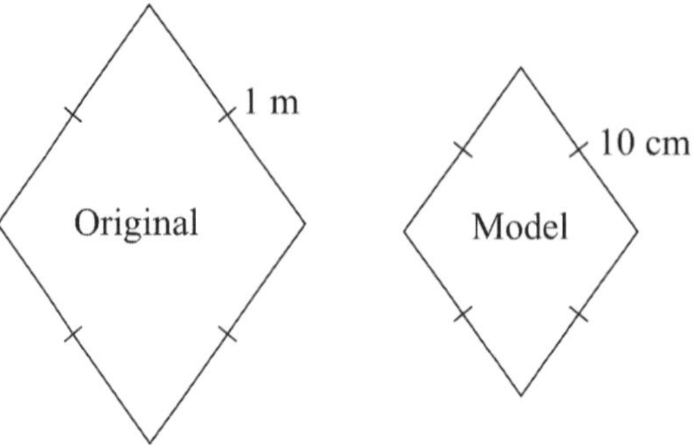

✓ Solution

Working	Explanation
$1\text{ m} = 100\text{ cm}$ $k = \frac{10}{100} = \frac{1}{10}$	To make the units the same, convert 1 m to 100 cm. Determine the scale factor.

Example

Cindy bought a replica of the Eiffel Tower when she visited Paris. She knows that the height of the actual Eiffel Tower is 300 m. If the replica is 1000th the size of the actual tower, how tall is Cindy's replica?

✓ Solution

Working	Explanation
$k = \frac{1}{1000}$ $300 \times \frac{1}{1000} = 0.3$ The height of the replica is 0.3 m (or 30 cm).	Write the scale factor in the form of a ratio. Multiply the actual height by the scale factor to obtain the height of the replica.

Exercise 8.2.1

An architect is building a model of the stage of a concert hall to show her client. The width of the proposed stage is 20 m. The width of the model is 80 cm. Determine the scale factor used in building the model.

Exercise 8.2.2

Pat is hiking through a national park and has a map of the park scaled at 1:250 000. On the map the hiking track is measured as 67.2 mm. What is the actual distance of Pat's hike?

8.3 Enlargement using scale factor

To enlarge a figure by a given scale factor, a centre of enlargement needs to be placed. It does not matter where it is placed.

Consider the following triangles: ABC and $A'B'C'$.

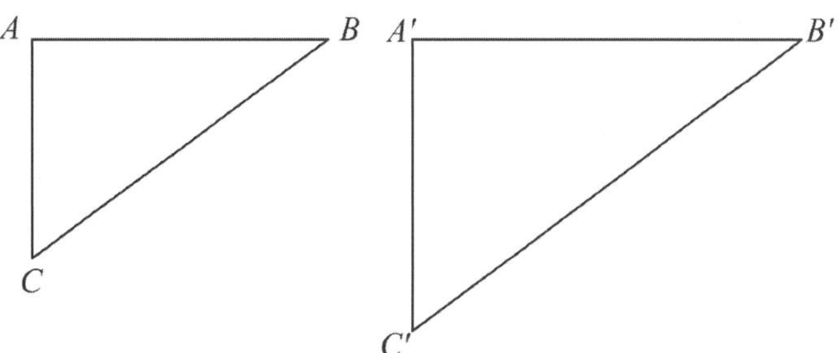

$\Delta A'B'C'$ is an enlargement of ΔABC by a scale factor of 2. In order to obtain $\Delta A'B'C'$, we specify a point as the centre of enlargement (point O in the diagram below).

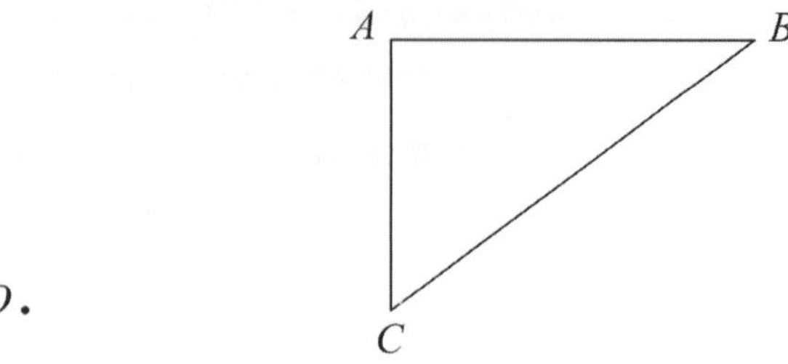

From point O, draw straight lines to points A, B and C and extend the lines beyond the points.

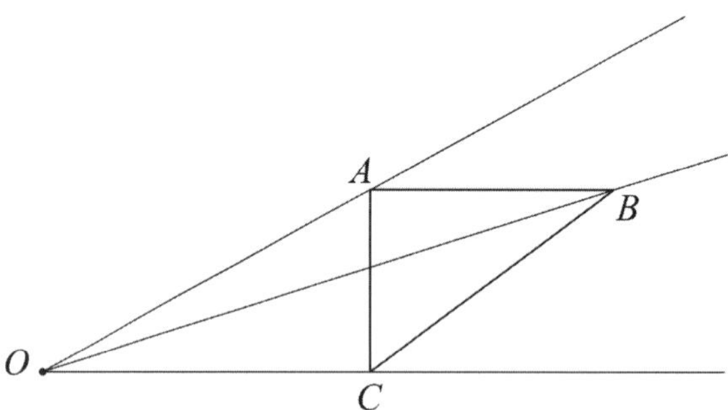

Measure the length OA and multiply it by the scale factor. This gives the distance from point O to point A'. Since the scale factor is 2, the length of OA' is double the length of OA. Mark the point A'.

Repeat the process to determine the locations of points B' and C'.

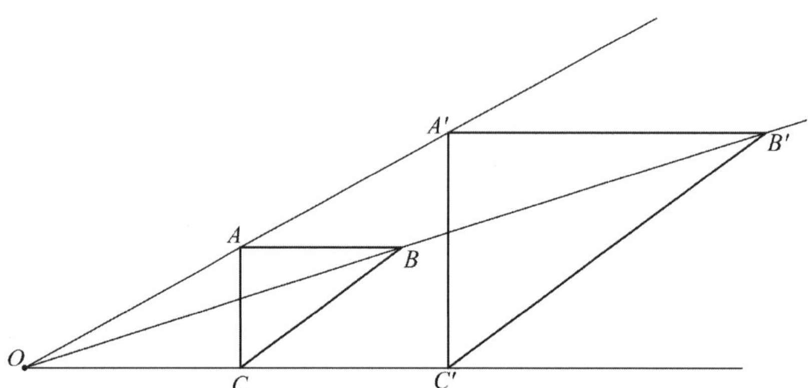

If you are asked to determine the centre of enlargement when two similar figures are given, you just need to reverse the process. Join A' to A, B' to B and C' to C and continue the lines. The point where the lines meet is the centre of enlargement. You do not need to know the scale factor to find the centre of enlargement.

Hint: in some cases, a grid will make enlargement easier.

Example

Enlarge the following triangle by a scale factor of $\frac{1}{2}$ from O, the centre of enlargement.

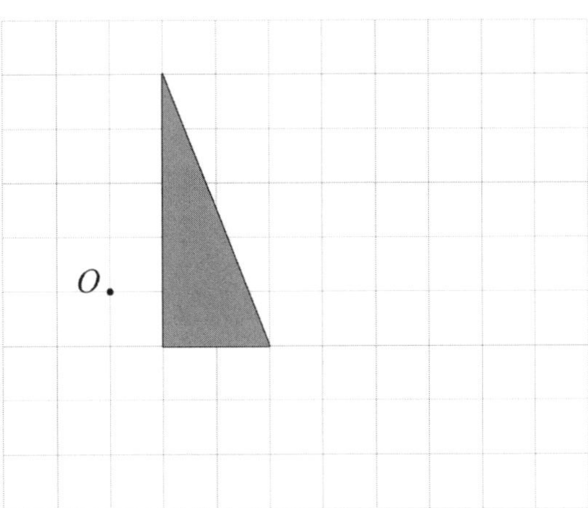

✓ Solution

Working	Explanation
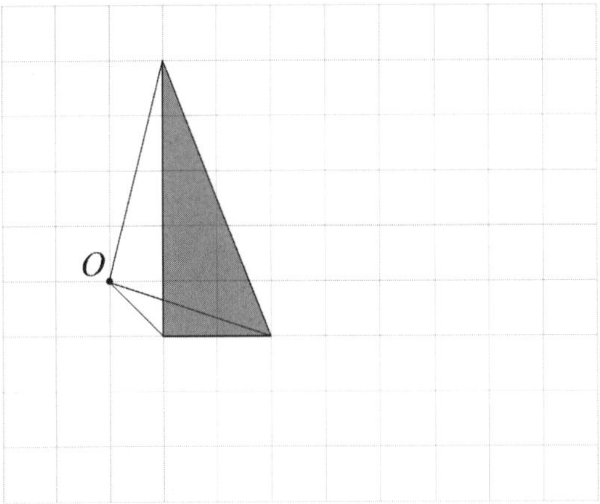	Draw a line from the centre of enlargement to each vertex.
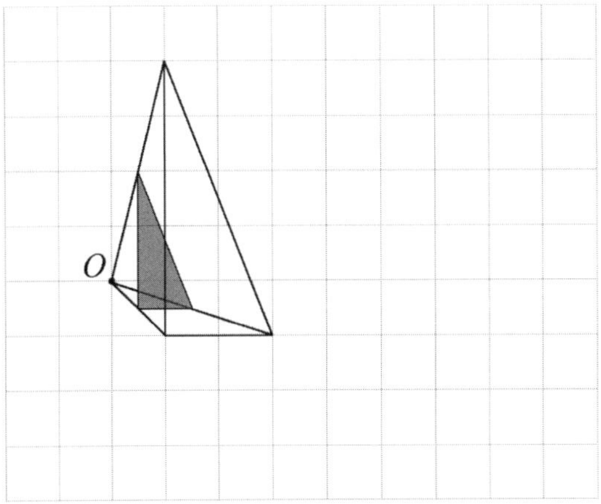	Measure the length of each line, multiply the length by the scale factor $\left(\frac{1}{2}\right)$ and mark a point on the line at that length. Connect the three new points to draw the enlarged triangle.

Example

Determine the centre of enlargement for the following triangles.

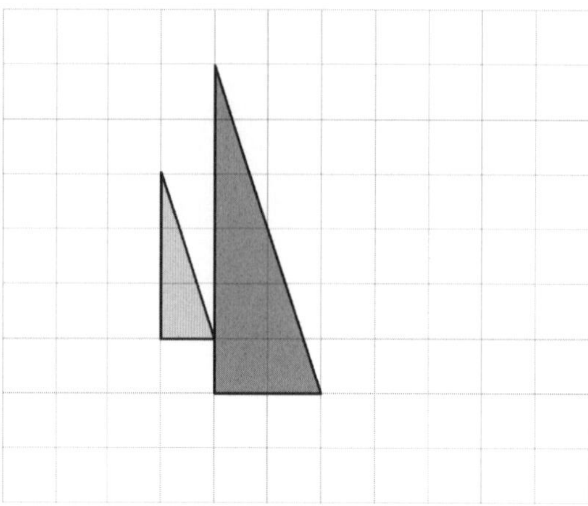

✓ *Solution*

Working	Explanation
	Draw straight lines connecting the corresponding vertices. Extend the lines until they meet. The point where they meet is the centre of enlargement.

Exercise 8.3.1

Enlarge the following parallelogram by a scale factor of 2.

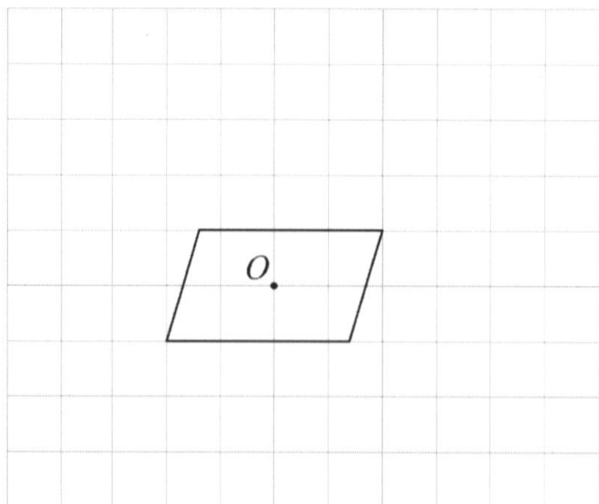

Exercise 8.3.2

Determine the centre of enlargement for the following figures.

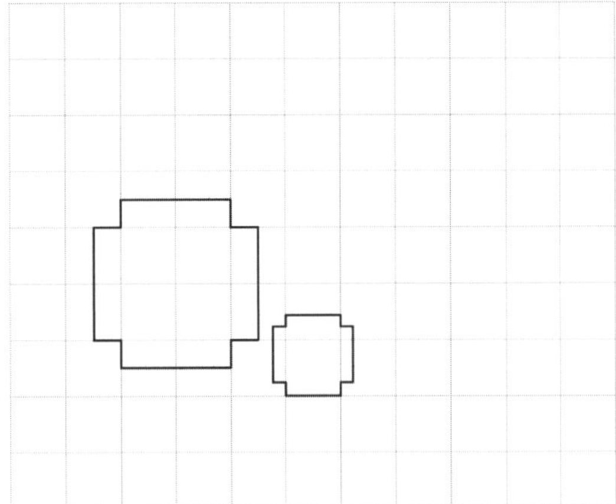

8.4 Applying the scale factor to area and volume

The scale factor, k, applies to the **length** of an enlarged shape or an enlarged three-dimensional object. Consider the following two squares. Square A has sides of 3 cm. Square B, which is an enlargement of square A, has sides of 9 cm.

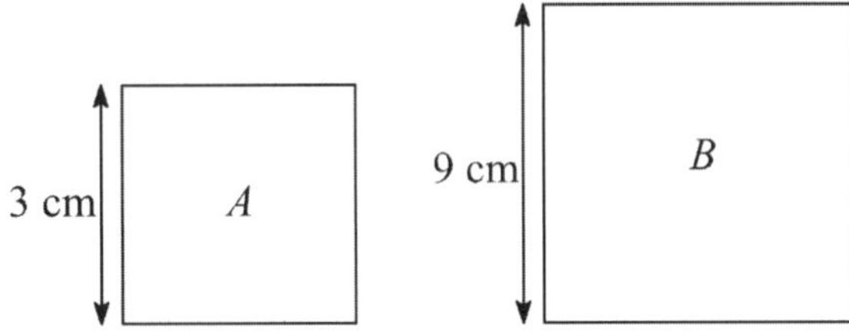

The scale factor is $k = \frac{9}{3} = 3$.

The area of square A is $9\ \text{cm}^2$ and the area of square B is $81\ \text{cm}^2$. The area has been scaled up by $\frac{81}{9} = 9$. Since $9 = 3^2$, we can say that if the length is enlarged by k, the area will be enlarged by k^2.

Similarly, consider two cubes. Cube C has sides of 3 cm and cube D has sides of 9 cm. The scale factor is again 3.

The volume of cube C is $27\ \text{cm}^3$ and the volume of cube D is $729\ \text{cm}^3$. The volume is scaled up by $\frac{729}{27} = 27$. Since $27 = 3^3$, we can say that if the length is enlarged by k, the volume will be enlarged by k^3.

Example

The total surface area and the volume of prism A below are 92 cm^2 and 48 cm^3 respectively. Prisms B and C are both enlargements of prism A. By first determining the scale factors, calculate the total surface area and volume of prism B and prism C.

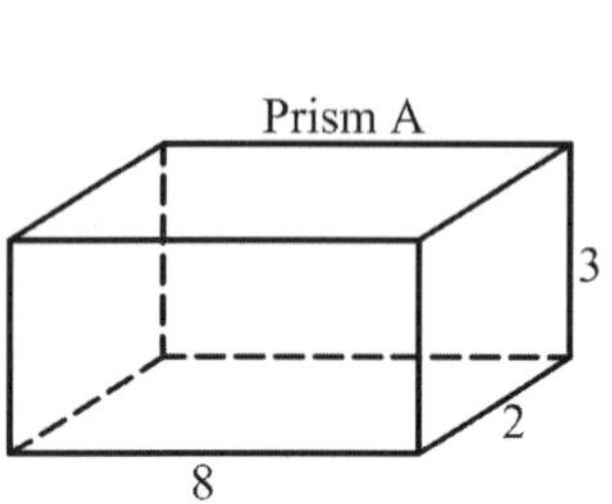

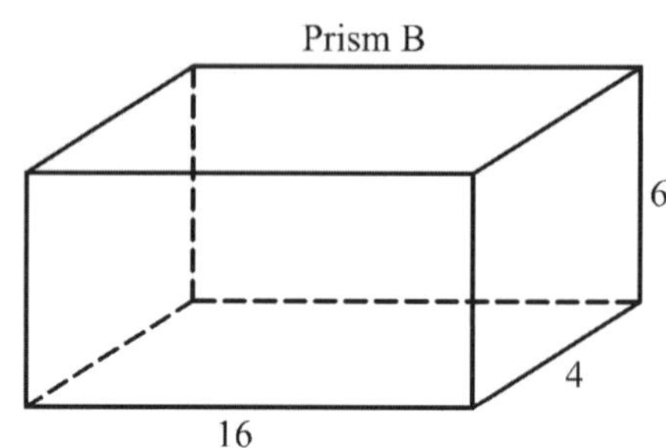

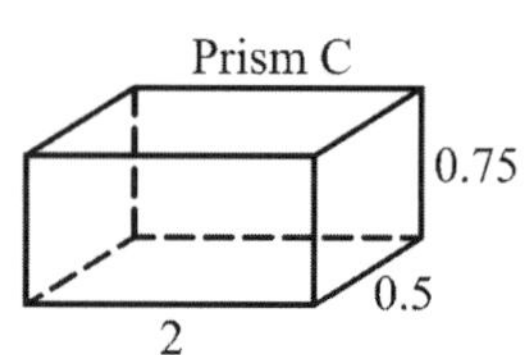

✓ *Solution*

Working	Explanation
Prism B Scale Factor $= k = \frac{16}{8} = 2$ TSA $= 92 \times 2^2 = 368$ cm^2 Volume $= 48 \times 2^3 = 384$ cm^3 **Prism C** Scale Factor $= k = \frac{2}{8} = \frac{1}{4}$ TSA $= 92 \times \left(\frac{1}{4}\right)^2 = 5.75$ cm^2 Volume $= 48 \times \left(\frac{1}{4}\right)^3 = 0.75$ cm^3	For each prism: • Determine the scale factor, k. • Multiply the total surface area of prism A by k^2 to obtain the total surface area of the prism. • Multiply the volume of prism A by k^3 to obtain the volume of the prism.

Exercise 8.4.1

While visiting the National Gallery of Australia in Canberra, Mike bought a replica of the painting *Blue Poles* by Jackson Pollock. The width and length of the original painting are 2.1 m and 4.86 m respectively. The replica is $\frac{1}{3}$ the size of the original painting. Determine the area and perimeter of the replica.

Exercise 8.4.2

In the diagram below, solid D is a scaled model of solid C.

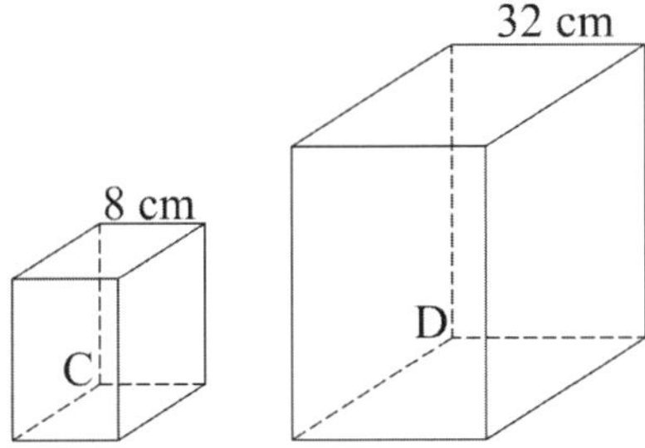

a. Determine the scale factor used to enlarge solid C to solid D.

b. Determine the surface area of solid D if the surface area of solid C is 448 cm^2.

c. Determine the volume of solid C if the volume of solid D is $40\ 960$ cm^3.

Exercise 8.4.3

When Tom was in Paris a few years ago, he visited the Rodin Museum and bought a small replica of the famous sculpture called *The Thinker*. He was told that the replica is $\frac{1}{6}$ the size of the original sculpture in all its dimensions.

a. Given that the replica is 31 cm high, what is the height of *The Thinker*?

b. If the surface area of the original sculpture is approximately $116\ 000$ cm^2, calculate the surface area of the replica to the nearest 10 cm^2.

c. Given that the volume of the replica is 3000 cm^3, calculate the volume of *The Thinker*.

Answers

Exercise 8.1.1

All sides of a square are the same length. For $ABCD$, all sides have length d and for $EFGH$, all sides have length l. Therefore, the ratio of corresponding sides will always be $\frac{d}{l}$ $\left(\text{or } \frac{l}{d}\right)$. Moreover, since both are squares, all corresponding angles are the same, i.e. $90°$. Hence all squares are similar.

Exercise 8.1.2

$ABCDE$ is similar to $PQRST$ because all the corresponding sides have the same ratio $\left(4 \text{ or } \frac{1}{4}\right)$ and all corresponding angles are $108°$.

Exercise 8.2.1

scale factor $= \frac{1}{25}$

Exercise 8.2.2

16.8 km

Exercise 8.3.1

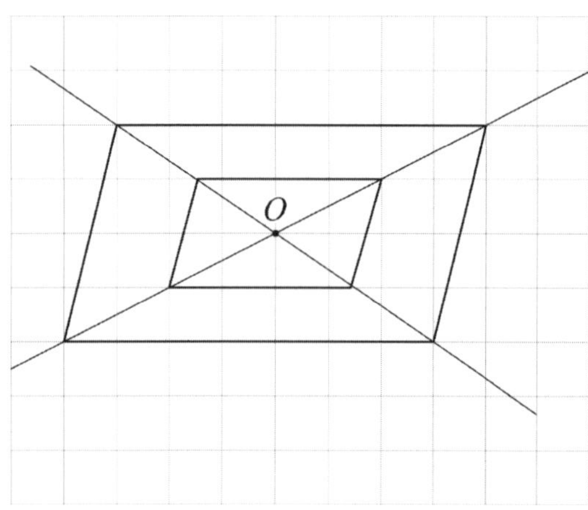

Exercise 8.3.2

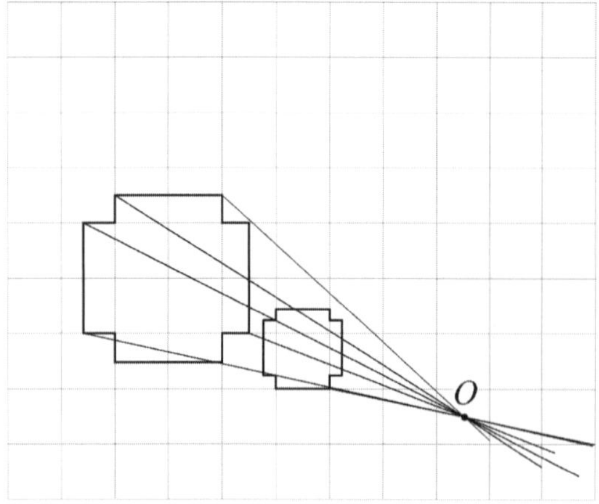

Exercise 8.4 1

perimeter $= 4.64$ m   area $= 1.13$ m^2

Exercise 8.4 2

a. $k = 4$ b. 7168 cm^2 c. 640 cm^3

Exercise 8.4 3

a. 186 cm   b. 3220 cm^2 c. $648\ 000$ cm^3

Chapter 9 – Geometric reasoning

9.1 Review of angles

Types of single angles that you should know are listed below.

Type of angle	Illustration	Range of angle
Acute	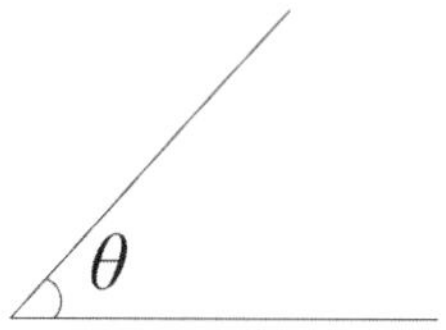 θ	$0° < \theta < 90°$
Right	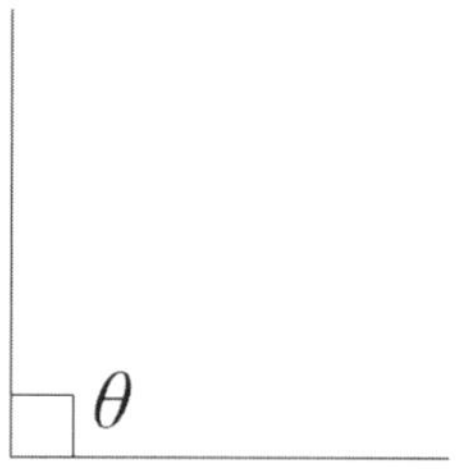 θ	$\theta = 90°$
Obtuse	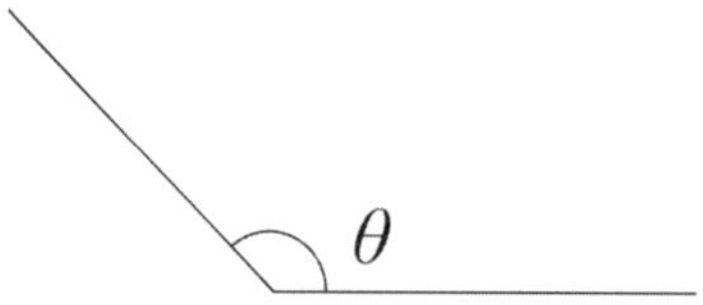 θ	$90° < \theta < 180°$
Straight	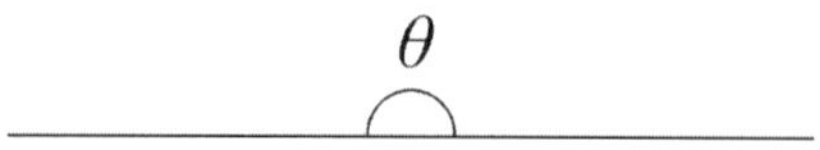 θ	$\theta = 180°$
Reflex	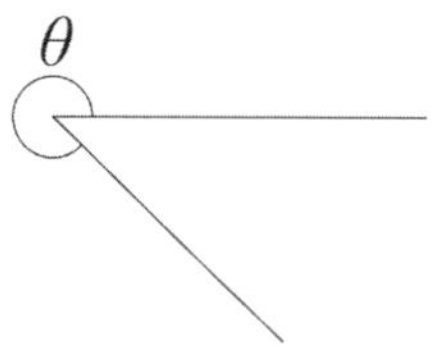 θ	$180° < \theta < 360°$
Full rotation	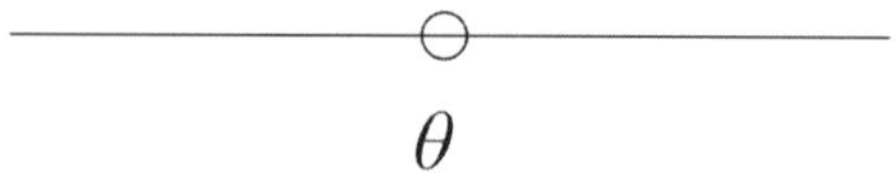 θ	$\theta = 360°$

The area contained within a right angle, straight angle or full-revolution angle can be separated into smaller areas. These areas have their own angles. The names of these angles, and their relationships to other angles, are described in the following table.

Type of angle	Illustration	Explanation
Complementary angles	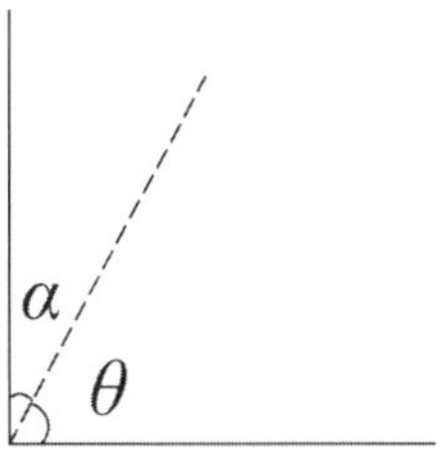 α θ	$\alpha + \theta = 90°$
Supplementary angles	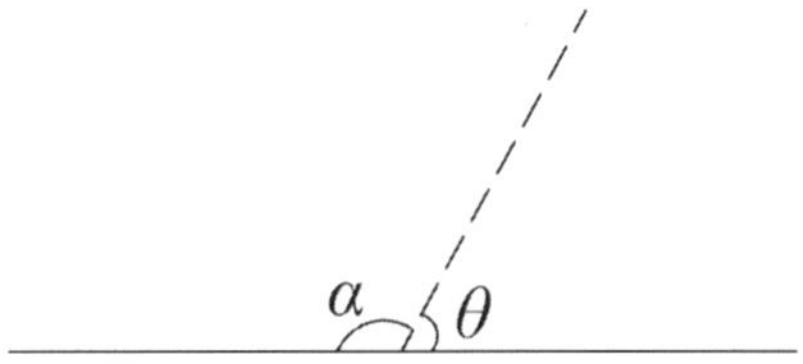 α θ	$\alpha + \theta = 180°$
Vertically opposite angles	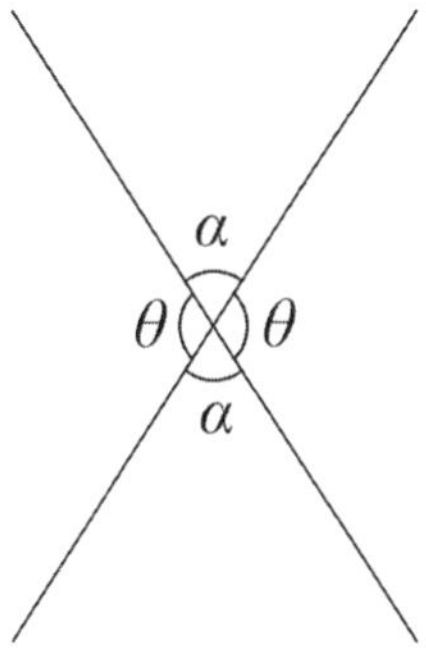 α θ θ α	When two straight lines intersect, the opposite angles formed are equal.

The angles formed when a line crosses two parallel lines are described in the following table.

Type of angle	Illustration	Explanation
Corresponding angles	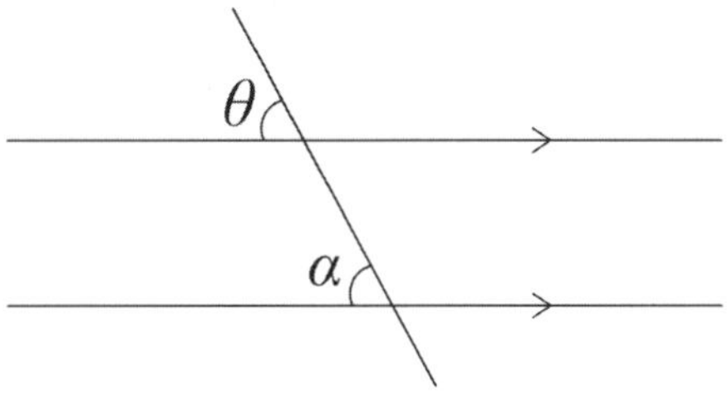 θ α Or 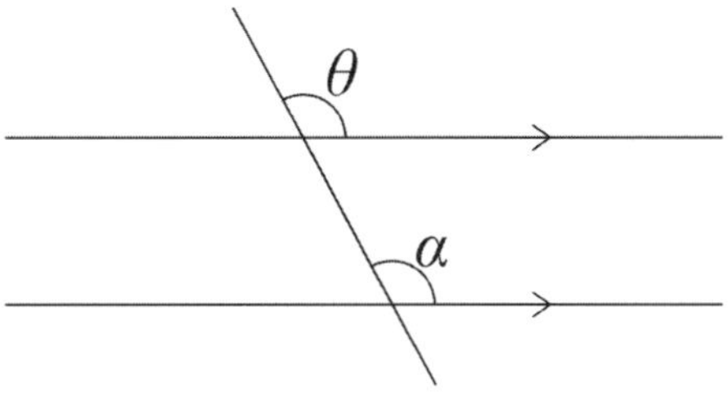 θ α	$\alpha = \theta$

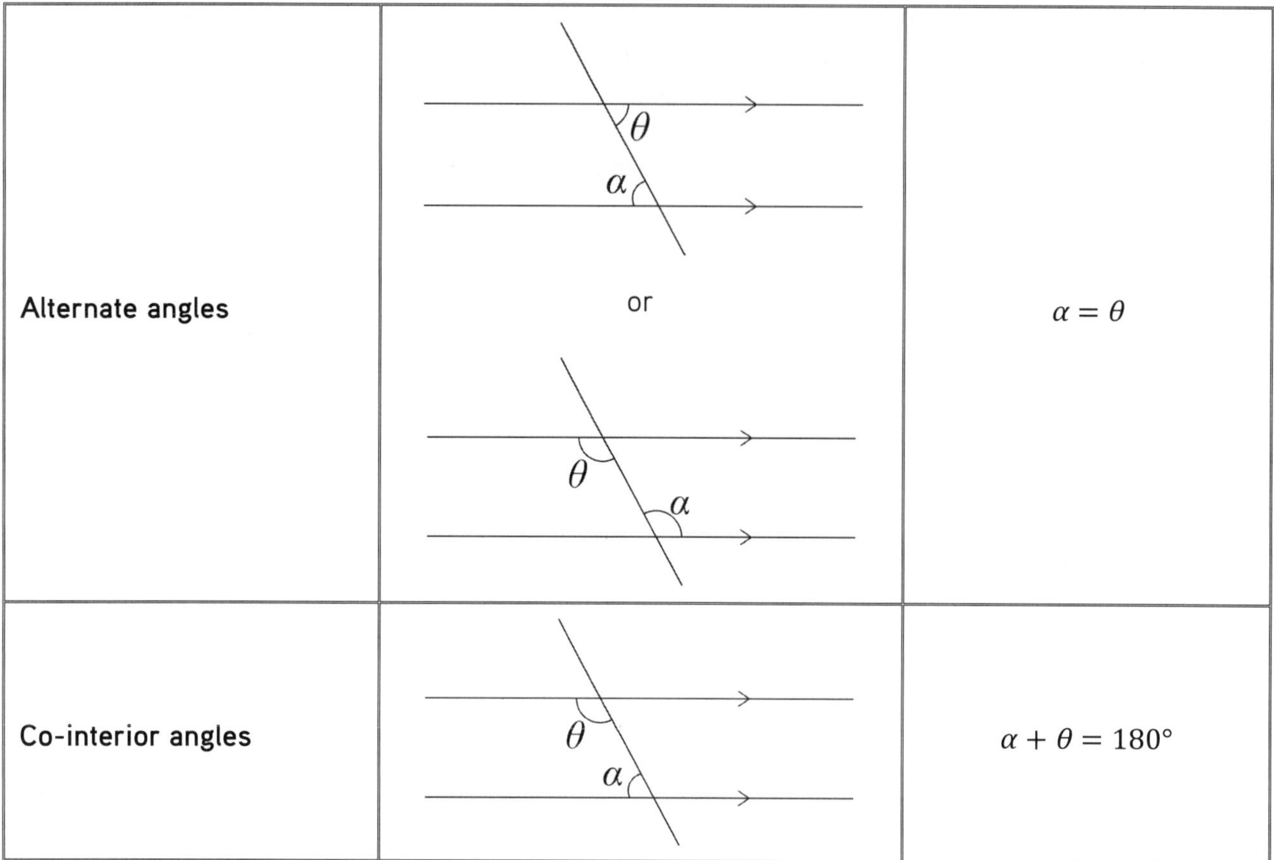

Alternate angles	or	$\alpha = \theta$
Co-interior angles		$\alpha + \theta = 180°$

We can use the properties of known angles to determine the values of unknown angles.

Example

Determine the values of the unknown angles in the following diagrams.

a.

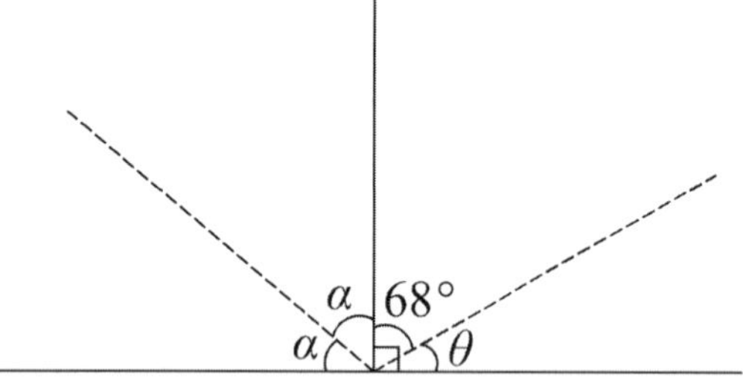

b.

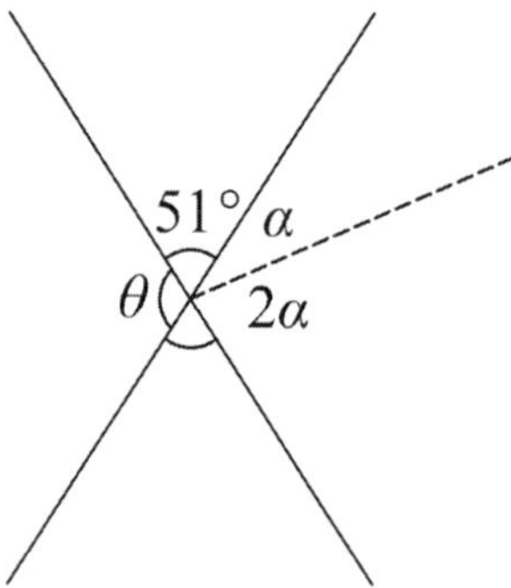

c.

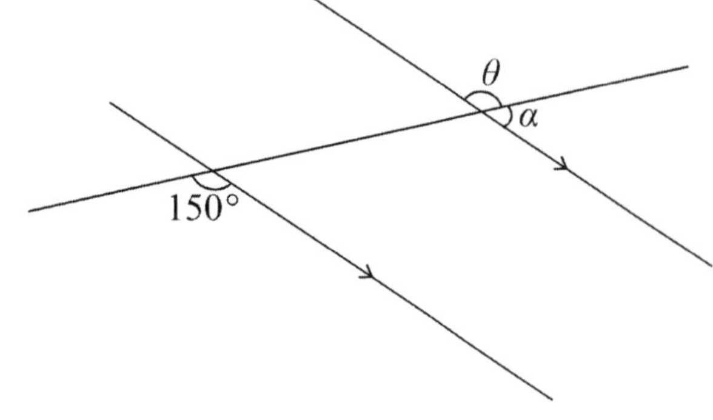

✓ *Solution*

Working	Explanation
a. $68° + \theta = 90°$ $\theta = 90° - 68°$ $\theta = 22°$	From the right angle given, 68° and θ are complementary angles, which add up to 90°.
$2\alpha = 90°$ $\alpha = 45°$	Since the horizontal line is a straight line and there are two equal angles that form a right angle, the value of α can be determined.
b. $51° + \theta = 180°$ $\theta = 180° - 51°$ $\theta = 129°$	We can see that $51°$ and θ are supplementary angles, which add up to $180°$.
$3\alpha = 129°$ $\alpha = 43°$	The two angles that make up 3α and θ are vertically opposite angles.
c.	Identify the corresponding angle to $150°$. This is indicated by the dot in the diagram on the left. The angle vertically opposite the dot is θ. Hence $\theta = 150°$.
$\alpha + 150° = 180°$ $\alpha = 30°$	α and θ are supplementary angles, which must add up to $180°$.

Example

Prove that $\alpha + \beta = 90°$ in the diagram below.

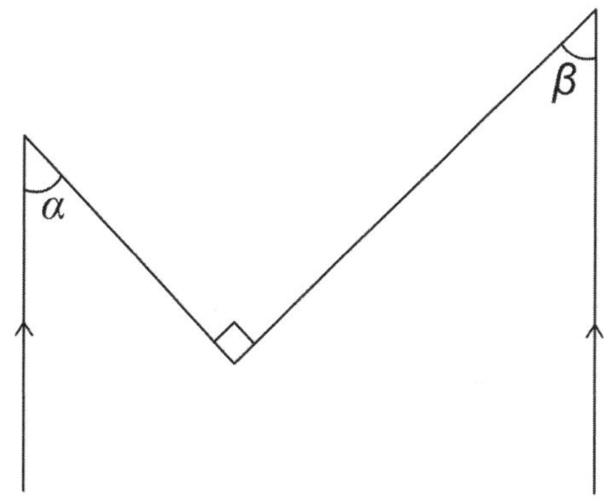

✓ ***Solution***

Working	Explanation
Therefore: • $\alpha = \gamma$ (alternate angles) • $\beta = \theta$ (alternate angles) Since $\gamma + \theta = 90°$, $\alpha + \beta = 90°$.	Draw a line parallel to both parallel lines and passing through the right angle (dashed in the diagram on the left). Label the angles between the dashed line and the sides of the right angle: γ and θ. Use the fact that alternate angles are equal to prove that $\alpha + \beta = 90°$.

Exercise 9.1.1

Determine the values of the unknown angles in the following diagrams.

a.

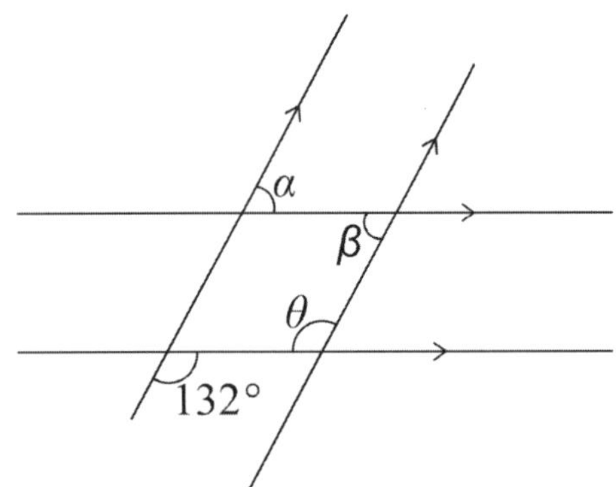

b.

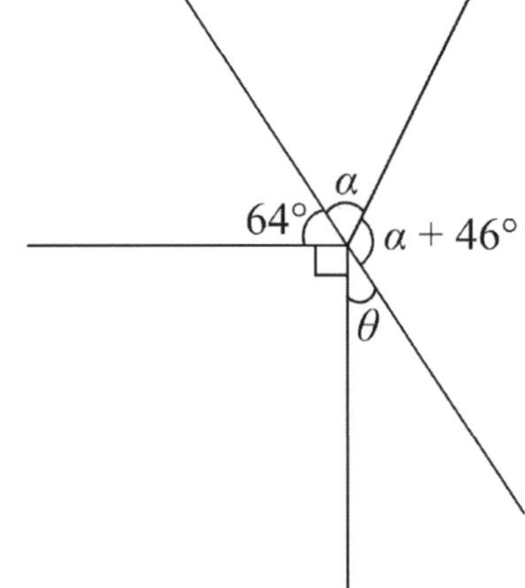

c.

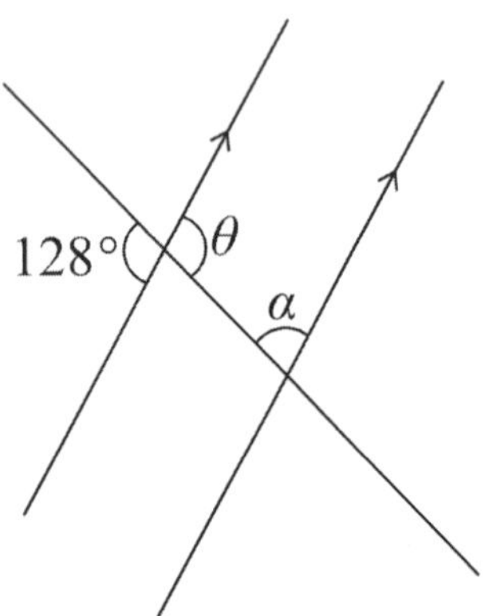

Exercise 9.1.2

Prove that $\alpha + \beta - \gamma = 180°$ in the following diagram.

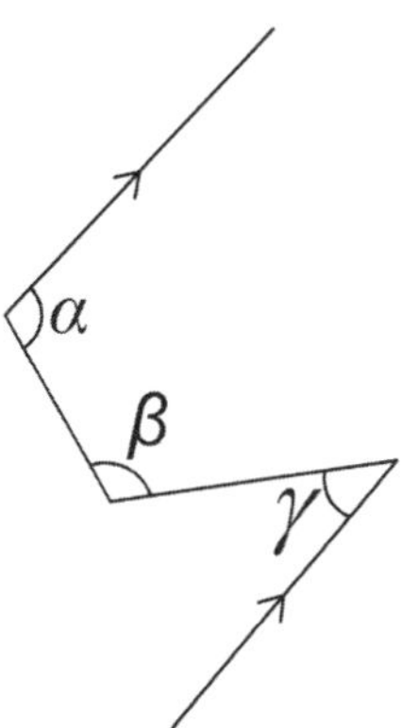

9.2 Review of triangles

A triangle is a closed polygon with three sides. Types of triangles are summarised in the table below.

Note the two unique cases:

- equilateral triangles, where each internal angle is $60°$
- isosceles triangles that are also right-angled triangles, where two of the angles are $45°$ and one of the angles is a right angle ($90°$).

		Classified by length of sides		
		Equilateral triangles (three sides of equal length)	**Isosceles triangles** (two sides of equal length)	**Scalene triangles** (no sides are of equal length)
Classified by internal angles	**Acute-angled triangles** (all internal angles are acute, i.e. less than $90°$)	$60°$, $60°$, $60°$	θ, θ	
	Obtuse-angled triangles (one internal angle is obtuse, i.e. greater than $90°$)	not possible	θ, θ	
	Right-angled triangles (one internal angle is a right angle, i.e. $90°$)	not possible	$45°$, $45°$	

The properties of angles and triangles can both be applied in solving problems in geometry. Consider the diagram below.

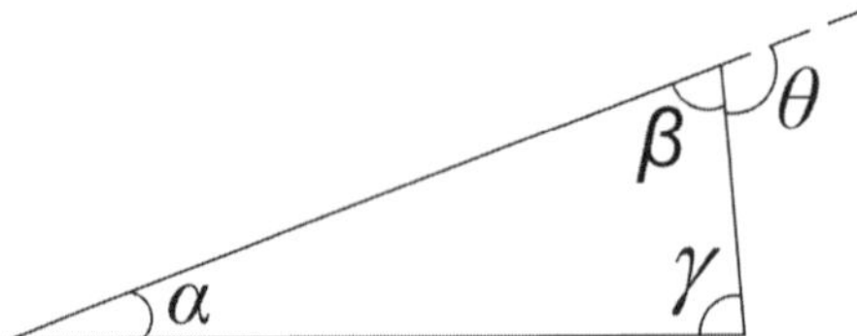

The sum of the internal angles of a triangle is always 180°. Hence $\alpha + \beta + \gamma = 180°$, from which it follows that $\beta = 180° - \alpha - \gamma$. Further, $\beta + \theta = 180°$ (since they are supplementary angles). We can therefore conclude, by substitution, that the exterior angle (in this case, θ) equals the sum of the two opposite interior angles (i.e. α and γ).

$$\boldsymbol{\theta = \alpha + \gamma}$$

9.3 Similar triangles

Two triangles are said to be similar if they are the same shape but different in size. Corresponding angles will be the same (i.e. congruent) and corresponding side lengths will be in the same ratio. Recall from the previous chapter that this ratio is called the scale factor.

There are four tests for determining whether two triangles are similar. They are summarised in the following table.

Similarity test	Explanation	
Angle, Angle, Angle (AAA)		$\angle ABC = \angle DEF = 70°$ $\angle BCA = \angle EFD = 72°$ $\angle CAB = \angle FDE = 38°$ All angles are the same, therefore ΔABC is similar to ΔDEF (AAA).
Side, Side, Side (SSS)		$\frac{AB}{DE} = \frac{BC}{EF} = \frac{CA}{FD} = \frac{1}{2}$ All corresponding sides have the same ratio, therefore ΔABC is similar to ΔDEF (SSS).
Side, Angle, Side (SAS)		$\angle ABC = \angle DEF = 85°$ $\frac{AB}{DE} = \frac{BC}{EF} = 3$ An angle is the same and two pairs of corresponding sides have the same ratio, therefore ΔABC is similar to ΔDEF (SAS). **Note:** for the SAS test to apply, the angle must be between the two sides that are in the same proportion (1:3 in the example above).

Right angle, Hypotenuse, Side (RHS)	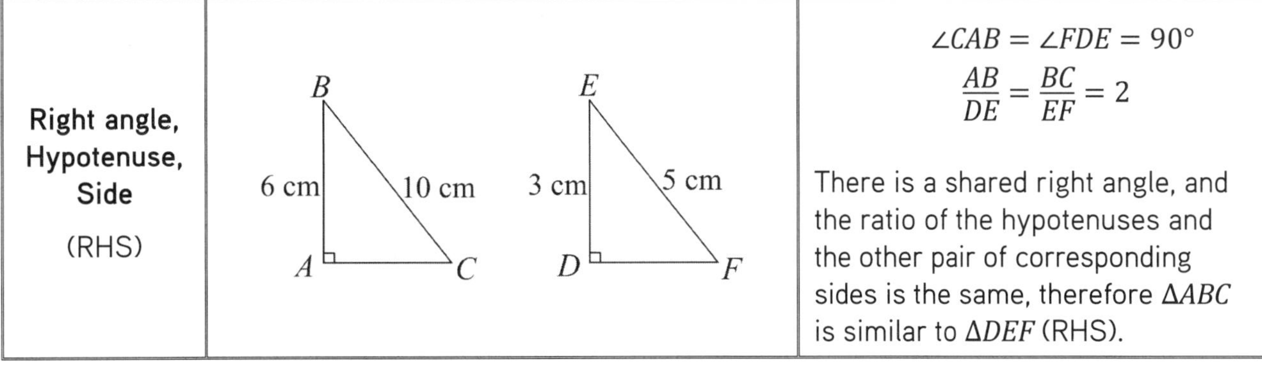	$\angle CAB = \angle FDE = 90°$ $\frac{AB}{DE} = \frac{BC}{EF} = 2$ There is a shared right angle, and the ratio of the hypotenuses and the other pair of corresponding sides is the same, therefore ΔABC is similar to ΔDEF (RHS).

The notation used to indicate that triangles are similar is

$$\Delta ABC \sim \Delta DEF \text{ or } \Delta ABC \ ||| \ \Delta DEF$$

You need to be able to write proofs and provide reasons as to why two triangles are similar. For example, suppose you had to prove that the following triangles are similar.

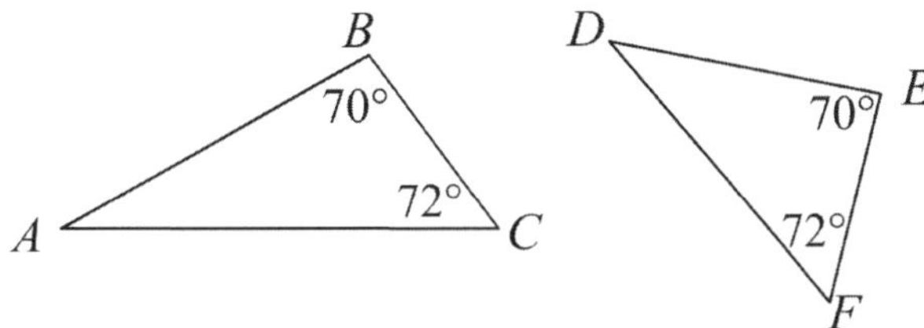

The table below shows the structure you should follow in providing your proof.

Structure	What is required
Introduction What needs to be proven?	Required to prove (RTP) that $\Delta ABC \sim \Delta DEF$
Statements and reason	In ΔABC and ΔDEF: • $\angle ABC = \angle DEF = 70°$ (given) • $\angle BCA = \angle EFD = 72°$ (given) • $\angle CAB = \angle FDE = 38°$ (as the sum of the internal angles in a triangle is 180°) The corresponding angles in both triangles are the same.
Conclusion and the test that was used	$\therefore \Delta ABC \sim \Delta DEF$ (AAA)

Example

Prove that the following two triangles are similar.

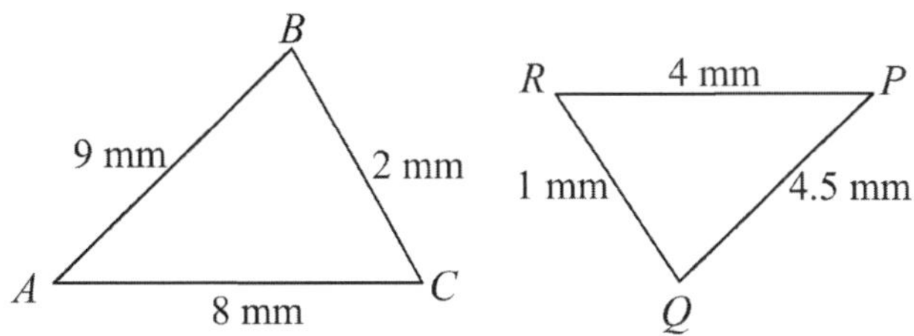

✓ Solution

Working	Explanation
RTP: $\Delta ABC \sim \Delta PQR$	Write what you are required to prove.
In ΔABC and ΔPQR: • $\frac{AB}{PQ} = \frac{9}{4.5} = 2$ • $\frac{BC}{QR} = \frac{2}{1} = 2$ • $\frac{CA}{RP} = \frac{8}{4} = 2$	Since the measurements of the sides are given, this indicates that you need to calculate the ratios. State the ratios.
Or you can write: $\frac{AB}{PQ} = \frac{BC}{QR} = \frac{CA}{RP} = 2$	Provide a reason for drawing your conclusion.
The ratio of the corresponding sides of the two triangles is the same. $\therefore \Delta ABC \sim \Delta PQR$ (SSS)	Conclude that the two triangles are similar and state the test you used.

Example

Prove that the following two triangles are similar.

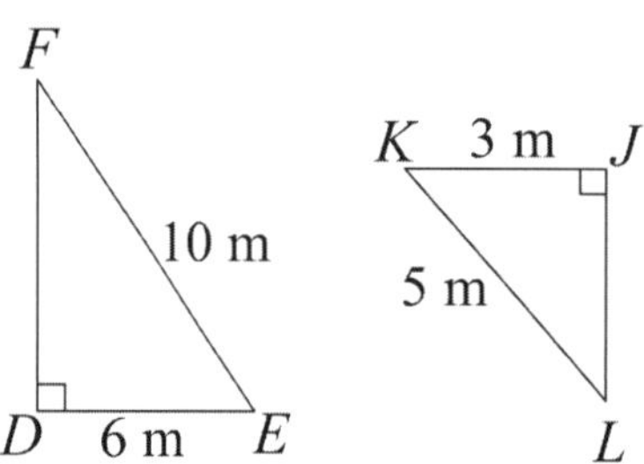

✓ Solution

Working	Explanation
RTP: $\Delta DEF \sim \Delta JKL$	Write what you are required to prove.
In ΔDEF and ΔJKL: • $\Delta FDE = \Delta LJK = 90°$ (given) • $\frac{DE}{JK} = \frac{6}{3} = 2$ (ratio of the given sides) • $\frac{EF}{KL} = \frac{10}{5} = 2$ (ratio of the hypotenuses)	For each triangle, the information given is one angle and two sides. The angle is 90° and one of the sides is the hypotenuse. Hence the RHS test can be used. Write the statements that support your conclusion.
Both triangles have a right angle, and the ratio of the hypotenuses and the other corresponding sides is the same. $\therefore \Delta DEF \sim \Delta JKL$ (RHS)	Provide a reason for drawing your conclusion. Conclude that the two triangles are similar and state the test you used.

Example

Prove that the following triangles are similar.

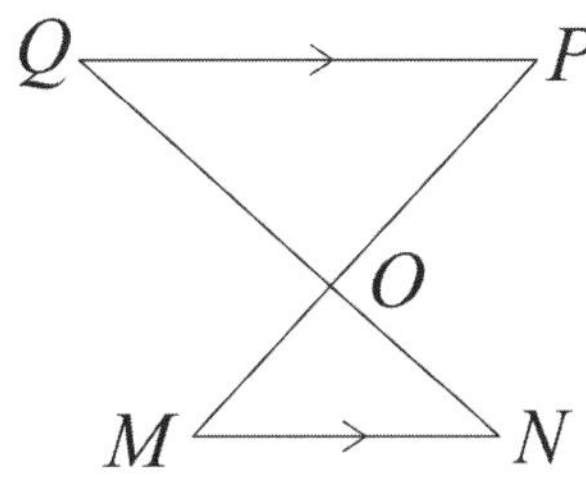

✓ ***Solution***

Working	Explanation
RTP: $\Delta OPQ \sim \Delta ONM$	Write what you are required to prove.
In ΔOPQ and ΔONM: • $\angle QOP = \angle MON$ (vertically opposite angles) • $\angle OPQ = \angle OMN$ (alternate angles, $QP \parallel MN$) • $\angle PQO = \angle ONM$ (alternate angles, $QP \parallel MN$)	No measurements or angles are given but we can use our knowledge of parallel lines and intersecting lines to provide a proof. Write the statements that support your conclusion. **Note:** $QP \parallel MN$ means QP is parallel to MN.
All corresponding angles are the same.	Provide a reason for drawing your conclusion.
$\therefore \Delta OPQ \sim \Delta ONM$ (AAA)	Conclude that the two triangles are similar and state the test you used.

Example

Prove that the following two triangles are similar.

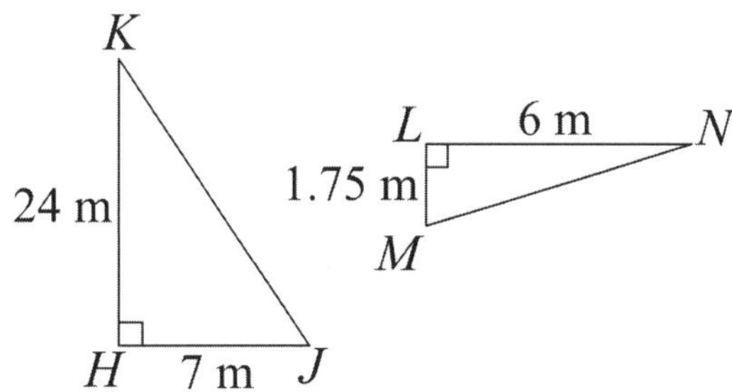

✓ *Solution*

Working	Explanation
RTP: $\Delta HKJ \sim \Delta LNM$	Write what you are required to prove.
In ΔHKJ and ΔLNM: • $\angle JHK = \angle MLN = 90°$ (given) • $\frac{HK}{LN} = \frac{24}{6} = 4$ (ratio of one pair of corresponding sides) • $\frac{JH}{ML} = \frac{7}{1.75} = 4$ (ratio of the other corresponding sides)	For each triangle, the information given is one angle and two sides (neither of which is the hypotenuse). Further, the angle is between the two given sides. Hence the test to use is SAS. Write the statements that support your conclusion. Provide a reason for drawing your conclusion.
The triangles share an angle, and the ratio of corresponding sides is the same. $\therefore \Delta HKJ \sim \Delta LMN$ (SAS)	Conclude that the two triangles are similar and state the test.

Exercise 9.3.1

Prove that the following triangles are similar.

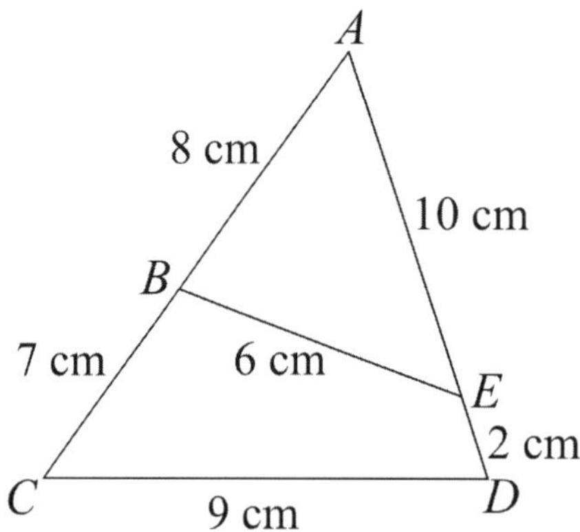

Exercise 9.3.2

Prove that the following triangles are similar.

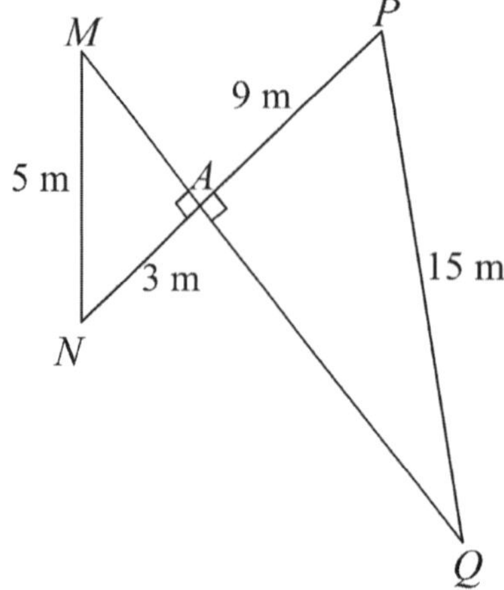

Exercise 9.3.3

Prove that the following triangles are similar.

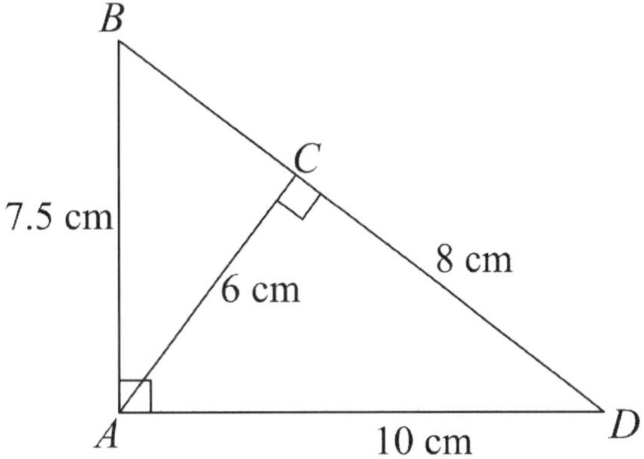

Exercise 9.3.4

Prove that the following triangles are similar.

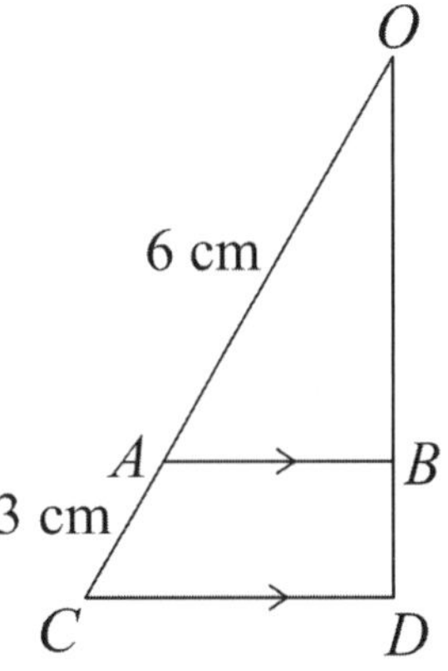

9.4 Applying similar triangles

The similarity of triangles can be put to many uses. For example, once you have established that two triangles are similar, you can determine the dimensions and angles of one triangle from the dimensions and angles of the other triangle.

Example

a. Prove that the two triangles in the diagram on the right are similar.

b. Determine the value of x to 1 decimal place.

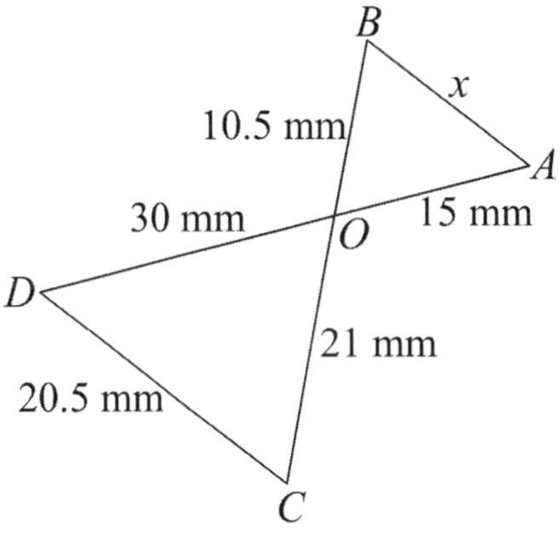

✓ Solution

Working	Explanation
a. RTP: $\Delta OAB \sim \Delta ODC$ In ΔOAB and ΔODC: • $\angle BOA = \angle COD$ (vertically opposite angles) • $\frac{OC}{OB} = \frac{21}{10.5} = 2$ (ratio of one pair of corresponding sides) • $\frac{OD}{OA} = \frac{30}{15} = 2$ (ratio of the other corresponding sides) The two triangles share an angle, and the corresponding sides share the same ratio. $\therefore \Delta OAB \sim \Delta ODC$ (SAS)	Write what you are required to prove. At least two sides are given for each triangle, and we can tell that they must share an angle: the vertically opposite angles where the triangles meet. Therefore the SAS test can be used. Write the statements that support your conclusion. Provide a reason for drawing your conclusion. Conclude that the two triangles are similar and state the test you used.
b. $\frac{DC}{AB} = \frac{20.5}{x} = 2$ $x = 10.25$ $x = 10.3$ mm	Since the ratio of the corresponding sides of similar triangles is also the scale factor, we can use the scale factor to determine the length of AB (x) by considering the ratio of AB to its corresponding side (DC).

Example

The diagram on the right shows a triangular structure supported by a vertical column QT.

T is at the centre of PS.

a. Prove that the two triangles are similar.

b. Determine the height of the column QT.

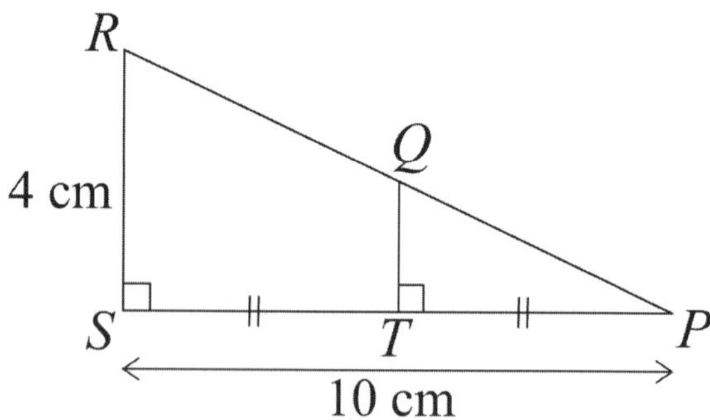

✓ *Solution*

Working	Explanation
a. RTP: $\Delta PQT \sim \Delta PRS$ In ΔPQT and ΔPRS: • $\angle TPQ = \angle SPR$ (common) • $\angle QTP = \angle RSP = 90°$ (given) • $\angle PQT = \angle PRS$ (the sum of the internal angles in a triangle is $180°$)	Write what you are required to prove. No measurements are given but it can be shown that the three angles in each triangle are the same. Hence the AAA test can be used. Write the statements that support your conclusion.
The two triangles share corresponding angles. $\therefore \Delta PQT \sim \Delta PRS$ (AAA)	Provide a reason for drawing your conclusion. Conclude that the two triangles are similar and state the test you used.
$\frac{PT}{PS} = \frac{5}{10} = \frac{1}{2}$ Therefore $\frac{QT}{RS} = \frac{QT}{4} = \frac{1}{2}$ $QT = 2$ The height of the column is 2 cm.	Since $PT = TS$, the scale factor can be determined. Use the scale factor to determine the height of the column.

Example

William is 1.3 m tall and stands 7 m away from a tree, as shown in the diagram below. The shadow he casts is 1.8 m long. The top of the shadow cast by the tree is at the same point as the top of the head of William's shadow.

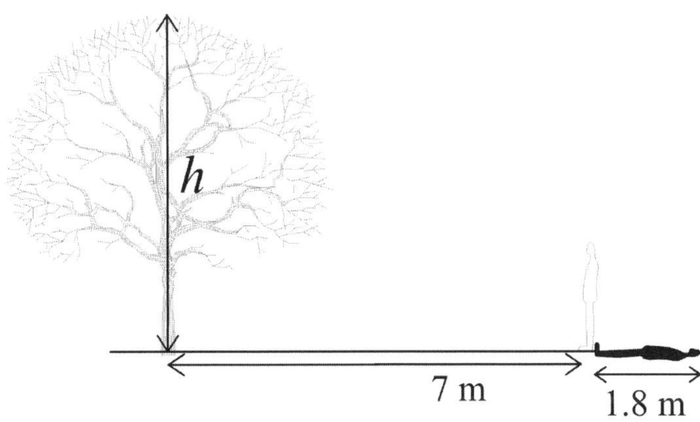

a. Draw a pair of triangles showing this situation and prove that they are similar.

b. Determine the height of the tree, h, to the nearest metre.

✓ *Solution*

Working	Explanation
a. RTP: $\Delta ABC \sim \Delta ADE$ In ΔABC and ΔADE: • $\angle CAB = \angle EAD$ (common) • $\angle BCA = \angle DEA = 90°$ (given) • $\angle ABC = \angle ADE$ (sum of the internal angles in a triangle is 180°)	Draw the triangles. The height of the tree, h, is one side of a right-angled triangle. William is standing 7 m away and casts a shadow of 1.8 m. Always label the vertices of the triangles. **Note**: you can assume that the tree and William are standing at 90° to the ground. There are some measurements given, and a right angle can be assumed. However, there is a common angle for both triangles at vertex A. Hence the AAA test can be used. Write the statements that support your conclusion.
The two triangles share corresponding angles. $\Delta ABC \sim \Delta ADE$ (AAA)	Provide a reason for drawing your conclusion. Conclude that the two triangles are similar and state the test you used.
b. Since $\Delta ABC \sim \Delta ADE$ $\frac{AE}{AC} = \frac{7+1.8}{1.8} = \frac{8.8}{1.8} = 4.\dot{8}$ Therefore $h = 4.\dot{8} \times 1.3 = 6.3\dot{5}$ The height of the tree is 6 m.	Use the scale factor to determine the height of the tree to the nearest metre.

Exercise 9.4.1

Consider the diagram to the right.

a. Prove that the two triangles are similar.

b. Determine the value of x to 1 decimal place.

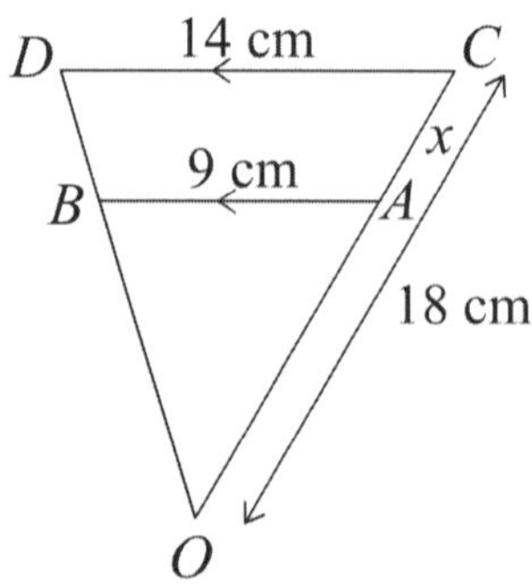

Exercise 9.4.2

A surveyor is measuring the width of a 6-lane freeway. She is unable to cross the freeway due to heavy traffic. She identifies 4 markers on her side of the highway (points A, B, C and D in the diagram below, which is not drawn to scale). A tree on the other side of the freeway directly opposite point D is marked as point E. She then measures the distances between the points on her side of the freeway.

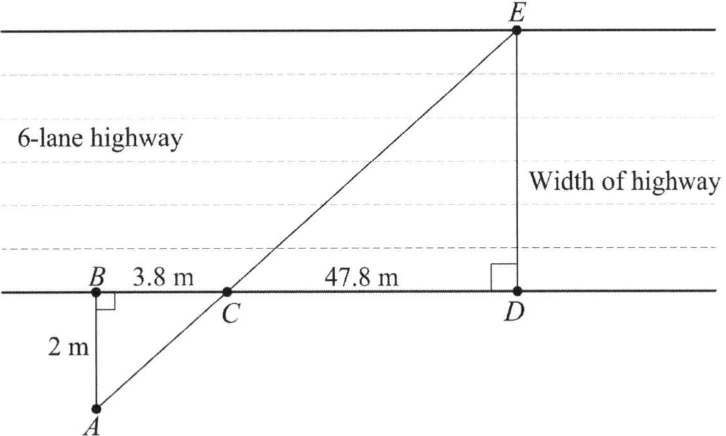

a. Prove that the two triangles formed by connecting the points as shown in the diagram are similar triangles.

b. Determine the width of a single lane of the highway (to the nearest cm).

Exercise 9.4.3

A tower casts a shadow 35 m long. At the same time, a stick is placed vertically in the ground at the farthest point of the shadow. The stick protrudes 2.5 m from the ground and casts a shadow of 6 m.

a. Draw a clearly labelled diagram to represent this situation.

b. Identify the similar triangles in the diagram and name the test that proves that they are similar. (You do not need to write down the proof.)

c. Determine the height of the tower.

Answers

Exercise 9.1.1

a. $\alpha = 48°$; $\beta = 48°$; $\theta = 132°$

b. $\alpha = 67°$; $\theta = 26°$

c. $\theta = 128°$; $\alpha = 52°$

Exercise 9.1.2

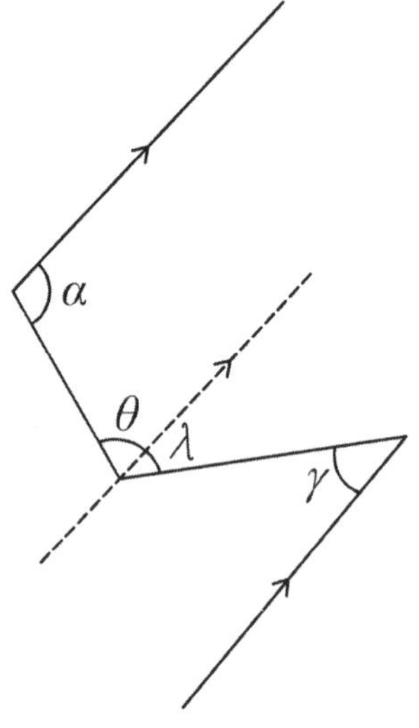

Construct a line parallel to the two parallel lines that splits β into two angles: θ and γ.

Therefore, $\theta + \gamma = \beta$ and hence $\theta = \beta - \gamma$.

$\alpha + \theta = 180°$ (co-interior angles) and hence $\theta = 180° - \alpha$.

We now have two equations for θ. Equating both expressions and rearranging the terms gives $\alpha + \beta - \gamma = 180°$.

Exercise 9.3.1

RTP: $\Delta ADC \sim \Delta ABE$

In ΔADC and ΔABE

- $\frac{AD}{AB} = \frac{12}{8} = 1.5$
- $\frac{DC}{BE} = \frac{9}{6} = 1.5$
- $\frac{CA}{EA} = \frac{15}{10} = 1.5$

The ratios of the corresponding sides of the two triangles are the same.

$\therefore \Delta ADC \sim \Delta ABE$ (SSS)

Exercise 9.3.2

RTP: $\Delta AMN \sim \Delta AQP$

In ΔAMN and ΔAQP:

- $\angle NAM = \angle PAQ = 90°$ (given)
- $\frac{PA}{NA} = \frac{9}{3} = 3$ (ratio of the given sides)
- $\frac{QP}{MN} = \frac{15}{5} = 3$ (ratio of the hypotenuses)

The triangles share a right angle, and the hypotenuses and the given sides share the same ratio.

$\therefore \Delta AMN \sim \Delta AQP$ (RHS)

Exercise 9.3.3

RTP: $\Delta CAD \sim \Delta ABD$

In ΔCAD and ΔABD:

- $\angle DCA = \angle DAB = 90°$ (given)
- $\frac{AB}{CA} = \frac{7.5}{6} = 1.25$ (ratio of two corresponding sides)
- $\frac{DA}{DC} = \frac{10}{8} = 1.25$ (ratio of the other corresponding sides)

The two triangles share an angle, and the corresponding sides share the same ratio.

$\therefore \Delta CAD \sim \Delta ABD$ (SAS)

Exercise 9.3.4

RTP: $\Delta OAB \sim \Delta OCD$

In ΔOAB and ΔOCD:

- $\angle BOA = \angle DOC$ (common angle for both triangles)
- $\angle OAB = \angle OCD$ (corresponding angles, $AB \parallel CD$)
- $\angle ABO = \angle CDO$ (corresponding angles, $AB \parallel CD$)

Note: for the last statement you could also state that the sum of the internal angles of a triangle is $180°$.

$\therefore \Delta OAB \sim \Delta OCD$ (AAA)

Exercise 9.4.1

a. RTP: $\Delta OAB \sim \Delta OCD$

In ΔOAB and ΔOCD:

- $\angle BOA = \angle DOC$ (common)
- $\angle OAB = \angle OCD$ (corresponding angles, $AB \parallel DC$)
- $\angle ABO = \angle CDO$ (corresponding angles, $AB \parallel DC$)

$\therefore \Delta OAB \sim \Delta OCD$ (AAA)

b. $x = 6.43$ cm

Exercise 9.4.2

a. RTP: $\Delta BCA \sim \Delta DCE$

In ΔBCA and ΔDCE:

- $\angle ABC = \angle EDC = 90°$ (given)
- $\angle ACB = \angle ECD$ (vertically opposite angles)
- $\angle CAB = \angle CED$ (sum of the internal angles in a triangle $= 180°$)

$\therefore \Delta BCA \sim \Delta DCE$ (AAA)

b. The width of a lane is 419 cm.

Exercise 9.4.3

a. 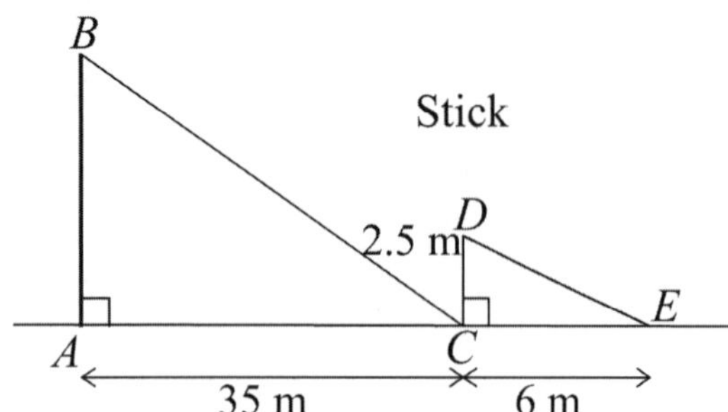

b. $\Delta ABC \sim \Delta CDE$ (AAA)

c. The height of the tower is 14.58 m.

Chapter 10 – Probability

10.1 Key concepts of probability

Probability is the branch of mathematics that deals with the occurrence of random events. The probability of a random event is between 0 and 1 (inclusive). A probability of 0 implies that the event is impossible, while a probability of 1 implies that the event is certain to happen.

For example, if we have a regular six-sided die, we can never roll a 7 with it. Hence, the probability of rolling a 7 on a regular die is 0. Tossing a coin will give us an even chance (i.e. a probability of 0.5) of getting a head (or a tail). We know for certain that the sun will set every day and so the probability of the sun setting today is 1.

Key terms

probability	the likelihood of a particular event occurring; e.g. the probability of rolling a six with a regular six-sided die is $\frac{1}{6}$
experiment (or **trial**)	a situation involving chance or probability that leads to one or more outcomes; e.g. rolling a die
outcome	the result of a single trial of an experiment; e.g. the occurrence of a six appearing on a die
event	one or more outcomes of an experiment
sample space	the set of all possible outcomes of an experiment; e.g. the sample space when rolling a six-sided die is $\{1, 2, 3, 4, 5, 6\}$

The probability of an event occurring is defined as

$$Pr(event) = \frac{\text{number of possible outcomes}}{\text{total number of outcomes}}$$

$$0 \leq Pr(event) \leq 1$$

Probability can be expressed in three ways: as a number between 0 and 1 (inclusive), as a percentage or as a fraction. So, the probability that a flipped coin lands heads up can be expressed as 0.5, 50% or $\frac{1}{2}$.

Example

A regular six-sided die is rolled. State:

a. the sample space

b. the probability of rolling an odd number

c. the probability that the number is divisible by 3.

✓ *Solution*

Working	Explanation
a. Sample space = $\{1, 2, 3, 4, 5, 6\}$	This is the complete set of the numbers that can be shown when rolling a regular six-sided die.
b. $\text{Pr(odd)} = \frac{3}{6}$	There are 3 odd numbers, i.e. 1, 3 and 5. Therefore, the probability of rolling an odd number is $\frac{3}{6}$.
c. $\text{Pr(divisible by 3)} = \frac{2}{6}$	Only 2 possible numbers are divisible by 3: 3 and 6. Therefore, the probability of rolling a number divisible by 3 is $\frac{2}{6}$.

Note: in answering questions on probability, you do not need to simplify fractions.

Example

The characters of the word 'PROBABILITY' are written on 11 cards of similar size. The cards are shuffled and laid on a table with the characters facing downwards. A card is randomly drawn. State the probability of:

a. drawing a B

b. drawing a consonant

c. drawing a vowel.

✓ *Solution*

Working	Explanation
a. $\text{Pr(drawing a B)} = \frac{2}{11}$	There are 11 characters and 2 Bs.
b. $\text{Pr(drawing a consonant)} = \frac{7}{11}$	There are 7 consonants.
c. $\text{Pr(drawing a vowel)} = \frac{4}{11}$	There are 4 vowels.

Exercise 10.1.1

Mary has 14 marbles: 3 are red, 4 are blue and the rest are green. The marbles are all of the same mass and size. She places them inside a pouch and draws one out randomly. State the probability that the marble she draws is:

a. red

b. green.

Exercise 10.1.2

Dean has a spinner, as shown in the diagram at the right.
State the probability of Dean spinning:

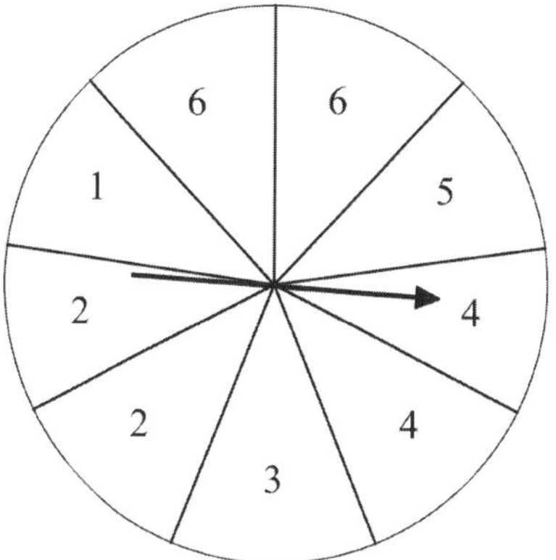

a. an odd number

b. a number divisible by 2

c. a number greater than 4

d. a number less than or equal to 3.

Exercise 10.1.3

Consider the numbers 1, 7, 12, 18, 24, 35, 51, 62, 78 and 81.

One of these numbers is picked at random. What is the probability that the number is:

a. odd?

b. greater than 7 but less than or equal to 51?

c. a prime number?

d. divisible by 3 and 9?

10.2 Venn diagrams and set notation

The sample space is also called the **universal set**, U. In the context of rolling a regular six-sided die, the sample space can be written in set notation as $U = \{1, 2, 3, 4, 5, 6\}$

This can be represented in a diagram, as shown on the right.

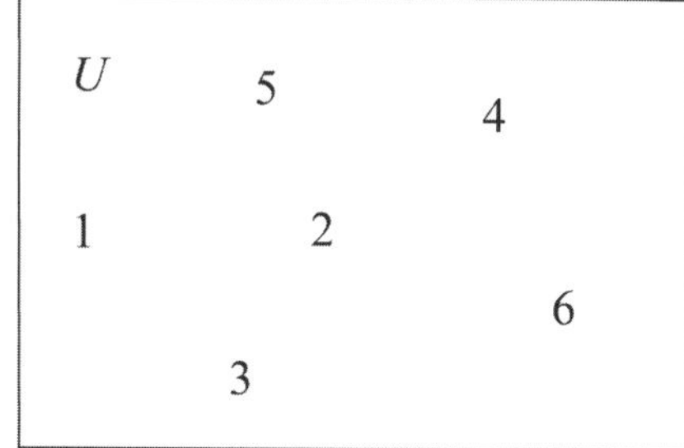

We know that there are 6 possible outcomes and we can use the following notation to indicate the number of outcomes.

$$n(U) = 6$$

Consider the trial of rolling a regular six-sided die. Let:

- A be the event of rolling an even number
- B be the event of rolling a prime number.

The various outcomes can be represented by a Venn diagram and in set notation, as the following table shows.

Situation	Venn diagram	Set notation
A only		$A = \{2, 4, 6\}$
B only		$B = \{2, 3, 5\}$
A AND B (intersection)		$A \cap B = \{2\}$
A OR B (union)		$A \cup B = \{2, 3, 4, 5, 6\}$
NOT A (complement)		$A' = \bar{A} = A^{c} = \{1, 3, 5\}$

Let C be the event that an odd number occurs, that is, $C = \{1, 3, 5\}$.

The Venn diagram showing both A and C is shown on the right.

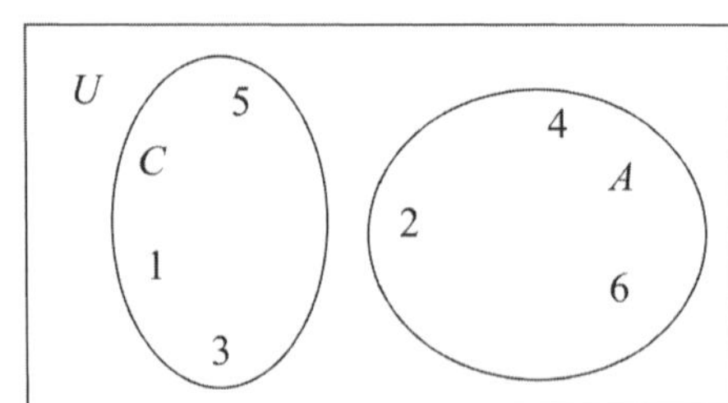

Note that these two events have nothing in common. We can write their intersection as

$$A \cap C = \{\ \} \text{ or } A \cap C = \phi$$

The sign { } and Ø are signs for the null set.

Events that have no common elements are called **mutually exclusive** events.

You shade various areas (or regions) of a Venn diagram to indicate the relationship between the sets being compared.

Some examples of shading are shown below.

 $A \cap B$ 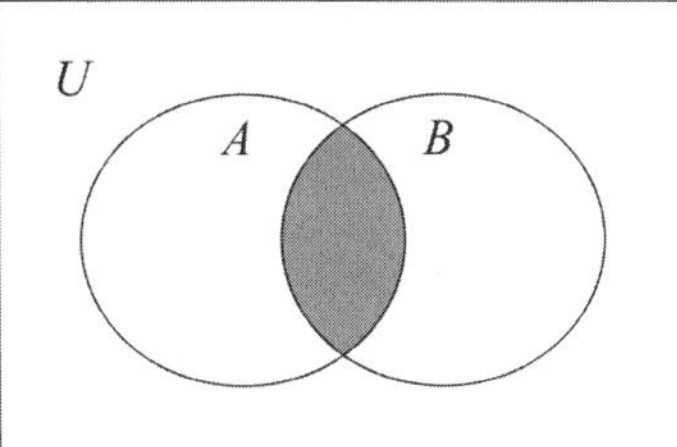 Shading = the area that is common to both A and B, i.e. just their intersection.	$A \cup B$ 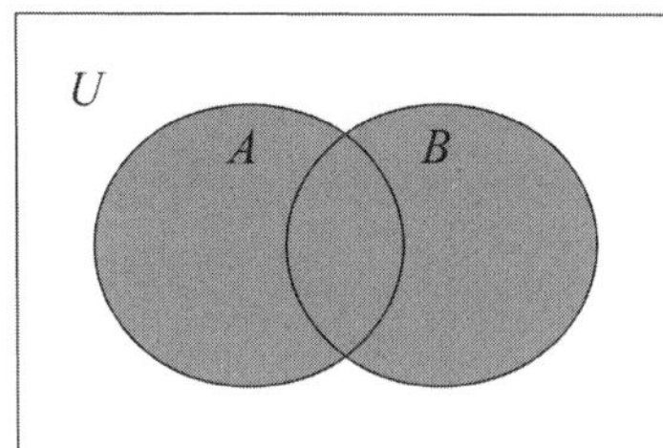 Shading = A and B, including their intersection.
A 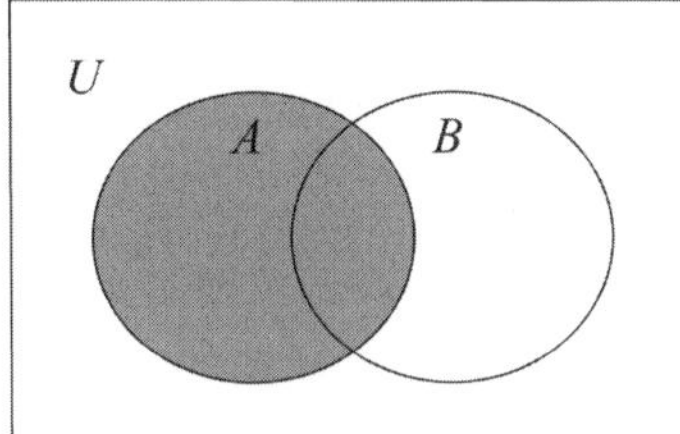 Shading = all of A, including the intersection of A and B.	A' 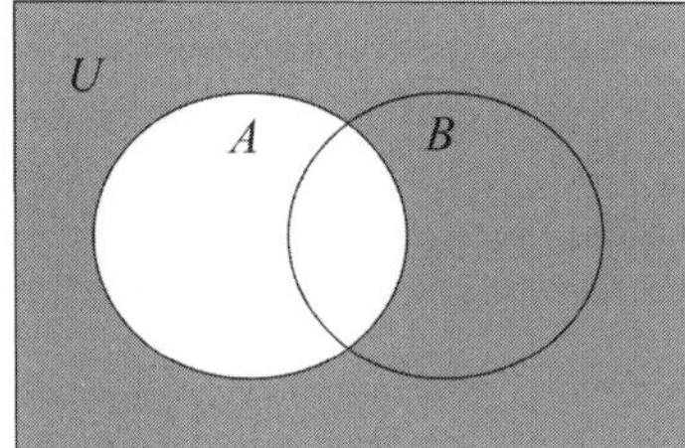 Shading = the area that is the complement of A, i.e. not A.
$A \cap B'$ 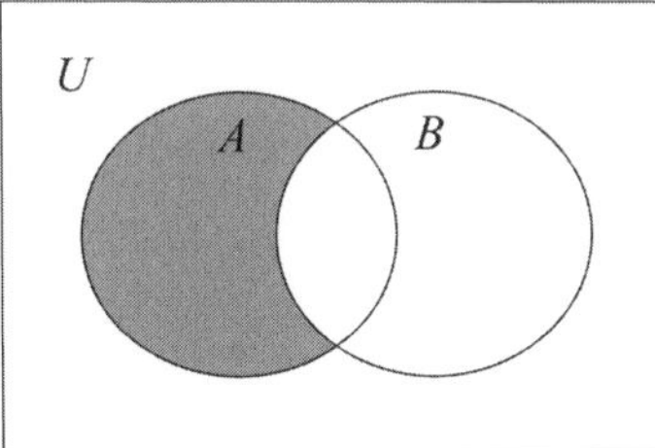 Shading = A but excluding the intersection of A and B.	$A \cup B'$ 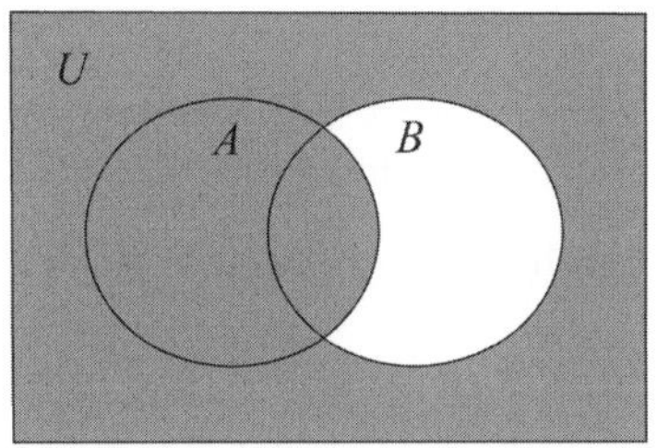 Shading = everything that is not just B, including the part of A that intersects B.
$(A \cap B)'$ or $A' \cup B'$ 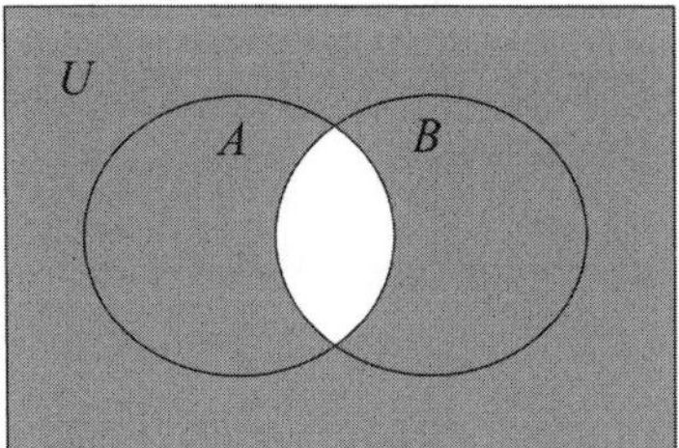 Shading = the complement of $A \cap B$ (i.e. everything that is not A or everything that is not B).	$(A \cup B)'$ or $A' \cap B'$ 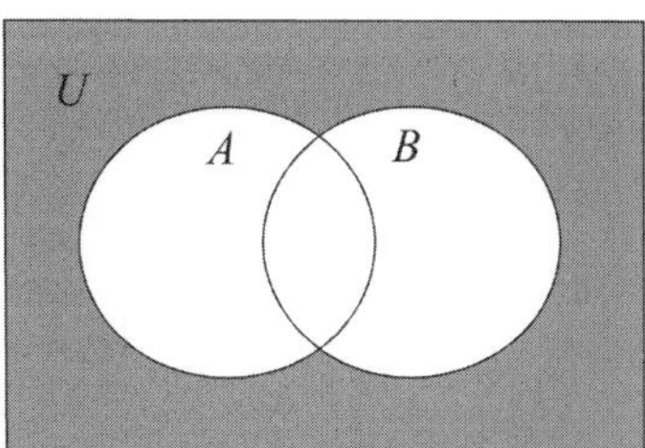 Shading = the complement of $A \cup B$ (i.e. everything that is not A and not B).

Example

A fair 20-sided die with sides numbered 1 to 20 is rolled.

a. Determine the probability of rolling an odd number or a number greater than 16.

b. Determine the probability of rolling an even number and a number divisible by 3.

✓ *Solution*

Working	Explanation
a. $U = \{1, 2, 3, 4, 5, \ldots 18, 19, 20\}$ $n(U) = 20$	Define the universal set and the total number of outcomes in the universal set.
Let A = rolling an odd number. Let B = rolling a number greater than 16.	Define the two events specified in the questions.
$A = \{1, 3, 5, 7, 9, 11, 13, 15, 17, 19\}$ $B = \{17, 18, 19, 20\}$	List the possible outcomes of each event.
$A \cup B = \{1, 3, 5, 7, 9, 11, 13, 15, 17, 18, 19, 20\}$	The word 'or' in the question indicates that either of the events could occur. Therefore, the appropriate relationship to consider between the two events is **union** (i.e. $A \cup B$). List the outcomes that represent the union of the two events (i.e. the outcomes in both sets).
$n(A \cup B) = 12$	Count the number of possible outcomes in the union.
$\Pr(A \cup B) = \dfrac{12}{20}$	State the probability as the number of possible outcomes over the total number of items in the universal set.
b. Let C = rolling an even number. Let D = rolling a number divisible by 3.	Define the two events specified in the question.
$C = \{2, 4, 6, 8, 10, 12, 14, 16, 18, 20\}$ $D = \{3, 6, 9, 12, 15, 18\}$	List the possible outcomes of each event.
$C \cap D = \{6, 12, 18\}$	The word 'and' in the question indicates that both events must occur together. Therefore, the appropriate relationship to consider between the two events is **intersection** (i.e. $C \cap D$). List the outcomes that represent the intersection of the two events (i.e. the outcomes that are common to both sets).
$n(C \cap D) = 3$	Count the number of possible outcomes in the intersection.
$\Pr(C \cap D) = \dfrac{3}{20}$	State the probability as the number of possible outcomes over the total number of items in the universal set.

Example

Fifty Year 9 students were surveyed to find out if they play a musical instrument. Twenty-four students said they play the piano (P), 12 said they play the violin (V) and 3 said they play both instruments.

a. Represent the results of the survey in a clearly labelled Venn diagram.

b. How many students do not play either of the instruments mentioned?

c. Determine the probability that a student randomly chosen from the group:

i. plays only the violin

ii. plays only one instrument

iii. does not play the piano

iv. plays both instruments.

✓ Solution

Working	Explanation
a. 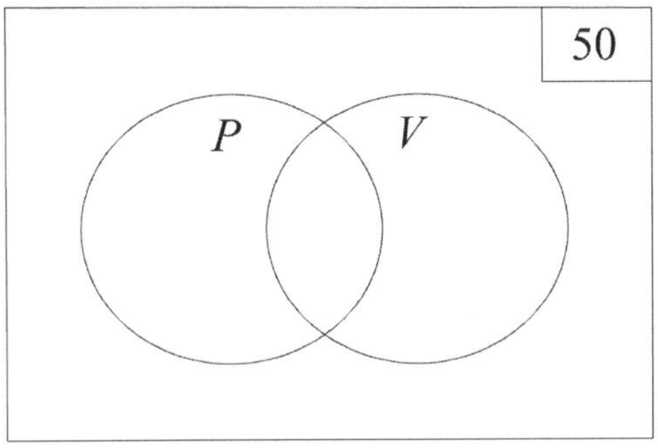 50 P V	Draw two overlapping ellipses, each representing an instrument. Label one ellipse P and the other V. Place the total number of students surveyed in the top right corner (as shown).
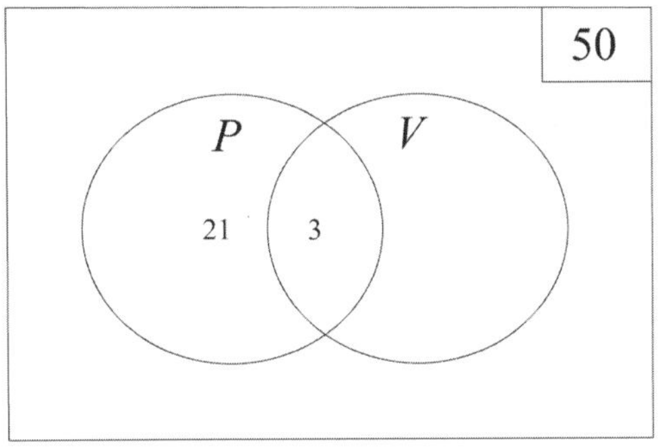 50 P V 21 3	Let's start by calculating the number of students who play only the piano. Since we know that the total number of students who play the piano is 24 and that 3 students play both instruments, it follows that the number of students who play only the piano is $n(P \text{ only}) = 24 - 3 = 21$ Add this value to the appropriate area of the Venn diagram, along with the number of students who play both instruments.

<table>
<tr>
<td>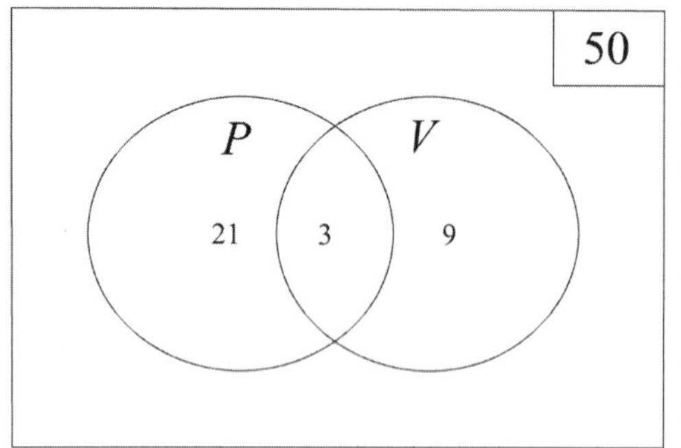

Or

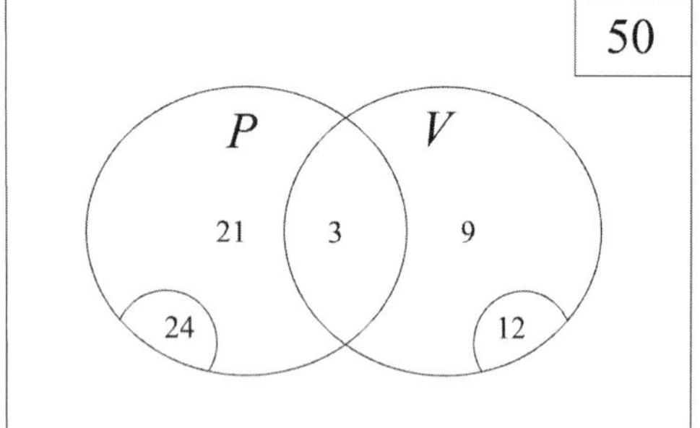
</td>
<td>Similarly, the number of students who play only the violin is

$$n(V \text{ only}) = 12 - 3 = 9$$

Add this value to the appropriate area of the Venn diagram.

Note: you can also include $n(P)$ and $n(V)$ in the relevant ellipse (as shown at the left).</td>
</tr>
<tr>
<td>**b.** 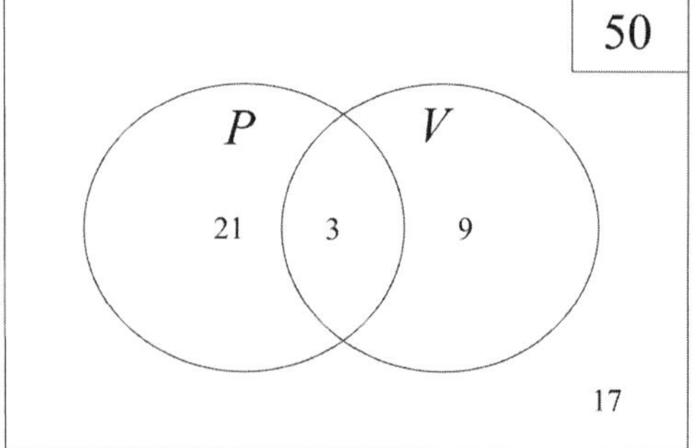

17 students do not play either musical instrument.</td>
<td>From the Venn diagram we can see that the total number of students who play the piano **or** the violin is

$$n(P \cup V) = 21 + 3 + 9 = 33$$

Therefore, the complement of this – i.e. the number of students who do not play the piano or the violin – is $50 - 33$ which is 17.

Add this to the Venn diagram.</td>
</tr>
<tr>
<td>**c.** **i.** $\Pr(V \text{ only}) = \frac{9}{50}$
ii. $\Pr(P \text{ only or } V \text{ only}) = \frac{30}{50}$
iii. $\Pr(P') = \frac{26}{50}$
iv. $\Pr(P \cap V) = \frac{3}{50}$</td>
<td>Consult the Venn diagram to calculate the probabilities.</td>
</tr>
</table>

Exercise 10.2.1

Consider the following sets.

$$U = \{11, 12, 13, 14, 15, 16, 17, 18, 19, 20\}$$
$$K = \{11, 13, 15, 17, 19\}$$
$$M = \{13, 14, 15, 16\}$$

a. Construct a Venn diagram representing the sets.

b. List the elements in the following sets.

i. K' ii. $K \cup M$ iii. $K' \cap M$ iv. $(K \cap M)'$

c. Determine the following.

i. $\Pr(K \cap M)$ ii. $\Pr(M')$ iii. $\Pr(K \cap M')$ iv. $\Pr(K' \cup M)$

Exercise 10.2.2

Mr Smith's Year 9 Mathematics class has 32 students. Twenty students were born overseas and 8 of them speak a second language at home. Nine students were born in Australia and do not speak a second language at home. Let B represent the set of students who were born overseas and L represent the set of students who speak a second language at home.

a. Construct a Venn diagram representing the students.

b. Determine the following.

i. $n(L \text{ only})$ ii. $n(L \cup B)$ iii. $\Pr(L')$ iv. $\Pr(B \cap L)$

Exercise 10.2.3

Two-hundred students were surveyed about the food they enjoyed at the annual school fete. The results showed that 98 enjoyed chocolate fudge (F), 40 enjoyed mango jelly (J) and 20 students enjoyed both.

a. Construct a Venn diagram representing the survey results.

b. Determine the following.

i. $\Pr(J \cup F)$ ii. $\Pr(J')$ iii. $\Pr(F \cap J)$

iv. $\Pr(F \cap J')$ v. $\Pr(J \cup F)'$

c. Matt said that enjoying chocolate fudge and enjoying mango jelly are mutually exclusive. Do you think that his comment is correct? Justify your answer.

10.3 Two-way tables

The information in a Venn diagram can also be represented in a two-way table. The general form of a two-way table is shown below.

	A	A'	**Total**
B	$A \cap B$	B only	Total for B
B'	A only	Neither A nor B	Total for not B (B')
Total	Total for A	Total for not A (A')	Total

To illustrate how a two-way table can represent sets, consider the situation where Ms Chong, the Mathematics teacher, surveyed her class of 30 students. She found that 16 students have a cat (C) as a pet and 19 students have a dog (D). She also found that 11 students have both a dog and a cat.

We can represent this information in a Venn diagram as shown below:

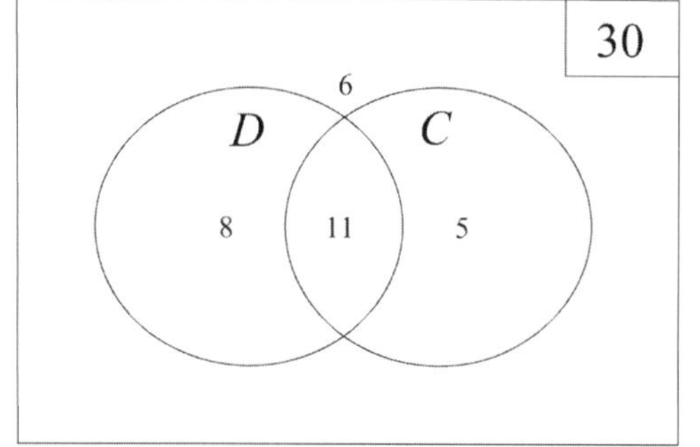

We can also represent the situation as a two-way table as shown below:

	D	D'	**Total**
C	11	5	16
C'	8	6	14
Total	19	11	30

Example

The local supermarket offers free apples and bananas to children. On a particular day, 180 children went to the supermarket with their parents. Of the 180 children, 102 took an apple (A), 89 took a banana (B) and 30 took both.

a. Display the information in a two-way table.

b. Determine the number of children who did not take any fruit.

c. What is the probability that a child selected at random took a banana but not an apple?

✓ Solution

<table>
<tr><th>Working</th><th>Explanation</th></tr>
<tr><td>a.
<table><tr><td></td><td>A</td><td>A'</td><td>Total</td></tr><tr><td>B</td><td>30</td><td>59</td><td>89</td></tr><tr><td>B'</td><td>72</td><td>19</td><td>91</td></tr><tr><td>Total</td><td>102</td><td>78</td><td>180</td></tr></table></td><td>Construct a two-way table, filling in the cells with the information provided.</td></tr>
<tr><td>b. The number of children who took neither is 19.</td><td>The number of children who took neither an apple nor a banana can be determined from the table. This situation is represented by $A' \cap B'$.</td></tr>
<tr><td>c. $\Pr(\text{banana only}) = \frac{59}{180}$</td><td>The number of children who took only a banana is 59. This is represented by $A' \cap B$. So the probability of randomly selecting a child who took only a banana is 59 out of the total number of children.</td></tr>
</table>

Exercise 10.3.1

During a sports carnival, of the 28 students in Mrs Duncan's class, 18 students participated in the cross-country race (C) and 16 participated in the 100 metres sprint (S). Four students participated in the 100 metres sprint but did not take part in the cross-country race.

a. Represent this information in a two-way table.

b. How many students did not take part in either event?

c. If a student is chosen at random, what is the probability that the student participated in both events?

Exercise 10.3.2

Customers can order either a burger (B), chips (C) or both from the local café. On one particular day, 88 customers ordered both burgers and chips, 3 ordered chips only, 9 ordered a burger only and 25 customers did not order either a burger or chips.

a. Represent this information in a two-way table.

b. How many customers did the café have that day?

c. If a customer is chosen at random, what is the probability that the customer ordered a burger?

10.4 Relative frequency

Theoretically, we know that if we toss a fair coin, the chance of it landing heads or tails is the same. The probability is $\frac{1}{2}$ (or 50% or 0.5). However, in real life, if we toss a coin 1000 times it is possible that we end up with a result that is not exactly 500 heads and 500 tails. We could, for example, get 551 heads and 449 tails. This variation could have a number of causes, such as the way the coin is tossed or a difference in the distribution of mass on the surface of the coin. For this particular coin we can say that

$$\Pr(\text{head}) = \frac{551}{1000} = 55.1\% \text{ and } \Pr(\text{tail}) = \frac{449}{1000} = 44.9\%$$

Based on these probabilities we can predict that the next toss of this coin has a 55.1% probability of landing heads up.

Probability based on an actual number of outcomes is called **experimental probability** or **relative frequency**. We can define experimental probability as

$$\textit{experimental probability} = \frac{\textit{number of times the outcome has occurred}}{\textit{total number of trials in the experiment}}$$

As with standard probability, experimental probability falls between 0 and 1 (inclusive).

Experimental probability can be used as an estimate of theoretical probability if there has been a large number of trials.

Example

Jonathan rolled a regular die 3000 times and obtained the following results.

Outcome	1	2	3	4	5	6
Frequency	578	495	425	534	462	506

Use the table to calculate the probability (to 4 decimal places) that the next roll of the die will be:

a. a 3 **b.** an odd number **c.** a number less than 3.

✓ *Solution*

Working	Explanation
a. $\Pr(3) = \frac{425}{3000} = 0.1417$	Use the experimental probability formula to determine the probability of obtaining a 3.
b. $\Pr(\text{odd}) = \frac{578 + 425 + 462}{3000} = 0.4883$	There are three odd numbers (1, 3 and 5), so you need to add up the frequencies of these numbers to obtain the probability.
c. $\Pr(<3) = \frac{578 + 495}{3000} = 0.3577$	There are 2 numbers less than 3 (1 and 2). You need to add up the frequency of both. **Note:** we normally quote the probability to 4 decimal places. This is because we will still have 2 decimal places if the probability is converted to a percentage.

Example

During his time playing soccer, Simon scored 5 goals from 11 penalty kicks.

a. State the relative frequency of Simon scoring a goal from a penalty kick.

b. Determine the expected number of goals Simon would score from 37 penalty kicks.

✓ Solution

Working	Explanation
a. $\text{Pr(goal)} = \frac{5}{11}$	The experimental probability is the number of goals as a fraction of the number of penalty kicks.
b. $\frac{5}{11} \times 37 = 16.82$ The expected number of goals is 17 from 37 penalty kicks.	Use this probability to estimate the expected number of goals. Give your answer to the nearest whole number, as there can only be a whole number of soccer goals.

Exercise 10.4.1

Every year for the past 10 years, Dr Quinn has gone on a field trip to collect samples of four types of herbs for her research. From the data collected over the past 10 years, she knows that out of 200 herb samples collected, she is likely to obtain the following quantities of herbs.

Herb	Number
angelica	90
boneset	50
chickweed	5
damiana	55

a. State the relative frequency of boneset.

b. This year, Dr Quinn went on another field trip and collected 1000 herbs.

  i. What is the probability that angelica is the first herb she collects?

  ii. How many samples of damiana would she expect to collect?

  iii. At the end of the field trip, she found that she had collected 200 chickweeds. Determine the relative frequency of chickweed for this field trip.

Exercise 10.4.2

A biased 5-sided spinner has numbers 1 to 5. The probability that the spinner will land on a particular number is given in the table below.

Number	1	2	3	4	5
Relative Frequency	$2x$	x	0.2	0.25	0.1

a. What is the relative frequency of spinning a 2?

b. The spinner is spun 300 times. What is the expected number of times it will land on an odd number?

10.5 Multi-stage experiments

A multi-stage experiment is one where we repeat the experiment several times, such as tossing a coin a number of times or rolling a die twice (or rolling two dice). An array table or a tree diagram can be used to represent the results of these experiments. The **array table** below shows the outcomes from rolling two dice.

		Die 2					
		1	2	3	4	5	6
Die 1	1	(1, 1)	(1, 2)	(1, 3)	(1, 4)	(1, 5)	(1, 6)
	2	(2, 1)	(2, 2)	(2, 3)	(2, 4)	(2, 5)	(2, 6)
	3	(3, 1)	(3, 2)	(3, 3)	(3, 4)	(3, 5)	(3, 6)
	4	(4, 1)	(4, 2)	(4, 3)	(4, 4)	(4, 5)	(4, 6)
	5	(5, 1)	(5, 2)	(5, 3)	(5, 4)	(5, 5)	(5, 6)
	6	(6, 1)	(6, 2)	(6, 3)	(6, 4)	(6, 5)	(6, 6)

We can use this array table to obtain the probability of, for example, rolling a 6 on at least one of the dice. We know that there are 36 possible outcomes all together and out of the 36 outcomes, there are 11 outcomes in which at least one 6 appears. The probability is therefore $\frac{11}{36}$. Another way of displaying outcomes is with a **tree diagram**. The following tree diagram shows the possible outcomes from tossing a fair coin three times.

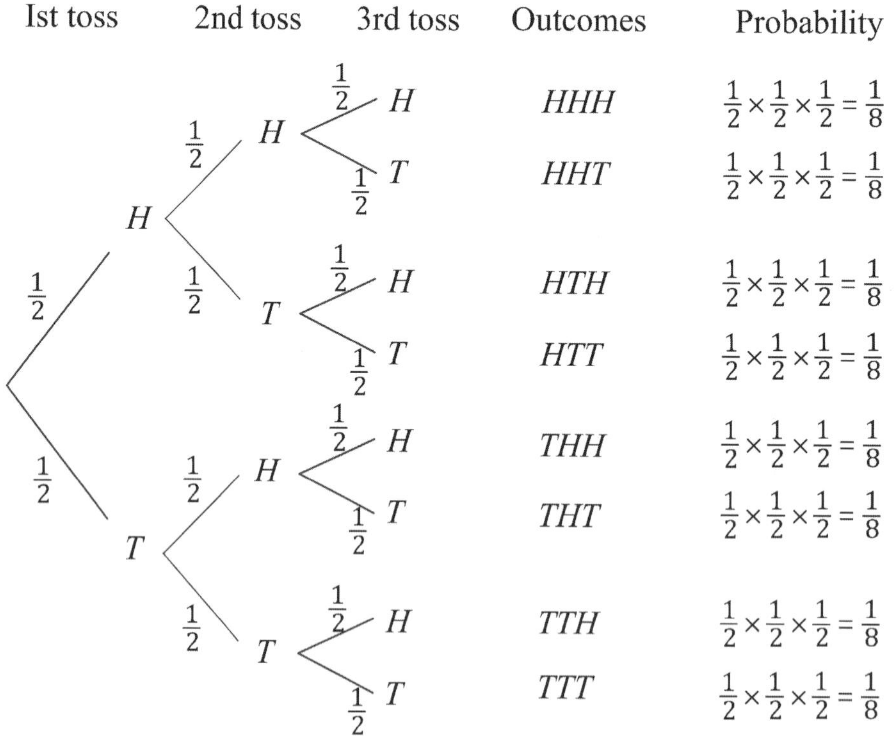

In a tree diagram you should list all the possible outcomes in the sample space, label each branch with its probability and give the probability of each outcome. The sum of the probabilities of all outcomes should equal 1.

Multi-stage experiments with and without replacement

Consider the following two situations.

Situation 1: Each of the letters of the word S T A R T is written on a card. The cards are placed face down on a table and jumbled. A card is chosen at random, its letter revealed before being placed face down back on the table. The cards are rejumbled and a second card is chosen.

Situation 2: Each of the letters of the word S T A R T is written on a card. The cards are placed face down on a table and jumbled. A card is chosen at random, its letter revealed and the card is put to one side. Then a second card is chosen from the cards remaining on the table.

We can represent these situations using tree diagrams (see below). Note that in this case we have simplified the tree. There are two Ts in S T A R T, and instead of adding a branch for each possible T, we added just one branch but specified a probability of $\frac{2}{5}$ when it was possible that two Ts could be selected.

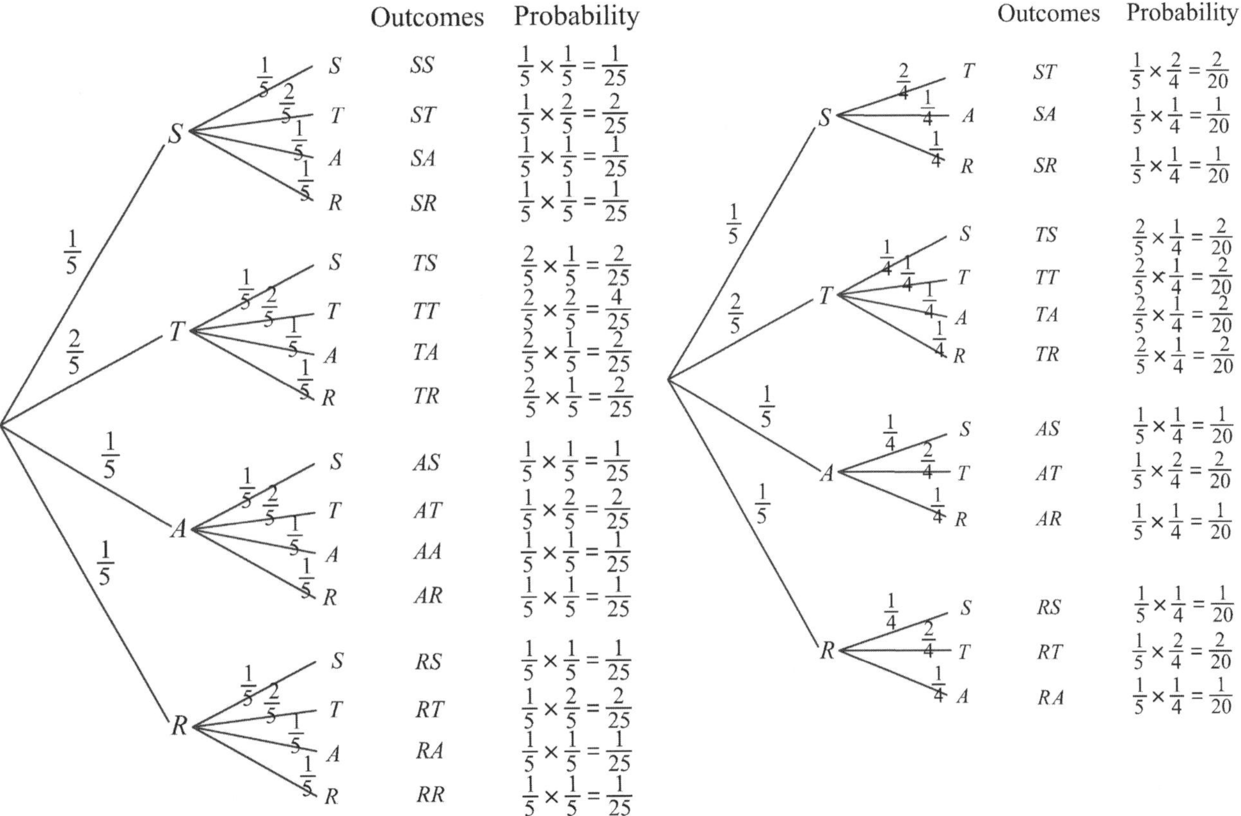

The difference between situation 1 and situation 2 is whether the first card is replaced. In situation 1, the draw of the second is not affected by any card having been put to one side. In situation 2, the draw of the second card is affected by the fact that the first card has not been replaced, as there is now one card fewer from which to choose.

The probabilities for the second draw in situation 1 have not changed, but the probabilities for the second draw in situation 2 have changed. We can also see from the tree diagram that there are more possible outcomes in situation 1 than in situation 2.

In summary, two events are **independent** if the result of one event has no effect on the probability of the second event. Two events are **dependent** if the result of one event affects the probability of the second event.

Example

Two regular dice are rolled. Determine the probability that the sum of their uppermost faces is between 4 and 6 inclusive.

✓ *Solution*

<table>
<tr><th>Working</th><th>Explanation</th></tr>
<tr><td>
<table>
<tr><td></td><td></td><td colspan="6">Die 2</td></tr>
<tr><td></td><td></td><td>1</td><td>2</td><td>3</td><td>4</td><td>5</td><td>6</td></tr>
<tr><td rowspan="6">Die 1</td><td>1</td><td>2</td><td>3</td><td>4</td><td>5</td><td>6</td><td>7</td></tr>
<tr><td>2</td><td>3</td><td>4</td><td>5</td><td>6</td><td>7</td><td>8</td></tr>
<tr><td>3</td><td>4</td><td>5</td><td>6</td><td>7</td><td>8</td><td>9</td></tr>
<tr><td>4</td><td>5</td><td>6</td><td>7</td><td>8</td><td>9</td><td>10</td></tr>
<tr><td>5</td><td>6</td><td>7</td><td>8</td><td>9</td><td>10</td><td>11</td></tr>
<tr><td>6</td><td>7</td><td>8</td><td>9</td><td>10</td><td>11</td><td>12</td></tr>
</table>
</td><td>Construct an array table showing the sum of the uppermost face of each die.
Determine the total number of outcomes in the sample space: 36.
Count the number of outcomes where the sum is between 4 and 6. (These are shaded in the array table.)</td></tr>
<tr><td>Pr(sum lies between 4 and 6) $= \frac{12}{36}$</td><td>State the probability.</td></tr>
</table>

Example

A bag contains two green balls and one pink ball. One ball is selected at random and its colour noted. The ball is placed back in the bag. Another ball is selected and its colour noted. Draw a tree diagram to show all the outcomes and then determine the following.

a. Pr(drawing a pink and a green in any order)

b. Pr(both balls drawn are pink)

c. Pr(drawing a green followed by a pink)

✓ *Solution*

<table>
<tr><th>Working</th><th>Explanation</th></tr>
<tr><td>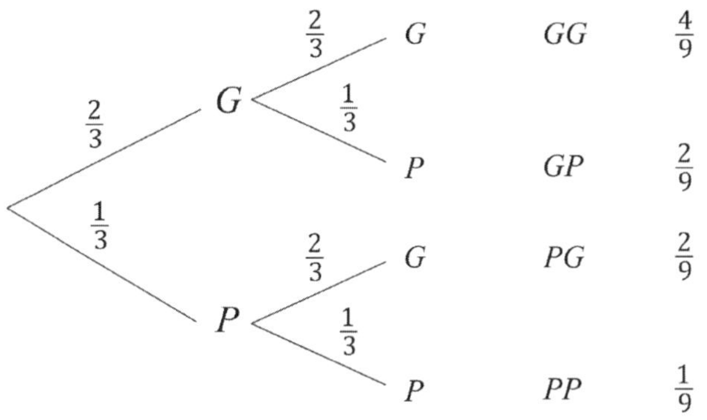
</td><td>Draw a tree diagram starting with two branches labelled G (green) and P (pink). Note that there are 3 balls in total, of which 2 are green and 1 is pink. Hence, the probability of drawing a green ball is $\frac{2}{3}$ and the probability of drawing a pink ball is $\frac{1}{3}$.

Label the branches with their probabilities.</td></tr>
<tr><td>a. $\Pr(PG \text{ or } GP) = \frac{2}{9} + \frac{2}{9} = \frac{4}{9}$</td><td>Since the order does not matter – it can be GP or PG – we add the two probabilities together.</td></tr>
<tr><td>b. $\Pr(PP) = \frac{1}{9}$</td><td rowspan="2">These probabilities can be read directly from the tree diagram.</td></tr>
<tr><td>c. $\Pr(GP) = \frac{2}{9}$</td></tr>
</table>

Example

Each of the letters M A T H is written on a separate card. The four cards are placed face down on a table and jumbled. A card is chosen, its letter revealed and the card is put to one side. Then a second card is chosen from the cards remaining on the table.

a. List all the possible outcomes in an array table.

b. Determine the probability that the two letters chosen are T and A in that order.

c. Determine the probability of choosing a card with M on it.

✓ *Solution*

<table>
<tr><th>Working</th><th>Explanation</th></tr>
<tr><td>a.
<table>
<tr><td colspan="2"></td><td colspan="4">Draw 2</td></tr>
<tr><td colspan="2"></td><td>M</td><td>A</td><td>T</td><td>H</td></tr>
<tr><td rowspan="4">Draw 1</td><td>M</td><td>-</td><td>(M, A)</td><td>(M, T)</td><td>(M, H)</td></tr>
<tr><td>A</td><td>(A, M)</td><td>-</td><td>(A, T)</td><td>(A, H)</td></tr>
<tr><td>T</td><td>(T, M)</td><td>(T, A)</td><td>-</td><td>(T, H)</td></tr>
<tr><td>H</td><td>(H, M)</td><td>(H, A)</td><td>(H, T)</td><td>-</td></tr>
</table></td><td>Draw an array table as shown. As the first card is not replaced, there are no outcomes in which a letter occurs twice; hence the dash in some cells.</td></tr>
<tr><td>b. $\Pr(\text{T, A}) = \frac{1}{12}$</td><td>There are 12 possible outcomes (i.e. the cells in the array table with letters in them). Only one outcome is T followed by A.</td></tr>
<tr><td>c. $\Pr(\text{outcomes with M}) = \frac{6}{12}$</td><td>Count all the cells with an M and state the probability.</td></tr>
</table>

Example

Jenny is participating in a tennis tournament where she has to play three other players. She estimates that she has a 60% chance of winning the first match, an equal chance of winning the second match and a 25% chance of losing the final match.

a. Construct a tree diagram to show the sample space, clearly showing all outcomes and their associated probabilities.

b. Determine the probability that Jenny wins at least two matches.

✓ Solution

Working	Explanation
a. 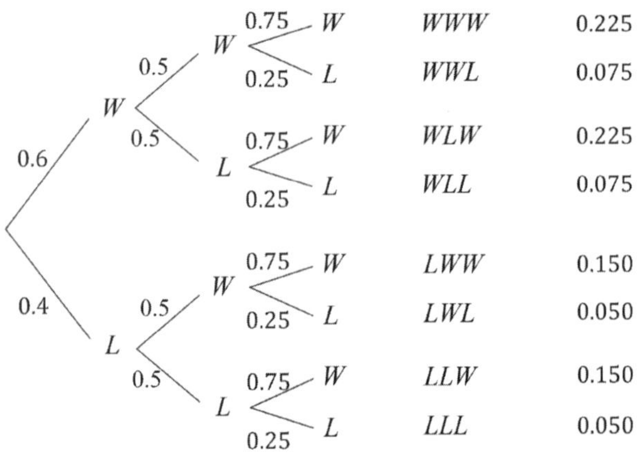 Tree diagram: first branch W (0.6), L (0.4); second branch W (0.5), L (0.5); third branch W (0.75), L (0.25). WWW 0.225 WWL 0.075 WLW 0.225 WLL 0.075 LWW 0.150 LWL 0.050 LLW 0.150 LLL 0.050	Each match is either a win (W) or a loss (L). Begin by calculating the probabilities in each match. **Match 1** – probability of W is 0.6 (60%), therefore the probability of L is 0.4 (40%). **Match 2** – equal chance of winning and losing, therefore the probability is 0.5 (50%) for each possible outcome. **Match 3** – probability of L is 0.25 (25%), therefore the probability of W is 0.75 (75%). Construct the tree as shown, clearly labelling all branches, and state the outcomes and their associated probabilities.
b. Pr(WWW or WWL or WLW or LWW) $= 0.225 + 0.075 + 0.225 + 0.150$ $= 0.675$	There are 4 outcomes that show Jenny winning at least 2 matches (including the outcome which shows her winning all three games). Add up all the probabilities to determine the probability of Jenny winning at least 2 games. **Note:** in this case it is easier to work with decimals than with percentages.

Exercise 10.5.1

Two fair six-sided dice are rolled and the sum of their face values is recorded. One die is numbered 4, 4, 5, 5, 6 and 6, and the other is numbered 1, 3, 5, 7, 9 and 10.

a. Construct a suitable display showing all possible outcomes.

b. Determine the probability that the sum is:

i. odd **ii.** divisible by 5 **iii.** more than 10 **iv.** not more than 8.

Exercise 10.5.2

Luke has two containers of chocolates. In container A there are three milk chocolates (M) and one dark chocolate (D). In container B there are two milk chocolates and two dark chocolates. Luke chose one container at random and then chose one chocolate at random from that container.

a. State the probability of selecting a dark chocolate from container B.

b. Draw a tree diagram to represent this situation, showing all possible outcomes and their probabilities.

c. Determine the probability of selecting container A and a dark chocolate.

d. Determine the probability of selecting a milk chocolate.

Exercise 10.5.3

Tanya wants to form a two-digit number from the numbers 5, 3 and 8. She writes each of the numbers on a card and then chooses two cards at random.

She decides that the number on the first card chosen will be the 10s digit and the number on the second card chosen will the 1s digit.

a. Construct two displays that are suitable for showing the outcomes for the following situations.

   i. After the first selection, Tanya places the card back for selection.

   ii. Tanya does not place the card back after the first selection.

b. Compare the probability of forming an odd number if the first card is replaced, to the probability of forming an odd number if the first card is not replaced.

Exercise 10.5.4

Harry is playing in a round robin chess tournament. He plays three matches and needs to win at least two if he is to progress to the next round. He has a probability of 0.8 of winning his first match. If he wins a match, his confidence increases and the probability of him winning the next match becomes 0.9. However, if he loses a match, the probability that he wins the next match becomes 0.3.

a. Construct a tree diagram from the information provided.

b. Determine the probability that:

   i. Harry wins all three matches

   ii. Harry loses only one match

   iii. Harry does not progress to the next round.

Answers

Exercise 10.1.1

a. $\frac{3}{14}$

b. $\frac{7}{14}$

Exercise 10.1.2

a. $\frac{3}{9}$

b. $\frac{6}{9}$

c. $\frac{3}{9}$

d. $\frac{4}{9}$

Exercise 10.1.3

a. $\frac{5}{10}$

b. $\frac{5}{10}$

c. $\frac{2}{10}$

d. $\frac{2}{10}$

Exercise 10.2.1

a.

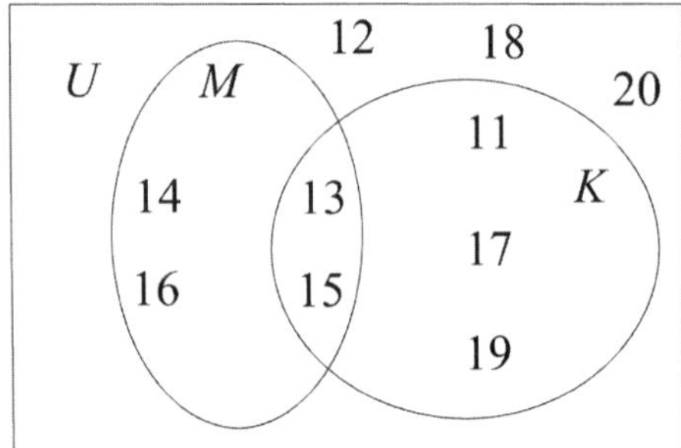

b. i. $\{12, 14, 16, 18, 20\}$

ii. $\{11, 13, 14, 15, 16, 17, 19\}$

iii. $\{14, 16\}$

iv. $\{11, 12, 14, 16, 17, 18, 19, 20\}$

c. i. $\frac{2}{10}$

ii. $\frac{6}{10}$

iii. $\frac{3}{10}$

iv. $\frac{7}{10}$

Exercise 10.2.2

a.

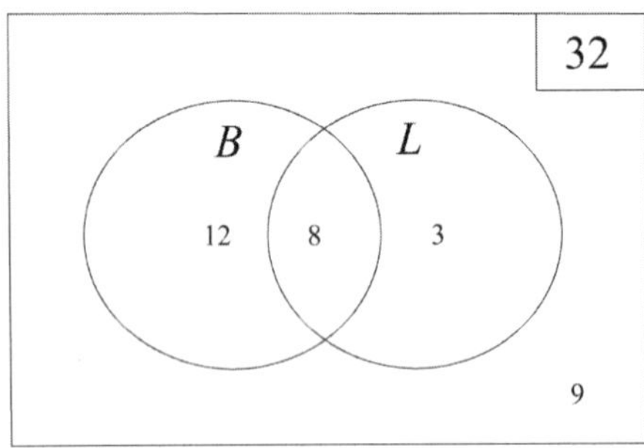

b. i. 3

ii. 23

iii. $\frac{21}{32}$

iv. $\frac{8}{32}$

Exercise 10.2.3

a.

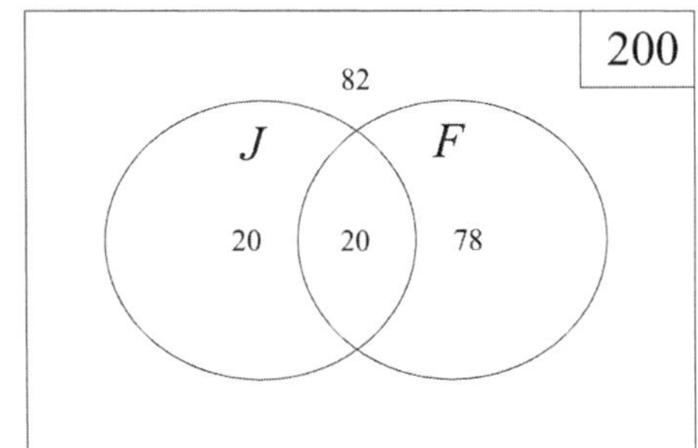

b. i. $\frac{118}{200}$ ii. $\frac{160}{200}$ iii. $\frac{20}{200}$ iv. $\frac{78}{200}$ v. $\frac{82}{200}$

c. Matt's comment is incorrect because $n(J \cap F) = 20$, i.e. the intersection is not a null set. Therefore, they are not mutually exclusive.

Exercise 10.3.1

a.

	C	C'	Total
S	12	4	16
S'	6	6	12
Total	18	10	28

b. 6 students

c. $\frac{12}{28}$

Exercise 10.3.2

a.

	B	B'	Total
C	88	3	91
C'	9	25	34
Total	97	28	125

b. 125 customers

c. $\frac{97}{125}$

Exercise 10.4.1

a. $\frac{50}{200}$ b. i. $\frac{90}{200}$ ii. 275 iii. $\frac{200}{1000}$

Exercise 10.4.2

a. 0.15 b. 180 times

Exercise 10.5.1

a.

		Die 2					
		4	4	5	5	6	6
Die 1	1	5	5	6	6	7	7
	3	7	7	8	8	9	9
	5	9	9	10	10	11	11
	7	11	11	12	12	13	13
	9	13	13	14	14	15	15
	10	14	14	15	15	16	16

b. i. $\frac{22}{36}$ ii. $\frac{8}{36}$ iii. $\frac{20}{36}$ iv. $\frac{10}{36}$

Exercise 10.5.2

a. $\frac{1}{4}$

b.

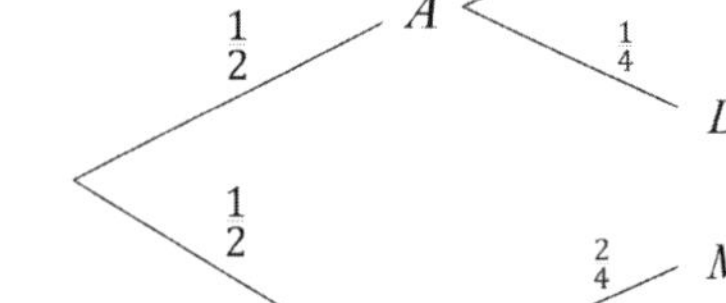

c. $\frac{1}{8}$

d. $\frac{5}{8}$

Exercise 10.5.3

a. i.

		With replacement		
		C2		
		5	3	8
C1	5	55	53	58
	3	35	33	38
	8	85	83	88

ii.

		Without replacement		
		C2		
		5	3	8
C1	5	-	53	58
	3	35	-	38
	8	85	83	-

b. **With replacement:**

Pr(odd) $= \frac{6}{9} = 0.6667$

Without replacement:

Pr(odd) $= \frac{4}{6} = 0.6667$

It is equally likely that an odd number is selected with or without replacement.

Exercise 10.5.4

a.

			Outcome	Probability
0.8 W	0.9 W	0.9 W	WWW	0.648
		0.1 L	WWL	0.072
	0.1 L	0.3 W	WLW	0.024
		0.7 L	WLL	0.056
0.2 L	0.3 W	0.9 W	LWW	0.054
		0.1 L	LWL	0.006
	0.7 L	0.3 W	LLW	0.042
		0.7 L	LLL	0.098

b. i. 0.648 ii. 0.150 iii. 0.202

Chapter 11 – Statistics

Statistics is concerned with collecting, analysing, interpreting and presenting information in ways that we can easily understand. It is useful in many areas of our life, such as business, science and economics. We will consider the process of statistical investigation in this chapter.

11.1 Data collecting

We can collect data from the entire population (a census) or from part of the population (a sample).

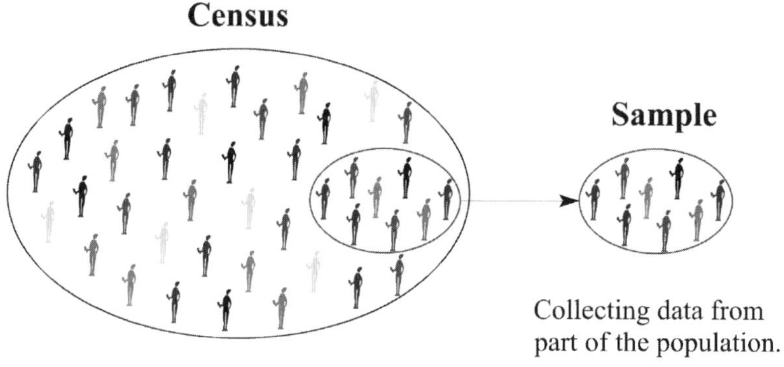

Collecting data from part of the population.

Collecting data from the entire population.

An entire population can be very large or difficult to access, making it impractical to conduct a census every time we want to collect data. Hence, we select a part of the population, called a sample, and collect the same information from each member of our sample.

Some examples of **census** data collection are:

- the census carried out by the Australian Bureau of Statistics every five years to collect information about the entire population of Australia
- a survey of all students in a school about their mode of transport in order to plan for a new bicycle parking area.

Some examples of **sample** data collection are:

- a survey by a market research company asking selected voters what party they intend to vote for in the upcoming state election
- a survey of only a selected number of the students about their mode of transport.

Some of the ways in which data can be collected are:

- surveys
- interviews
- forms (as in the five-yearly census)
- field observation (e.g. counting the number of cars passing through a particular intersection)
- experiments.

Data can be primary or secondary. **Primary data** is the data that you collect. **Secondary data** is the data you use that has been collected by others, such as when we use data collected by the Australian Bureau of Statistics in a school assignment.

Because of the cost and effort involved, it is sometimes impractical to collect data yourself; therefore we use data from other sources. One potential disadvantage is that often we do not know how the data was collected or how accurate it is.

There are two sampling methods – **probability sampling** and **non-probability sampling**. The probability sampling method involves random selection. This is a good way of reducing bias and obtaining a representative sample, as each member of the population has an equal chance of participating.

The non-probability sampling method involves non-random selection. An example is restricting a survey to a certain period (such as 8 am to 9 am) or at a particular location (such as outside a railway station). Only people who are present at that time or location are given an opportunity to participate in the survey. This can cause biases, as the population may not be accurately represented.

When collecting sample data, it is also important that the sample size is large enough to represent the entire population.

11.2 Types of data

Data can be classified as **categorical data** or **numerical data**. Categorical data can be divided into groups or categories. Numerical data can be measured.

Both types of data have two subcategories. These are summarised in the table below.

Data			
Categorical		Numerical	
Nominal	Ordinal	Discrete	Continuous
No order is implied by the name of the data	An order is implied by the name of the data	Only integers	Can be any value, not just an integer
Examples: • colours • overseas countries • fruit sold at a market	Examples: • pizza sizes (large, medium, small) • movie ratings (1 star to 5 stars)	Examples: • number of goals scored in a season • number of students who participated in a race	Examples: • the weight of newborn babies at a hospital • the height of students in Year 9

Exercise 11.2

Classify the following data.

a. the number of apples in a pre-packed 1 kg bag

b. the colour of the cars in a showroom

c. the types of smartphones that students have in a class

d. the reaction times of the students in a Year 9 class

e. the possible responses to a survey question: agree, no opinion, disagree

f. the number of students catching public transport to school every day

g. the number of jelly beans in a 180 g packet

h. the length of the hand span of students in a mathematics class

11.3 Statistical measures

Numerical data can be analysed mathematically. This enables us to precisely describe data sets and compare similar data sets. In Year 9 we focus on determining the mean, mode, median and range of data. In future years you will learn how to determine outliers and calculate standard deviation.

Mean

- The mean is the arithmetic average of the numerical data.
- It is one measure of the central tendency of the data in a data set.
- It is calculated using the formula

$$\textit{mean}(\bar{x}) = \frac{\textit{sum of the values}}{\textit{total number of values}} = \frac{x_1 + x_2 + x_3 + \ldots + x_n}{n}$$

where $\bar{x}$ = the mean of the data set

$x_1, x_2, x_3, \ldots, x_n$ are the values in the data set

n = the number of values in the data set.

For example, the mean of 2, 4, 7, 3 and 4 is 4.

Median

- The median is the middle value in an **ordered** set of values.
- To determine the median, you must arrange the data in order (the easiest way being from smallest to largest).
- For an **odd-numbered** data set, you can determine the median by taking the value of the $\left(\frac{n+1}{2}\right)^{\text{th}}$ term. For example, the median of 2, 4, 7, 3, 4 is 4.
- For an **even-numbered** data set, the median is the average of the two middle numbers. For example, the median of 5, 4, 7, 3, 8 and 9 is $\frac{5+7}{2} = 6$.

Mode

- The mode is the value that appears with the greatest frequency in a data set. For example, the mode of 2, 4, 7, 3 and 4 is 4.
- There can be multiple modes in a data set. For example, the modes of 7, 2, 4, 7, 3 and 4 are 4 and 7, as these appear with the equal highest frequency. (If there are two modes in a data set, the set is referred to as **bi-modal**. You can also have multi-modal data sets.)
- There is no mode in a data set if no data is repeated; for example, 2, 4, 7, 3, 5.

Range

The range is the difference between the largest and smallest data points. For example, the range of 2, 4, 7, 3, 5 is $7 - 2 = 5$. The range is also known as the **spread**.

Example

Determine the mean, median, mode and range of the following data sets.

a. 18, 25, 28, 29, 24, 19, 21, 22, 23, 24, 20

b. 23, 24, 23, 25, 23, 26, 27, 28, 28, 23, 28, 22, 26, 28, 25, 26

✓ Solution

Working	Explanation
a. mean $= \frac{18 + 25 + 28 + \ldots + 20}{11}$ $= \frac{253}{11}$ $= 23$	Add up all the data points (253) and divide by the total number of data points (11) to calculate the mean.
Order the data set: 18, 19, 20, 21, 22, 23, 24, 24, 25, 28, 29 $\left(\frac{n+1}{2}\right)^{\text{th}}$ term is $\frac{11+1}{2} = 6^{\text{th}}$ term $= 23$ The median is 23.	Order the data set from the smallest to the largest. There is an odd number of data points (11), therefore we can find the median using the formula $\left(\frac{n+1}{2}\right)$.
mode $= 24$	24 is the value that appears most often in the data set.
range $= 29 - 18 = 11$	The range is the value of the largest data point minus the value of the smallest data point.
b. mean $= \frac{405}{16} = 25.31$	Add up all the data points (405) and divide by the total number of data points (16) to calculate the mean.
Order the data set: 22, 23, 23, 23, 23, 24, 25, 25, 26, 26, 26, 27, 28, 28, 28, 28 The middle pair is 25 and 26. median $= \frac{25+26}{2} = 25.5$	Order the data set from the smallest to the largest. There are 16 data points, therefore we can find the median by taking the average of the two middle terms in the ordered set: term 8 (25) and term 9 (26).
There are two modes: 23 and 28 (and thus the data set is bi-modal).	23 and 28 are the two values that appear most often in the data set.
Range $= 28 - 22 = 6$	The range is the largest data point minus the smallest data point.

Exercise 11.3

Determine the mean, median, mode and range of the following data sets.

a. 122.5, 145.4, 122.2, 146.7, 138.5, 102.3, 98.9, 134.6, 136.5, 112.4

b. 1, 8, 7, 5, 9, 12, 10, 2, 14, 8, 7, 3, 5, 8, 4, 6, 7, 8, 1, 8, 2, 3, 9, 11, 12, 14, 10

c. 0.5, 0.5, 2.3, 1.2, 1.2, 3.5, 0.8, 0.9, 0.3, 4, 1.6, 3.1, 2.2, 3.5, 1.5

11.4 Displaying data

There are many ways of displaying data. For categorical data, we generally use bar graphs (also known as column graphs) or pie charts. For numerical data, we generally use histograms, stem-and-leaf plots or dot plots.

Bar graph

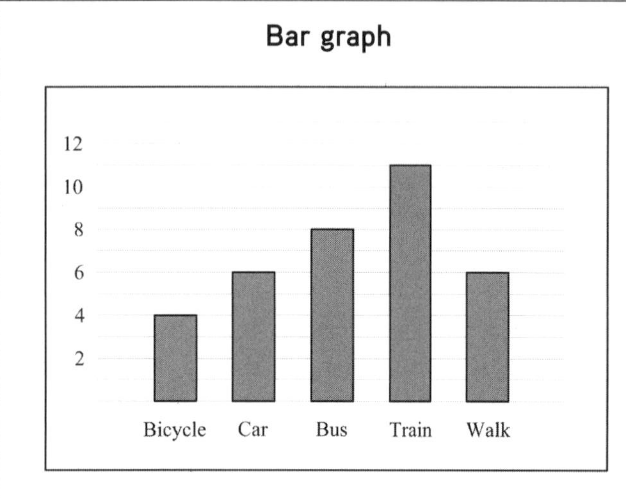

Pie chart

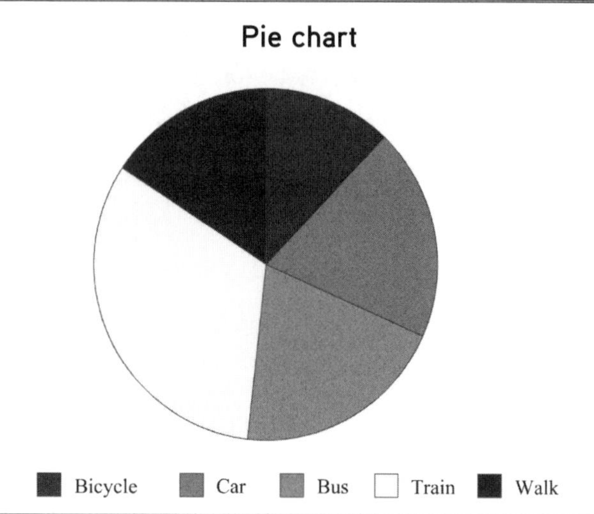

Histogram

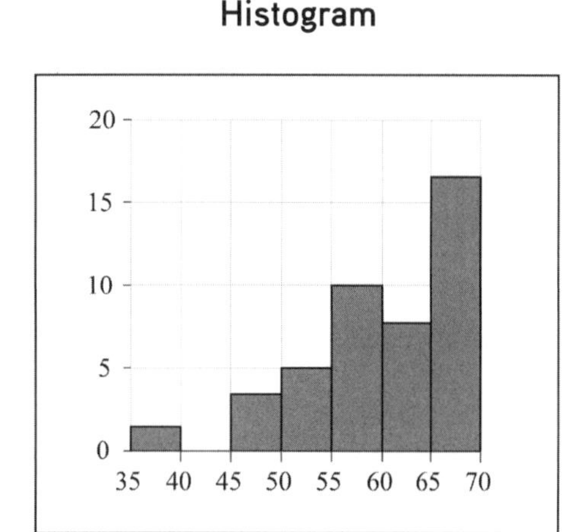

Dot plot

Stem-and-leaf plot

Stem	Leaf
0	6 8
1	4 6 7
2	3 3 3 8
3	5 8 9
4	8 9
5	8

Key: 1|7 means 17

A bar graph and a histogram look alike. In both cases the y-axis represents frequency, but there are key differences between the two. The main differences are:

- The bars along the x-axis of a histogram represent numerical values grouped by a common range, while the bars along the x-axis of a bar graph represent different categories.
- There should be no gaps between the bars of a histogram unless the frequency for the particular range of values is 0. Gaps are permitted in bar graphs.

For Year 9, we focus on histograms and stem-and-leaf plots.

Constructing a histogram

It is important to consider the following points when constructing a histogram.

- There should be no gaps between the bars unless the corresponding frequency is 0.
- The y-axis always represents frequency.
- The x-axis always represents numbers grouped into intervals.
- There are usually 6 to 10 equal groups along the x-axis.
- A tally table can be handy to work out the frequency of each group of numbers.

Let's consider an example. The following data gives the length of a particular type of fish (to the nearest cm) caught at a popular fishing spot in a single day.

11	43	57	25	48	32	48	53	45	22
31	63	45	44	48	54	37	43	51	31
40	24	43	37	30	49	33	37	38	40
38	45	38	36	46	50	32	30	42	58
54	43	34	42	54	45	41	43	33	38
34	38	18	47	48	33	27	47	32	43

To represent this data in a histogram, the data needs to be grouped into equal intervals. By inspecting the data set, we see that the shortest fish is 11 cm and the longest fish is 63 cm. To have between 6 and 10 equal intervals, we group the data into intervals of 10 cm. These intervals are known as the **class intervals.** A tally table can then be used to count the frequency of each class interval.

Length of fish (l)	Tally	Frequency
$10 \leq l < 20$	||	2
$20 \leq l < 30$	||||	4
$30 \leq l < 40$	~~||||~~ ~~||||~~ ~~||||~~ ~~||||~~ |	21
$40 \leq l < 50$	~~||||~~ ~~||||~~ ~~||||~~ ~~||||~~ ||||	24
$50 \leq l < 60$	~~||||~~ |||	8
$60 \leq l < 70$	|	1

The grouped data can now be represented as a histogram.

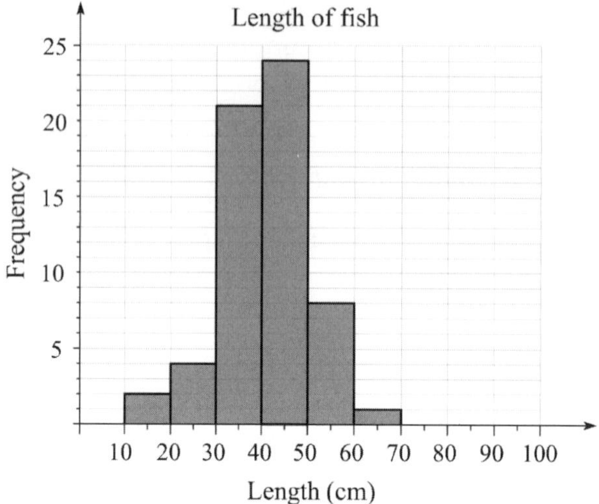

The height of a bar is the frequency of the corresponding class interval. For example, the first bar in the histogram above indicates that 2 of the fish caught were between 10 cm (inclusive) and 20 cm (exclusive).

When you are given a histogram, or a tally table without the original data, the mean of the data can be estimated from the midpoint of each class interval. The table below gives the midpoint of each class interval in the fish example introduced above. The corresponding frequency can be read from the histogram.

Length of fish (l)	Midpoint of class interval	Frequency
$10 \leq l < 20$	15	2
$20 \leq l < 30$	25	4
$30 \leq l < 40$	35	21
$40 \leq l < 50$	45	24
$50 \leq l < 60$	55	8
$60 \leq l < 70$	65	1

The mean can be estimated by multiplying each midpoint by the corresponding frequency, adding all the values and then dividing by the total number of data points.

$$\text{mean} = \frac{(2 \times 15) + (4 \times 25) + (21 \times 35) + (24 \times 45) + (8 \times 55) + (1 \times 65)}{60} = 40.8 \text{ cm}$$

If we use the actual data, we find that the mean is 40.2 cm. Therefore the mean found using the midpoint of each class interval is just an estimate.

We cannot determine the mode from the grouped data, but we can state the **modal class** (i.e. the class interval with the highest frequency). For the fish data discussed above, the modal class is $40 \leq l < 50$ cm. The actual mode derived from the raw data is 43 cm.

Stem-and-leaf plots

Stem-and-leaf plots (or stem plots) are commonly used to display a single data set or two related data sets. An example is shown below.

Stem	Leaf
0	6 8
1	4 6 7
2	3 3 3 8
3	5 8 9
4	8 9
5	8

Key: 1|7 means 17

The Stem column is the first digit of a two-digit number, or the first two digits of a three-digit number, and so on.

The Leaf column is usually the last digit of the value.

The stem-and-leaf plot shown above represents the total rainfall captured in a rain gauge for July 2010. The raw data being represented is shown below.

Total rainfall for July 2010 (cm):

$$16, 8, 17, 23, 28, 35, 58, 49, 6, 23, 48, 39, 23, 14, 38$$

The leaves are arranged in order, with the smallest closest to the stem and the largest furthest away from the stem.

You must always provide a key that explains how the stem and leaf combinations are to be interpreted. In the example above, the key indicates that a 1 in the Stem column and a 7 in the Leaf column should be interpreted as 17.

We can also have a back-to-back stem-and-leaf plot in which we can compare two sets of data. For example, if we want to compare the total rainfall for July 2020 to the total rainfall for July 2010, a back-to-back stem-and-leaf plot should be constructed. The raw data for July 2010 is given above and the raw data for July 2020 is shown below.

Total rainfall for July 2020 (cm):

$$57, 16, 54, 26, 46, 43, 36, 43, 40, 32$$

The back-to-back stem-and-leaf plot representing both sets of rainfall data is shown below.

July 2020	Stem	July 2010
	0	6 8
6	1	4 6 7
6	2	3 3 3 8
6 2	3	5 8 9
6 3 3 0	4	8 9
7 4	5	8

Key: 6|1|4 means 16 for July 2020 and 14 for July 2010

There are now three columns, with the middle column being the stem. The leaves are again arranged in order, from the smallest (closest to the stem) to the largest (furthest away).

Exercise 11.4.1

The heights (h), to the nearest cm, of a group of basketball players are given below.

185, 192, 175, 189, 178, 185, 193, 196, 189, 195, 197, 203, 201, 184, 198,
201, 178, 189, 186, 193, 187, 179, 195, 196, 185, 184, 189, 194, 194, 189

a. Create a tally table using class intervals of 5 cm: $175 \leq h < 180$, $180 \leq h < 185$, $185 \leq h < 190$ etc.

b. Construct a histogram to represent the height of the basketball players.

c. Estimate the mean height and state the modal class.

Exercise 11.4.2

Construct a back-to-back stem-and-leaf plot to display the results for two Year 9 classes who recently sat the same mathematics test.

Mr McGrath's class	63, 62, 51, 52, 55, 99, 49, 59, 45, 63, 65, 56
Ms McNeil's class	75, 76, 67, 78, 82, 69, 65, 82, 91, 93, 74, 80

11.5 Describing and comparing data

When you describe data or compare two data sets, you need to consider the location, spread and shape of the data.

- **Location**: a measure of central tendency. The main measures are mean, median and mode.
- **Spread**: range.
- **Shape**: symmetrical or skewed.

For the location you can choose to give the mean, median or mode of the data. The mean is most often used, but if there is a small number of very large or very small data points (called outliers) in the data set, the median is often used. (Outliers can skew the mean so that it is no longer a good indicator of central tendency.) Mode can be used when there is a score (i.e. a data value) that frequently occurs in the data set.

For the spread, calculate the range (i.e. the largest value minus the smallest value).

For the shape, describe whether the data is scattered, symmetrical, bi-modal or multi-modal, and if it is positively or negatively skewed. The table below illustrates some of these features.

Shapes of histograms

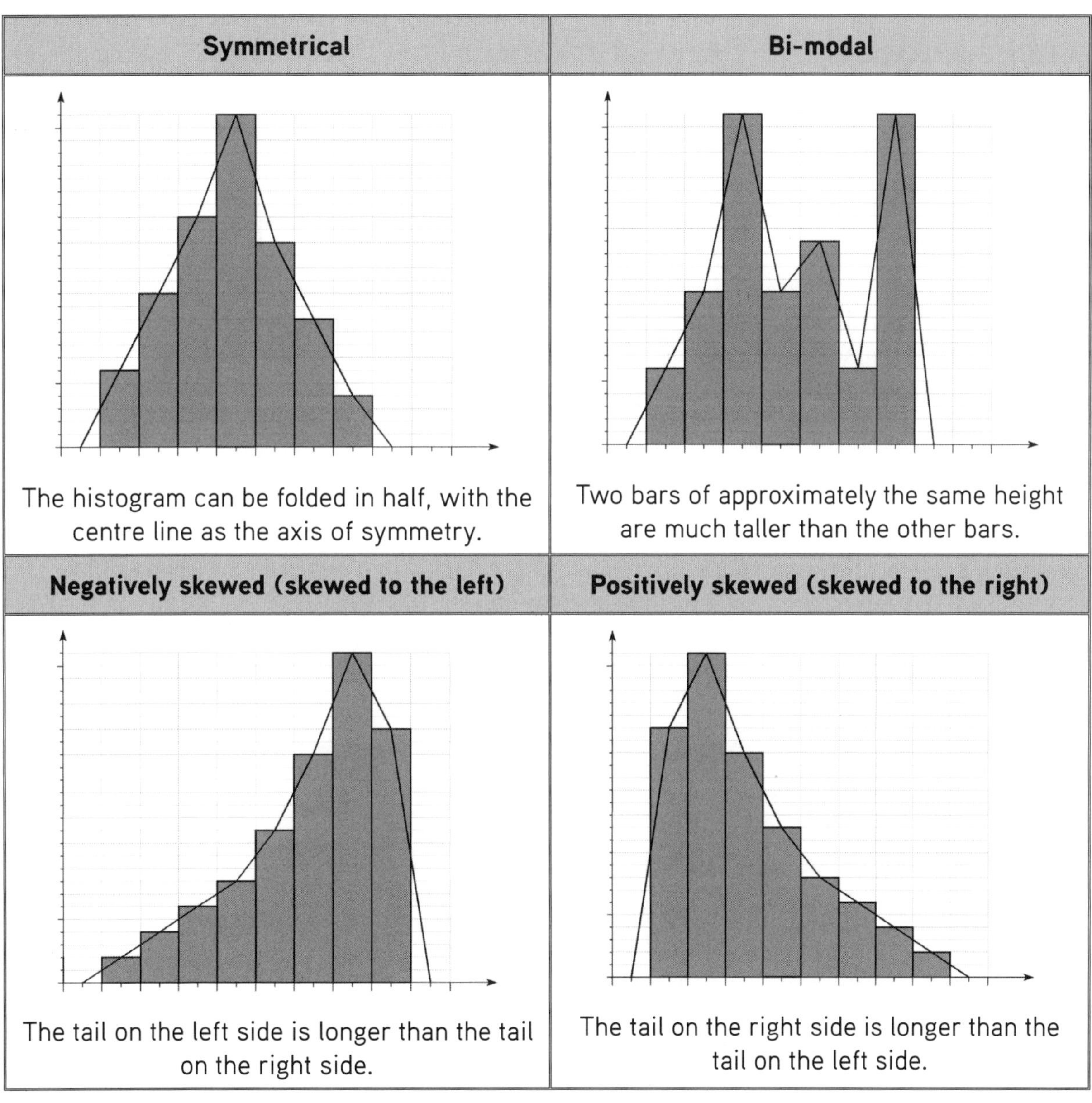

Note: a histogram could have more than one of the shapes described above; for example, it could be symmetrical and bi-modal.

Shapes of stem-and-leaf plots

Symmetrical

Stem	Leaf
0	5
1	4 6
2	3 3 8
3	2 4 6 8 9
4	2 3 4 4 5 8 9
5	1 3 6 8 8
6	4 5 6
7	6 8
8	9

A curve drawn along the edge of the leaves is evenly distributed around the stem with the most leaves.

Negatively skewed (skewed to the left)

Stem	Leaf
0	5
1	4
2	3 3
3	2 4 6
4	2 3 4 4 5
5	1 3 6 8 8 8 9
6	1 3 4 4 5 6
7	1 3 6 8 8
8	1 2 4 5 7

The tail of a curve drawn along the edge of the leaves is longer towards the smaller data points.

Positively skewed (skewed to the right)

Stem	Leaf
0	2 2 4 5 7
1	3 4 6 7 8
2	3 3 4 5 6 8 9
3	2 4 4 5 6 6
4	2 3 4 4 5
5	1 3 6
6	3 4
7	2
8	1

The tail of a curve drawn along the edge of the leaves is longer towards the larger data points.

Example

The histogram below shows the number of hours worked by 70 casual sales staff in a department store. Determine the location and spread of the data represented, and describe the shape of the histogram. Take the mean as the best indicator of location.

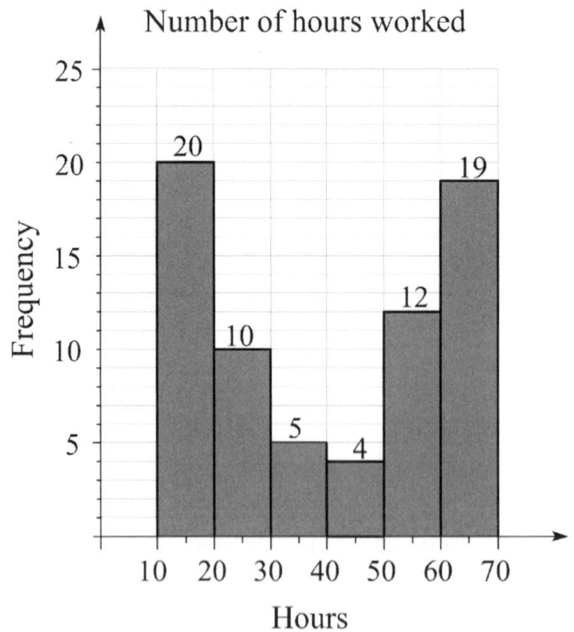

✓ ***Solution***

Working	Explanation
Location (i.e. central tendency) mean $= \dfrac{20 \times 15 + 10 \times 25 + 5 \times 35 + 4 \times 45 + 12 \times 55 + 19 \times 65}{70}$ $= 40$ hours	Determine the mean using the midpoint of each class interval.
The mean number of hours the casual sales staff worked is 40 hours.	Describe the histogram in terms of the mean.
Spread Spread = Range $= 70 - 10 = 60$	Determine the spread (i.e. the range of the data). For histograms, subtract the smallest number in the first bar from the largest number in the last bar.
The spread of the hours the casual sales staff worked is 60 hours.	Describe the histogram in terms of the spread.
Shape The data is approximately symmetrical.	Consider the shape of the histogram and describe it using the terms discussed earlier in this section.

Example

Consider the rainfall data (in cm) presented in the back-to-back stem-and-leaf plot below. Determine the location and spread of the data represented, and describe the shape of each plot. Take the mean as the best indicator of location.

July 2020	Stem	July 2010
	0	6 8
6	1	4 6 7
6	2	3 3 3 8
6 2	3	5 8 9
6 3 3 0	4	8 9
7 4	5	8

Key: 6|1|4 means 16 for July 2020 and 14 for July 2010

✓ *Solution*

Working	Explanation
Location (i.e. central tendency) Mean for July 2020 = 39.3 cm Mean for July 2010 = 28.3 cm	Determine the mean of each data set.
The mean rainfall for July 2020 is 39.3 cm and the mean rainfall for July 2010 is 28.3 cm.	Compare the data sets in terms of the mean.
Spread Spread = Range Range for July 2020 = 41 cm Range for July 2010 = 52 cm	Determine the range of each data set.
The range for July 2020 is 41 cm while the range for July 2010 = 52 cm.	Compare the data sets in terms of the range.
Shape The rainfall data for July 2020 is negatively skewed and the rainfall data for July 2010 is positively skewed.	Compare the shapes of the stem-and-leaf plots. The plot for July 2020 is negatively skewed because the tail is longer towards the smaller data points. The plot for July 2010 is positively skewed because the tail is longer towards the larger data points.

Exercise 11.5.1

For each of the following data displays, describe the shape of the data.

a.

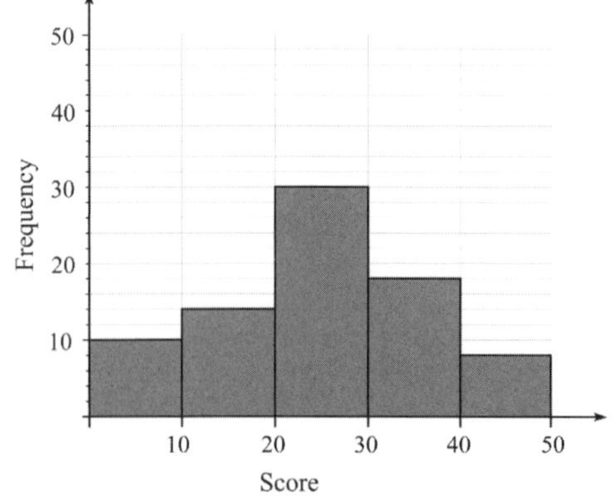

b.

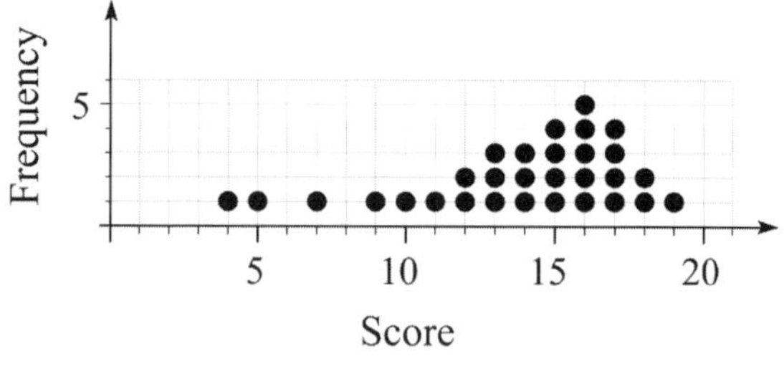

c.

Stem	Leaf
1	1 1 3 4 6 8 8 9
2	0 0 1 3 4 4 5 7 8 8
3	3 4 5 6 9
4	2 4 7 8
5	1 9
6	2 7
7	8

d.

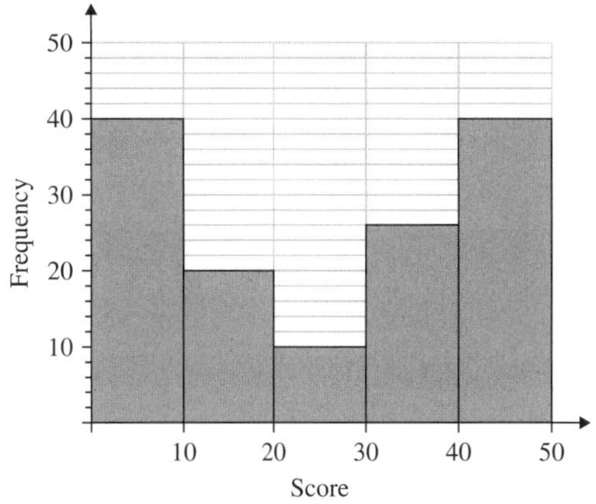

Exercise 11.5.2

The following histogram shows the travel time to school for 65 Year 9 students. Describe the data in terms of location, shape and range. State the modal class.

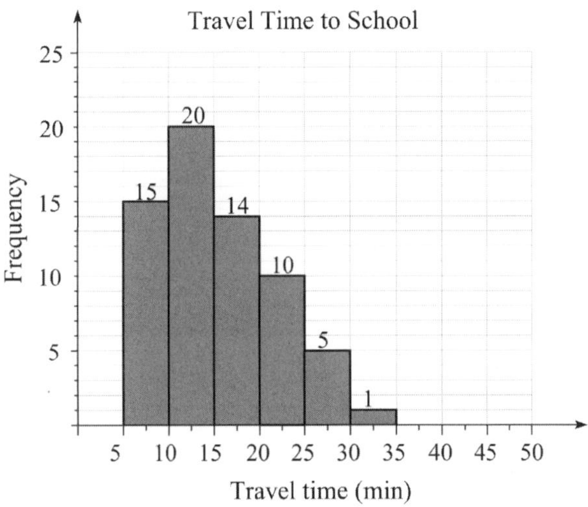

Exercise 11.5.3

The following table gives the results of a recent statistics test taken by students in Ms Lee's class and Mr Watson's class.

Ms Lee	49, 51, 52, 63, 70, 88, 76, 63, 65, 55, 45, 99, 56, 59, 62
Mr Watson	91, 48, 80, 52, 74, 75, 93, 65, 45, 82, 69, 67, 50, 52, 78, 76, 82

a. Construct a back-to-back stem-and-leaf plot to show the results for both classes.

b. Compare the results of both classes in terms of location, shape and spread.

11.6 Statistical investigations

It is important to understand the process by which statistical investigations are carried out. This process is represented in the diagram below.

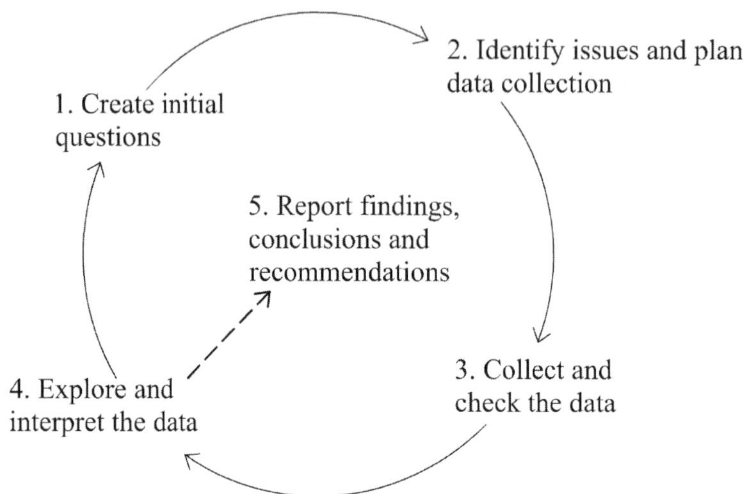

A statistical investigation typically begins by asking one or more relevant questions. For example, if the Year 11 student council is planning the Year 12 school ball for the following year, their initial questions might include:

- What is a suitable date?
- Where can we have the ball?
- How much are we willing to spend?
- Which band should we hire? Or should we use a DJ?

The next step is to think about the issues that need to be considered when planning a statistical investigation and then make sure the investigation addresses these issues. For example, thought needs to be given to the sample size, how to pick an appropriate sample and the appropriate measures or variables. To return to the Year 11 student council, their issues could include:

- How many current Year 11 students should we survey?
- Do we pick 10 students per class to answer our questions?
- How do we carry out the survey? Should we conduct an interview in person or use a Google form?

The next step is to think about collecting and checking the data. It is very important to check the data for any obvious mistakes (for example, the amount a student is willing to spend has been typed in as $10 000 instead of $100.00).

Once the data has been received, it needs to be explored and interpreted. The data could be displayed visually – as a stem-and-leaf plot or histogram, for example – and analysed using the statistical descriptors discussed in this chapter (i.e. location, spread and shape). The results of the analysis can then be used to make recommendations and decisions.

Note that this can be a cyclical process. Analysing the data may prompt more questions which lead to another investigation. In fact, there may be numerous iterations until the findings support a satisfactory recommendation.

11.7 Interpreting data in real life

We have to be careful in interpreting data that is presented to us. There are traps we have to avoid. Consider the following two graphs. They each represent the mean mark in a recent mathematics test taken by two classes.

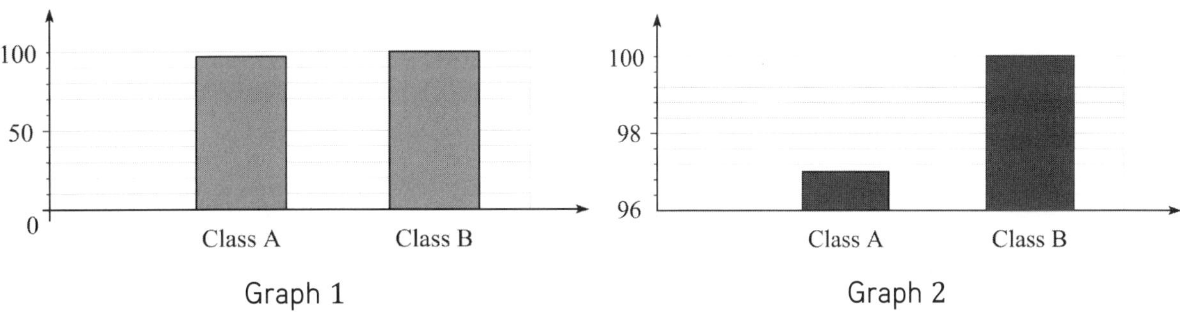

Graph 1

Graph 2

Looking at Graph 1, it seems that there is not much difference between the two classes. However, Graph 2 exaggerates the difference. If we do not pay attention to the scale on the vertical axis, we might conclude that Class B did much better than Class A. There are many examples like this, where the way in which data is displayed can easily mislead. Always take note of the scale and make sure that you understand what is being presented.

Answers

Exercise 11.2

a. numerical, discrete
b. categorical, nominal
c. categorical, nominal
d. numerical, continuous
e. categorical, ordinal
f. numerical, discrete
g. numerical, discrete
h. numerical, continuous

Exercise 11.3

a. mean $= 126$
median $= 128.55$
mode = none
range $= 47.8$

b. mean $= 7.19$
median $= 8$
mode $= 8$
range $= 13$

c. mean $= 1.81$
median $= 1.5$
mode $= 0.5, 1.2, 3.5$
range $= 3.7$

Exercise 11.4.1

a.

Height (h)	Tally	Frequency
$175 \leq h < 180$	||||	4
$180 \leq h < 185$	||	2
$185 \leq h < 190$	卌 卌	10
$190 \leq h < 195$	卌	5
$195 \leq h < 200$	卌 |	6
$200 \leq h < 205$	|||	3

b.

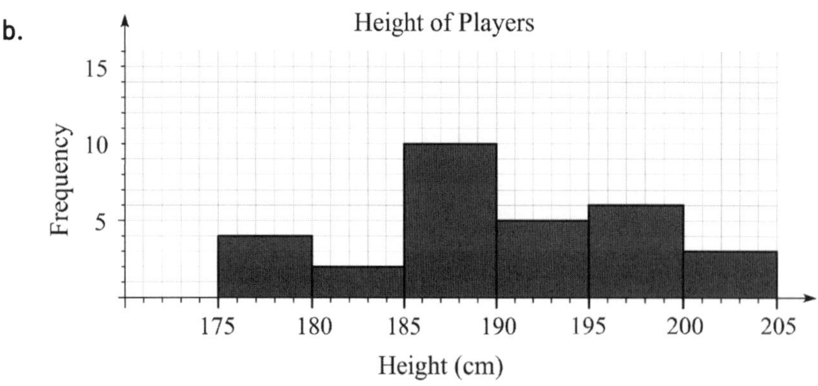

c. estimated mean height $= 190.2$ cm
modal class $= 185 \leq h < 190$ cm

Exercise 11.4.2

Mr McGrath's class	Stem	Ms McNeil's class
9 5	4	
9 6 5 2 1	5	
5 3 3 2	6	5 7 9
	7	4 5 6 8
	8	0 2 2
9	9	1 3

Key: 2|6|5 means 62 for Mr McGrath's class and 65 for Ms McNeil's class

Exercise 11.5.1

a. symmetrical
b. negatively skewed
c. positively skewed
d. symmetrical, bi-modal

Exercise 11.5.2

Location: The mean travel time for the 65 students is 15.4 minutes.

Shape: The histogram is positively skewed.

Range: The range of the travel time is 30 minutes.

Modal class: 10–15

Exercise 11.5.3

a.

Ms Lee's class	Stem	Mr Watson's class
9 5	4	5 8
9 6 5 2 1	5	0 2 2
5 3 3 2	6	5 7 9
6 0	7	4 5 6 8
8	8	0 2 2
9	9	1 3

Key: 1|5|2 means 51 for Ms Lee's class and 52 for Mr Watson's class

b. Location: The mean mark for Ms Lee's class is 63.53 while the mean mark for Mr Watson's class is 69.35.

Shape: The marks for Ms Lee's class are positively skewed while the marks for Mr Watson's class are symmetrical.

Spread: The spread for Ms Lee's class is 54 marks while the spread for Mr Watson's class is 48 marks.

Chapter 12 – Quadratic equations and graphs

12.1 Introduction

The general form of a quadratic equation is

$$y = ax^2 + bx + c$$

where a, b and c are constants. Note that a cannot be 0 because the equation will then be linear.

When $a = 1$, the equation is a **monic** quadratic equation (i.e. $y = x^2 + bx + c$).

The graph of a quadratic equation is called a **parabola**. The shape of a parabola can be seen in many real-life phenomena, such as satellite dishes and the trajectory of footballs.

12.2 The equation of the basic parabola and its graph

The equation of a basic parabola is

$$y = x^2$$

We can plot the graph of the basic parabola from the values in the following table.

x	-4	-3	-2	-1	0	1	2	3	4
y	16	9	4	1	0	1	4	9	16

The graph is shown below.

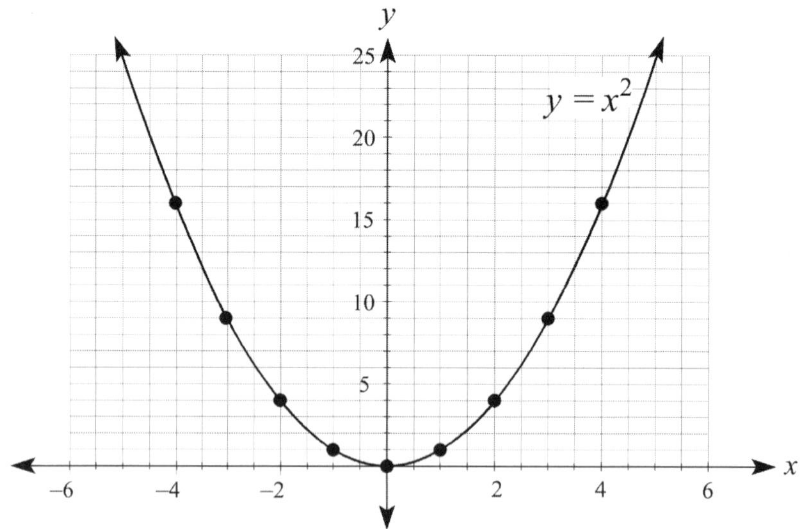

Note the following important features about the graph of the basic parabola.

- It is symmetrical about the y-axis (where $x = 0$).
- The x-intercept is the same as the y-intercept: at the origin, i.e. (0, 0).
- The minimum turning point (also known as the vertex) is at the origin: (0, 0). The turning point is always on the axis of symmetry (i.e. the y-axis).
- The range of y is greater than or equal to 0, because the **minimum** turning point is at $y = 0$.

These features are highlighted in the following graph.

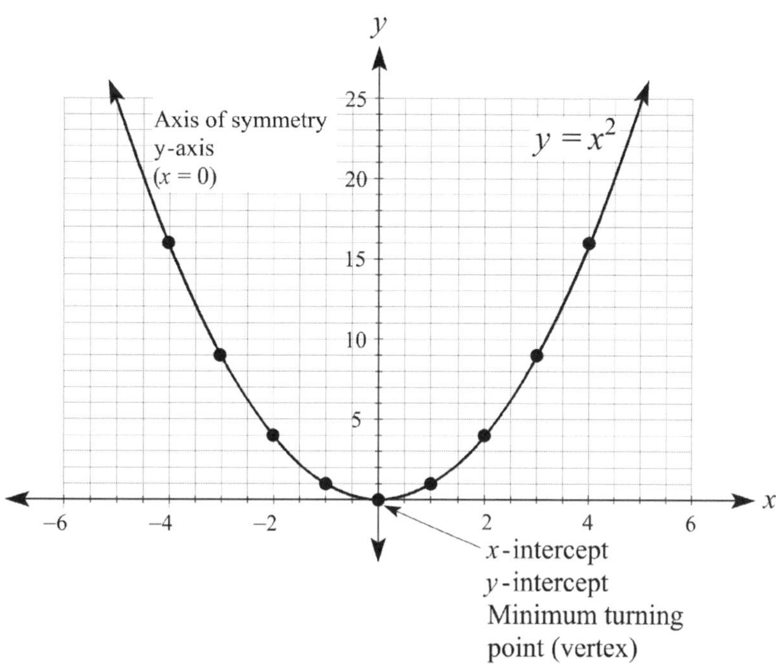

The basic parabola can be reflected about the x-axis (illustrated below). It has the same features, except that the minimum turning point is now the maximum turning point. Its equation is $y = -x^2$. The range of y is now less than or equal to 0, because the **maximum** turning point is at $y = 0$.

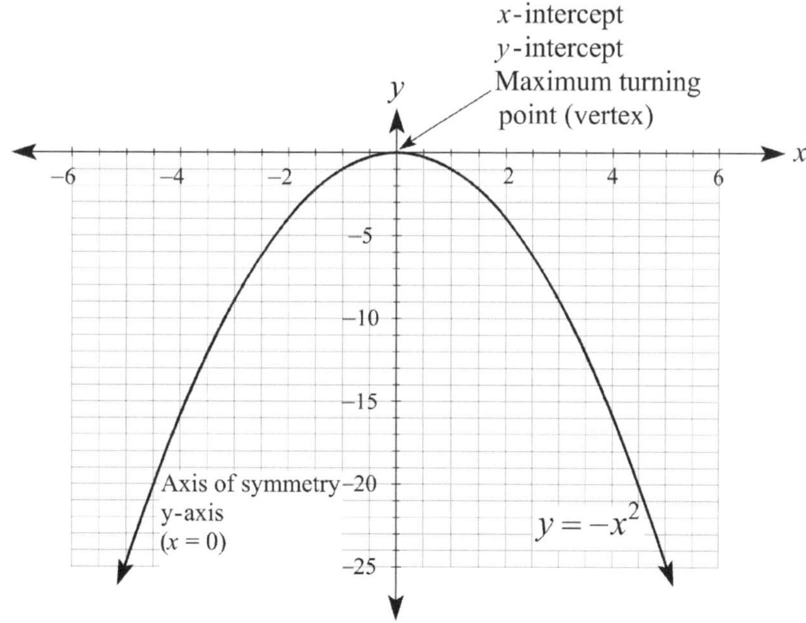

12.3 General equation of the parabola

The general quadratic equation of the parabola can take one of the following forms:

- **general form:** $y = ax^2 + bx + c$
- **root form:** $y = a(x \pm m)(x \pm n)$
- **turning-point form:** $y = a(x \pm h)^2 \pm k$

where a, b, c, m, n, h and k are all constants. Note that $a \neq 0$.

The following graph shows three parabolas plotted on the Cartesian plane.

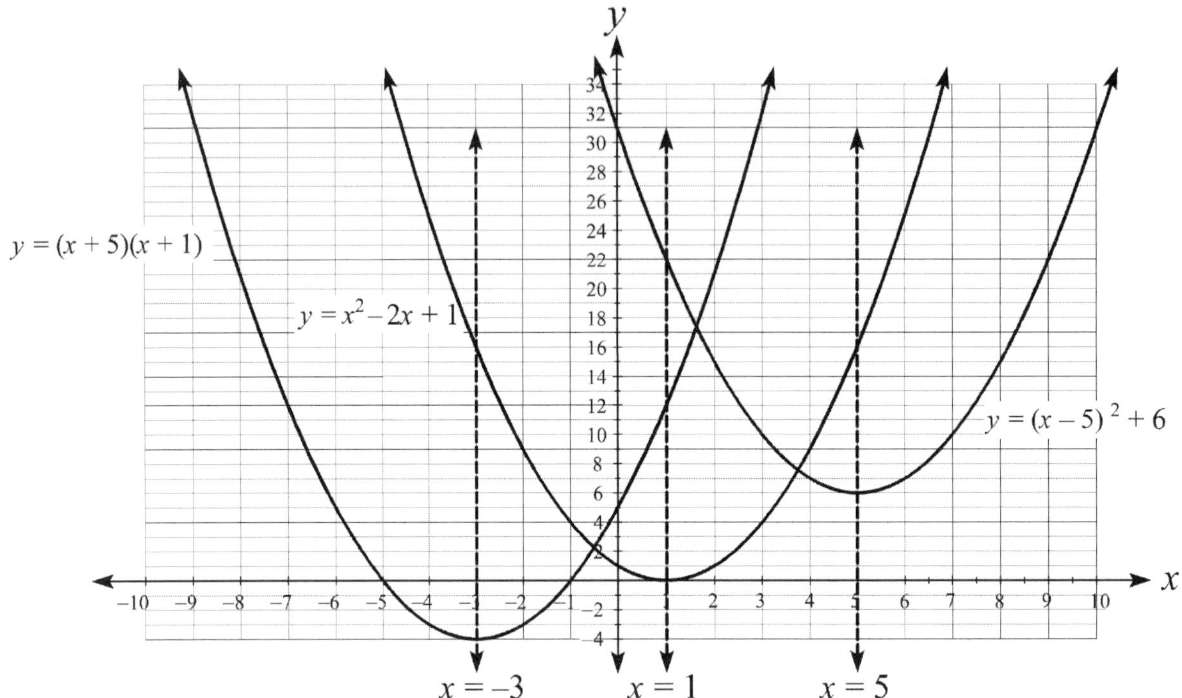

Note that the equations are labelled differently, each showing one of the three forms in which equations for parabolas can be written: the general form, root form and turning-point form.

Each parabola has a minimum turning point, an axis of symmetry and a y-intercept. Not every parabola has an x-intercept. The other term for an x-intercept is a **root**. From the graph above, you can see that a parabola can have 0, 1 or 2 roots.

The key features of each parabola are summarised in the following table.

Equation	Axis of symmetry	Turning point	y-intercept	x-intercept(s)
$y = x^2 - 2x + 1$	$x = 1$	$(1, 0)$	$(0, 1)$	$(1, 0)$
$y = (x + 5)(x + 1)$	$x = -3$	$(-3, -4)$	$(0, 5)$	$(-5, 0), (-1, 0)$
$y = (x - 5)^2 + 6$	$x = 5$	$(5, 6)$	$(0, 31)$	None

If you expand the quadratic equations expressed in root form or turning-point form, you will obtain the general form.

In Year 9, you do not need to know how to derive the turning-point form of a quadratic equation. The root form will be explained in a later section.

12.4 Identifying a parabola from a table of values

If you are given a table of values, it is possible to determine if the values represent a linear equation or a quadratic equation.

Linear equations

Determine the first-order differences, that is, the difference between the values of y when the values of x are increased by 1. If the values of the first-order differences are all the same, then the table of values represents a linear equation. An example is given below.

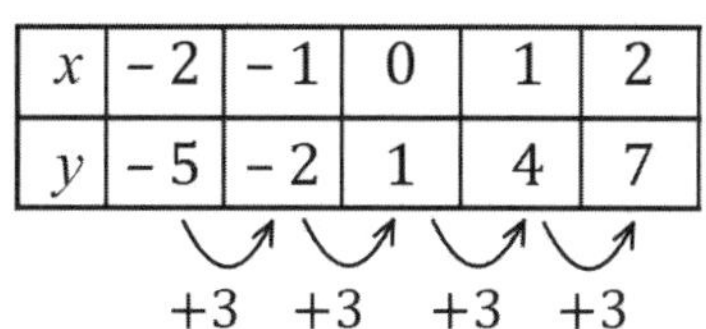

x	−2	−1	0	1	2
y	−5	−2	1	4	7

+3 +3 +3 +3

First-order differences are constant.

For every 1 unit increase in x, y increases by 3 units.

Quadratic equations

If a table of values represents a quadratic equation, the first-order differences will not be the same. If you calculate the second-order differences (i.e. the difference between consecutive first-order differences) and find that they are the same, then the table of values represents a quadratic equation. The values in the following table represent a quadratic equation.

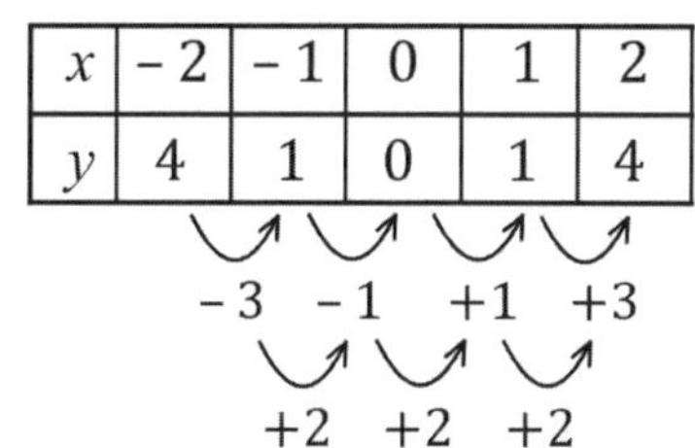

x	−2	−1	0	1	2
y	4	1	0	1	4

−3 −1 +1 +3

+2 +2 +2

Only second-order differences are constant.

Exercise 12.4

Determine if each of the following tables of values represent a linear equation, a quadratic equation or neither.

a.

x	−2	−1	0	1	2
y	10	7	4	1	−2

b.

x	−2	−1	0	1	2
y	5	2	0	2	5

c.

x	−2	−1	0	1	2
y	29	14	1	−10	−19

d.

x	−2	−1	0	1	2
y	44	12	0	8	36

e.

x	−2	−1	0	1	2
y	−6	−2	2	6	10

f.

x	−2	−1	0	1	2
y	2	14	22	18	14

12.5 Solving quadratic equations

Remember that a quadratic equation can have two, one or no roots (i.e. x-intercepts). Note that x-intercepts occur when $y = 0$, so you can find the roots of an equation by setting y to 0 and solving the equation.

Consider this quadratic equation: $y = x^2 - 4x - 5$

To find the roots we set y to 0: $x^2 - 4x - 5 = 0$

To solve this equation, first factorise the left-hand side of the equation: $(x + 1)(x - 5) = 0$

Now apply the **null factor law**, the law that states that if the product of two numbers equals zero, then either one or both numbers are zero. That is, if $m \times n = 0$ then $m = 0$, $n = 0$ or $m = n = 0$.

Therefore if $(x + 1)(x - 5) = 0$ it follows that $(x + 1) = 0$ or $(x - 5) = 0$.

Solving both equations gives $x = -1$ or $x = 5$.

Therefore the roots (i.e. the x-intercepts) of this quadratic equation are $(-1, 0)$ and $(5, 0)$.

Note: if the quadratic equation cannot be factorised, the equation has no roots.

From these considerations, it follows that $y = x^2 - 4x - 5$ can be written as $y = (x + 1)(x - 5)$. The graph of the equation, with the roots clearly marked, is plotted below.

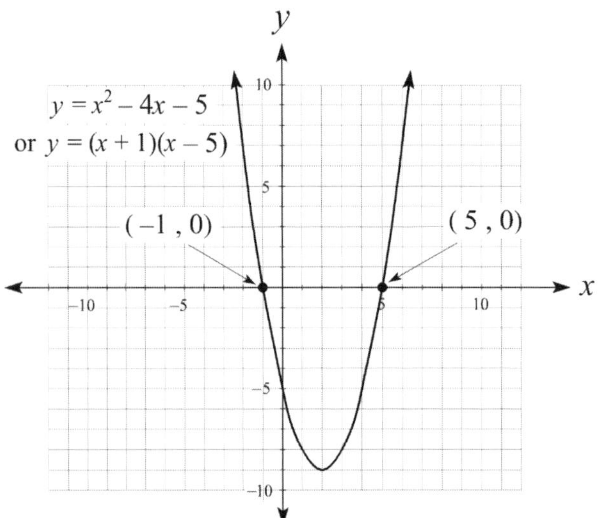

Example

Determine the roots of $y = (x - 5)(x + 8)$.

✓ Solution

Working	Explanation
$y = (x - 5)(x + 8)$	Note that the quadratic equation is already in the root form.
$(x - 5)(x + 8) = 0$	Equate the right-hand side (RHS) of the equation to 0.
$(x - 5) = 0$ or $(x + 8) = 0$	Apply the null factor law and solve for x.
$x = 5$ or $x = -8$ The roots are $(5, 0)$ and $(-8, 0)$.	State the roots of the equation.

Example

Determine the roots of $y = x^2 - 5x$.

✓ *Solution*

Working	Explanation
$y = x^2 - 5x$	Equate the RHS of the equation to 0.
$x^2 - 5x = 0$	Factorise the equation by taking out the common factor.
$x(x - 5) = 0$	Apply the null factor law and solve for x.
$x = 0$ or $(x - 5) = 0$	State the roots of the equation.
$x = 0$ or $x = 5$ The roots are $(0, 0)$ and $(5, 0)$.	**Note:** do not simplify the equation by dividing both sides by x, as you will miss one of the solutions, i.e. $x = 0$. Always factorise the quadratic expression.

Example

Determine the roots of $y = x^2 - 5x + 6$

✓ *Solution*

Working	Explanation
$y = x^2 - 5x + 6$	Equate the RHS of the equation to 0.
$x^2 - 5x + 6 = 0$	Factorise the equation (monic factorisation).
$(x - 2)(x - 3) = 0$	Apply the null factor law and solve for the values of x.
$(x - 2) = 0$ or $(x - 3) = 0$	State the roots of the equation.
$x = 2$ or $x = 3$	
The roots are $(2, 0)$ and $(3, 0)$.	

Example

Determine the roots of $y = x^2 + 5$.

✓ *Solution*

Working	Explanation
$y = x^2 + 5$	Equate the RHS of the equation to 0.
$x^2 + 5 = 0$	It is not possible to factorise this quadratic equation.
$x^2 = -5$ There are no solutions, therefore there is no root.	You can rearrange the equation by subtracting 5 from both sides. However, a square number cannot be negative, therefore there are no solutions (i.e. no roots).

Example

Determine the roots of $y = x^2 - 8x + 16$.

✓ ***Solution***

Working	Explanation
$y = x^2 - 8x + 16$	Equate the RHS of the equation to 0.
$x^2 - 8x + 16 = 0$	Factorise the equation (monic factorisation to a perfect square).
$(x - 4)(x - 4) = 0$	Apply the null factor law and solve for the values of x.
$x = 4$	State the roots of the equation.
The root is $(4, 0)$.	**Note:** where the equation is a perfect square, there is only one root.

Example

Determine the roots of $y = x^2 - 5x + 29$.

✓ ***Solution***

Working	Explanation
$y = x^2 - 5x + 29$	Equate the RHS of the equation to 0.
$x^2 - 5x + 29 = 0$	It is not possible to factorise this quadratic equation, therefore it has no roots.
The quadratic expression (LHS) cannot be factorised. Hence it has no roots.	

Example

Determine the roots of $y = x^2 - 81$.

✓ ***Solution***

Working	Explanation
$y = x^2 - 81$	Equate the RHS of the equation to 0.
$x^2 - 81 = 0$	Factorise the equation (monic factorisation – difference of perfect squares).
$(x - 9)(x + 9) = 0$	Apply the null factor law and solve for x.
$(x - 9) = 0$ or $(x + 9) = 0$	State the roots of the equation.
$x = 9$ or $x = -9$	
The roots are $(9, 0)$ and $(-9, 0)$.	

Alternatively: $x^2 - 81 = 0$ $x^2 = 81$ $x = \pm 9$ The roots are $(9, 0)$ and $(-9, 0)$.	Rearrange the quadratic equation by adding 81 to both sides of the equation. Since $x^2 = 81$, therefore $x = \pm 9$.

Example

Determine the roots of $y = 2x^2 + 4x - 16$.

✓ *Solution*

Working	Explanation
$y = 2x^2 + 4x - 16$	Equate the RHS of the equation to 0.
$2x^2 + 4x - 16 = 0$	Factorise the equation by taking out the common factor.
$2(x^2 + 2x - 8) = 0$	Factorise the bracketed terms (monic factorisation).
$2(x - 2)(x + 4) = 0$	Apply the null factor law and solve for x.
$(x - 2) = 0$ or $(x + 4) = 0$	State the roots of the equation.
$x = 2$ or $x = -4$	
The roots are $(2, 0)$ and $(-4, 0)$.	

Exercise 12.5

Determine the roots of the following quadratic equations.

a. $y = x^2 - 49$
b. $y = x^2 - 4x - 45$
c. $y = x^2 + 3x + 2$
d. $y = x^2 - 15x + 44$
e. $y = x^2 + 16$
f. $y = x^2 + 18x + 81$
g. $y = x^2 + 4x + 24$
h. $y = 3x^2 - 6x + 3$
i. $y = x^2 + 13x$
j. $y = x^2 + 8x - 9$
k. $y = 4x^2 + x$
l. $y = x^2 + 6x + 21$

12.6 Transforming a quadratic equation

The basic parabola ($y = x^2$) can be transformed by translation, reflection and dilation. It is important to observe graphically what happens to the basic parabola when it is transformed. Useful graphing tools are available online (e.g. at desmos.com or geogebra.org) and there are useful graphing calculators (e.g. the Casio ClassPad or the TI-Nspire). The online graphing tools are relatively easy to use and you will be using a graphing calculator in the future.

Translation of $y = x^2$

Vertical translation means moving the parabola up or down (i.e. in the direction of the positive y-axis or negative y-axis). Horizontal translation means moving the parabola to the right or left (i.e. in the direction of the positive x-axis or negative x-axis).

Vertical translation

Consider the following quadratic equations plotted on the Cartesian plane.

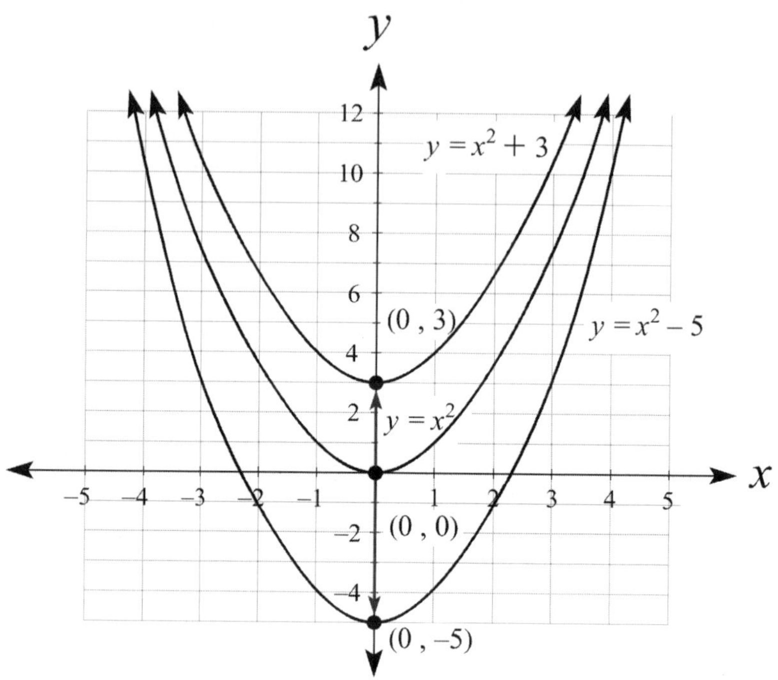

When $y = x^2$ is transformed to $y = x^2 + 3$, the entire parabola is translated up by 3 units. When $y = x^2$ is transformed to $y = x^2 - 5$, the entire parabola is translated down by 5 units. In general, if $y = x^2$ is transformed to $y = x^2 \pm k$, the parabola is translated up (+) or down (−) by k units.

Note: an easy way to observe the translation is to look at how the turning point moves.

Horizontal translation

Consider the following quadratic equations plotted on the Cartesian plane.

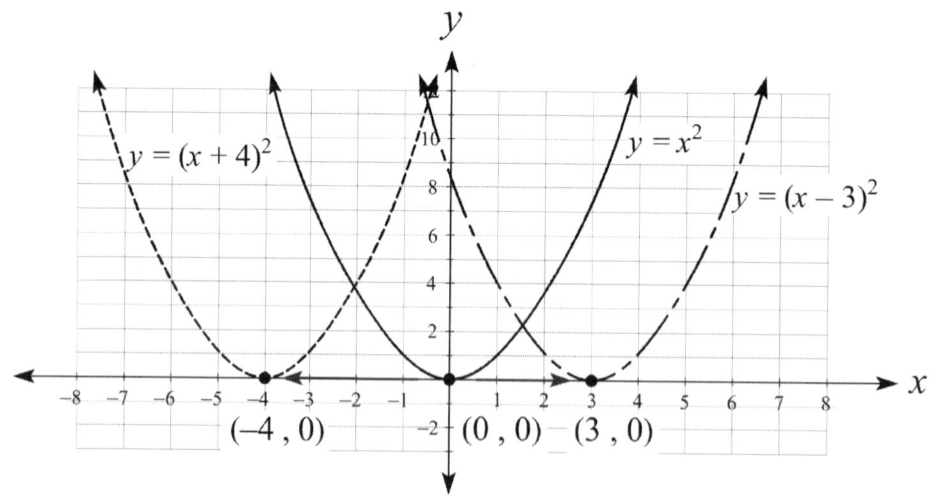

When $y = x^2$ is transformed to $y = (x + 4)^2$, the entire parabola is translated to the left by 4 units. When $y = x^2$ is transformed to $y = (x - 3)^2$, the entire parabola is translated to the right by 3 units. In general, if $y = x^2$ is transformed to $y = (x \pm h)^2$, the parabola is translated to the right (−) or to the left (+) by h units. Again, you can use the turning point to help you interpret the translation.

Note: for horizontal translation, the parabola moves in the opposite direction to the sign.

Combining both translations

Consider the following quadratic equations plotted on the Cartesian plane.

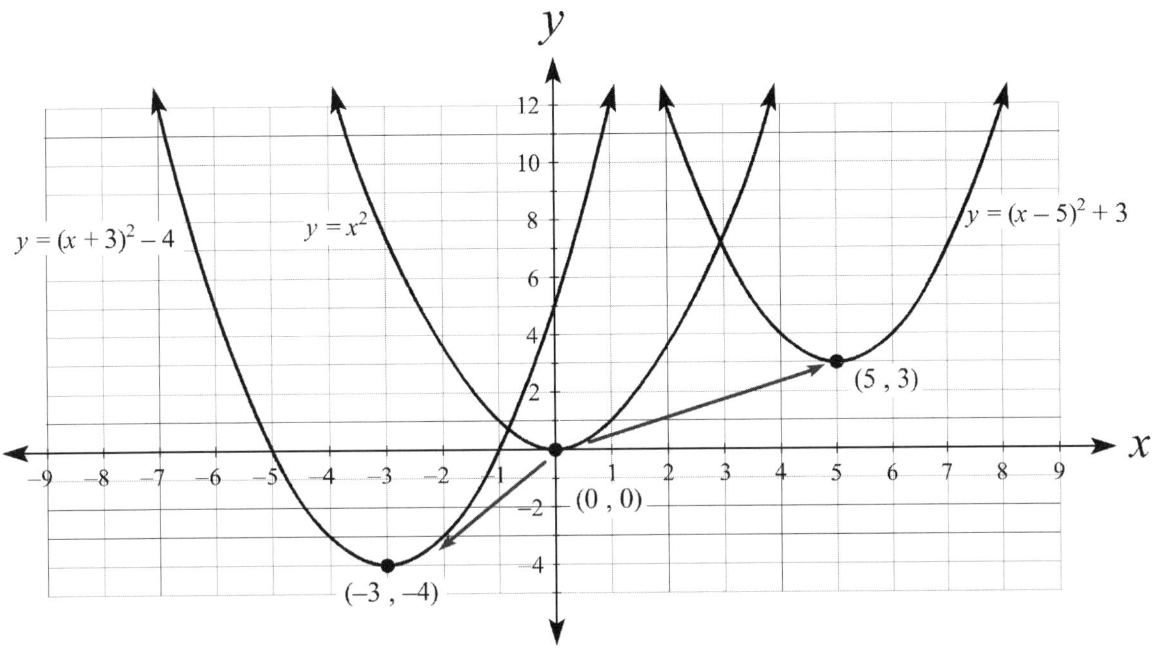

When $y = x^2$ is transformed to $y = (x + 3)^2 - 4$, the entire parabola is translated to the left by 3 units and translated down by 4 units. When $y = x^2$ is transformed to $y = (x - 5)^2 + 3$, the entire parabola is translated to the right by 5 units and translated up by 3 units. In general, if $y = x^2$ is transformed to $y = (x \pm h)^2 \pm k$, the parabola is translated to the right $(-)$ or to the left $(+)$ by h units, and translated up $(+)$ or down $(-)$ by k units. Again, use the turning point to help you interpret the effect of the translations.

When a quadratic equation is written in the turning-point form, $y = (x \pm h)^2 \pm k$, the turning point is $(\mp h, \pm k)$.

Dilation of $y = x^2$

Dilation of a parabola involves moving its arms closer to, or further away from, the axis of symmetry.

Consider the following quadratic equations plotted on the Cartesian plane.

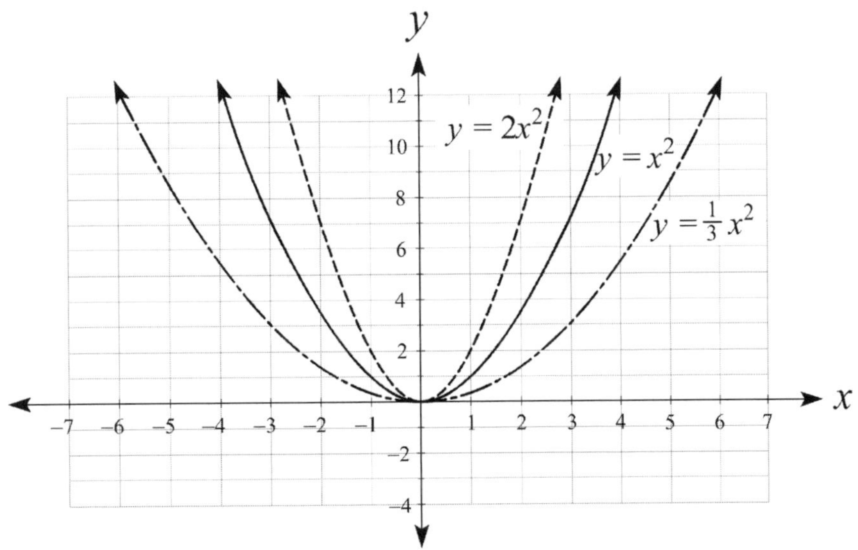

When $y = x^2$ is transformed to $y = 2x^2$, the arms of the parabola move closer to the axis of symmetry (the parabola becomes narrower). This is because the coefficient of 2 means that the y-coordinates are all multiplied by 2. When $y = x^2$ is transformed to $y = \frac{1}{3}x^2$, the arms of the parabola move away from the axis of symmetry (the parabola becomes wider). This is because the coefficient of $\frac{1}{3}$ means that the y-coordinates are all multiplied by $\frac{1}{3}$.

Reflection of $y = x^2$

A parabola can be reflected about the x-axis by preceding the equation with a negative sign. For example, $y = -x^2$ is the reflection of $y = x^2$.

Consider the following quadratic equations plotted on the Cartesian plane.

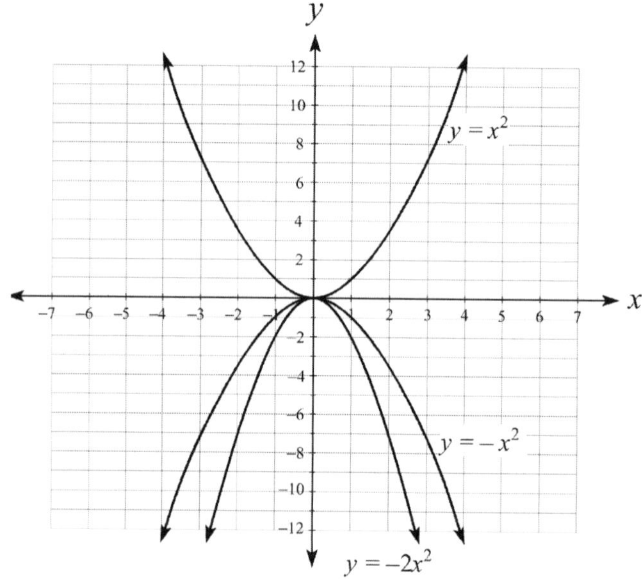

The negative sign indicates that the parabola is reflected about the x-axis. When $y = x^2$ is transformed to $y = -2x^2$, the factor of 2 applies to the y-coordinates, which are then reflected about the x-axis.

Combining transformations

Consider the following quadratic equations plotted on the Cartesian plane.

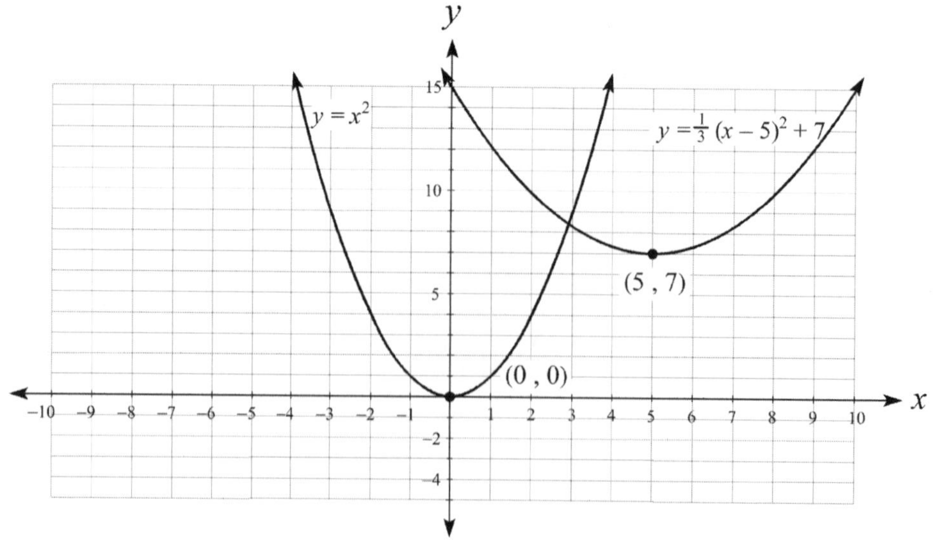

When $y = x^2$ is transformed to $y = \frac{1}{3}(x - 5)^2 + 7$, the parabola is translated 5 units to the right and 7 units up, and the arms move further apart.

Now consider the following parabolas.

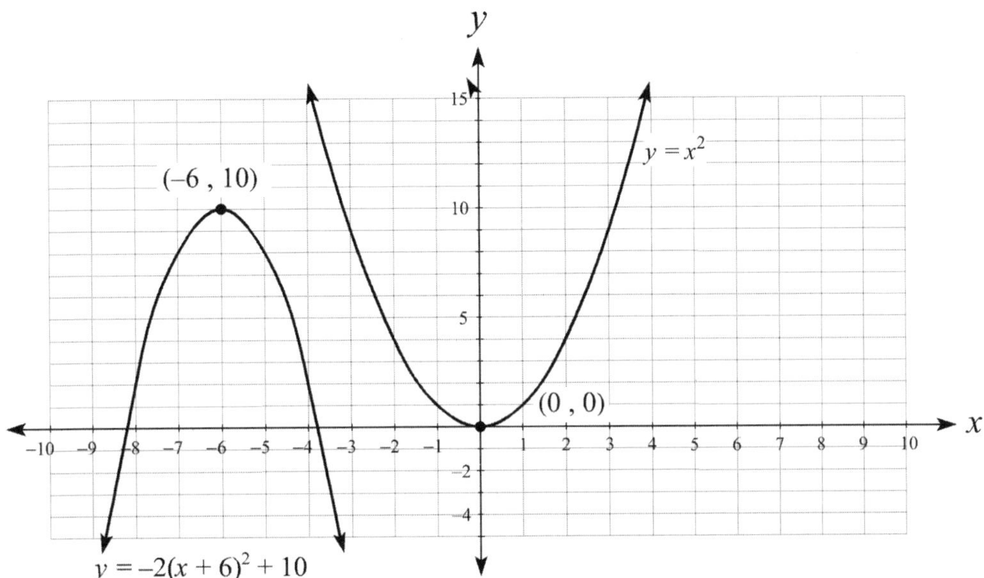

When $y = x^2$ is transformed to $y = -2(x + 6)^2 + 10$, the parabola is translated 6 units to the left and 10 units up, the arms move closer and the parabola is reflected about the x-axis.

To summarise, when $y = x^2$ is transformed to $y = a(x \pm h)^2 \pm k$, the parabola is:

- translated to the right $(-)$ or to the left $(+)$ by h units
- translated up $(+)$ or down $(-)$ by k units
- dilated by a factor of a (i.e. the y-coordinates are multiplied by a)
- reflected about the x-axis if the coefficient a is negative.

Note that:

- For $0 < a < 1$, the transformed parabola is wider than the basic parabola.
- For $a > 1$, the transformed parabola is narrower than the basic parabola.
- For $a = 1$, the parabola is the same shape as the basic parabola.

Answers

Exercise 12.4

a. linear
b. neither
c. quadratic
d. quadratic
e. linear
f. neither

Exercise 12.5

a. $(7, 0)$ and $(-7, 0)$
b. $(9, 0)$ and $(-5, 0)$
c. $(-1, 0)$ and $(-2, 0)$
d. $(4, 0)$ and $(11, 0)$
e. no roots
f. $(-9, 0)$
g. no roots
h. $(1, 0)$
i. $(0, 0)$ and $(-13, 0)$
j. $(-9, 0)$ and $(1, 0)$
k. $(0, 0)$ and $\left(-\frac{1}{4}, 0\right)$
l. no roots